To Tom,

Hope you have fun reading this.

Best Wishes.

Paul

GREAT BRITISH TRAINS

GREAT BRITISH TRAINS

An evocation of a memorable age in travel

By O. S. Nock

B.Sc., D.I.C., F.C.G.I., C. Eng., F.I.C.E., F.I.Mech.E.

Past President and Honorary Fellow
Institution of Railway Signal Engineers

PELHAM BOOKS

First published in Great Britain by
Pelham Books Limited
44 Bedford Square, London WC1B 3DP
1985

British Library Cataloguing in Publication Data

Nock, O.S.
    Great British trains.
    1. Locomotives——Great Britain——History——
    20th century
    I. Title
    625.2′6′0941   T J603.4.G7

    ISBN 0-7207-1580-6

Typeset, printed and bound in Great Britain by
Butler & Tanner Ltd, Frome and London

PICTURE CREDITS

The author and publishers are grateful to the following for permission to reproduce copyright illustrations: (**black and white**) British Railways pages 20, 21, 37, 40, 43, 59, 82, 85, 86, 127, 157, 198; H.C. Casserley Esq pages 94, 152, 153; the late D. Cross page 99; E.J. Bedford Esq page 28; Gibson & Co page 53; the late W.B. Greenfield pages 66, 185; the Locomotive Publishing Co pages 15, 55, 128, 168, 172; K.H. Leech Esq page 41; National Railway Museum, York, page 3; O.S. Nock Esq pages 11, 25, 30, 35, 46, 56, 71, 95, 119, 121, 156, 160, 161, 172, 176, 177, 178, 200, 204; the late R.J. Purves page 49; Rail Archive Stephenson pages 60, 64, 65, 70, 73, 81, 90, 91, 102, 105, 108, 109, 111, 114, 117, 133, 138, 139, 140, 141, 145, 148, 186, 190, 196, 197, 199; the late W.J. Reynolds page 147. (**colour**) From original paintings in the Author's possession: The Golden Arrow by F. Moore; Route of the Aberdonian, by V. Welch; On the Highland line, by V. Welch; The Southbound Corridor, by O.S. Nock; from colour transparencies from Rail Archive Stephenson: Cornish Riviera Express; The Torbay Limited; The Royal Scot locomotive; Southern 4-6-0 No. 739; LNER the 'Silver Link'. All the remainder are reproduced from original coloured postcards issued by the Locomotive Publishing Company.

CONTENTS

PREFACE

This is a story of the time before the private motor car and the internal airlines had supplanted the train as the premier means of long distance passenger travel in Great Britain, when family holidays involved the conveyance of mountains of luggage and several servants in attendance; when there was time on what would now be called an Inter-City express for important business to be negotiated over coffee and liqueurs after a leisurely meal in the restaurant car. But on reflection it must be admitted that a list of the great trains, at any rate those of which an aura of greatness has lingered around their memory, does not include very many that would be placed among 'big business' expresses. 'The Royal Scot', 'The Golden Arrow', the 'Queen of Scots' Pullman, and the 'Torbay Limited' were symbolic of leisured daytime travel for the passengers, if not for the engine crew, in contrast, for example, to the swift dash home in early evening for the Liverpool business man, who caught the Merseyside Express from Euston, after a long day's work in London.

In the earlier age of railway elegance the great express trains of this country had a manifold interest extending far beyond the speed, the coaching stock and the locomotives that hauled them. It is true that they tended to become the centre pieces of the business of travel. But in recalling those days one thinks of the innumerable preliminaries, asides, and incidents that went to make up the complex microcosm of a main line railway journey; and to me looking back over three-quarters of a century of such experience those memories certainly come crowding. In committing them to paper I have tried to provide something for all those who love railways. There is plenty about locomotives and carriages, much of the passing scene, points about architecture, railway history and archaeology, not forgetting the vignettes of fellow travellers, and railwaymen.

So far as the trains themselves are concerned, while writing almost entirely from personal experience, I have divided them into three broad categories; the first dealing with trains the character of which belongs essentially to the days before the first world war; the second concerns the inter-war period, and the first signs of the passing of the old elegance, and the third, the first essays into the breathless modern age.

My thanks are due to innumerable railwaymen, who, in the years between the two world wars, in every discipline from the highest to the lowest, have impressed and inspired me by their enthusiasm, and spirit of dedication to the service. No less has this been my experience with men in the supporting manufacturing industries. Most of them have now passed on, but I shall ever be grateful to them for the authority they gave me to roam their linesides and take photographs to my heart's content, to visit their workshops, and to appreciate the most prized privilege of all, to ride on the footplate of steam locomotives in traffic.

So far as the earlier period is concerned, although I am now getting somewhat 'long in the tooth', I cannot pretend to have seen 'The Flying Dutchman' in its broad gauge days; but I have certainly seen 'The Norfolk Coast Express' in its pre-1914 glory, and have travelled by 'The Southern Belle' and the 'West Coast Corridor', though not in the degree of privilege accorded to me in later years.

O. S. NOCK
August 1984
Batheaston
Bath

1

THE FLYING DUTCHMAN

In 1849 an outstanding racehorse owned by Lord Eglinton won both the Derby and the St Leger. It was named 'The Flying Dutchman'. Until the steam locomotive began to get into its stride a galloping horse was the fastest means of travel known to man, and when in the spring of 1862 in reply to competition from the London and South Western Railway, the broad gauge Great Western put on a new fast express to Bristol and South Devon, which began with a run from Paddington to Didcot at $55\frac{3}{4}$ mph, the new 'flyer' was quickly nicknamed after the legendary champion of the Turf, 'The Flying Dutchman'. On its inauguration it was fast only as far as Exeter, to which city it was highly competitive. Beyond there the Great Western had the country to itself, and there was no need for further hurry. That stylist among early railway authors, the Rev. W. J. Scott, chose it for the inauguration of a series of articles on 'World-Famous Trains' in the recently established *Railway Magazine* in 1899, and he opened in characteristic style:

'What memories that name, irrelevant and absurd in itself, awakens in the minds of "railwayacs" born somewhere about the century's middle years! To some of us for whom – while we found Cornelius Nepos an author who drew tears, and verbs in 'mi' a grievous burden – *Bradshaw* had no terrors, even 'Service Books' were not 'sealed', the putting on of the 11.45 am from Paddington was a joy too deep for words.' One feels however that the joys were of statistics rather than of the actual experience of travel in it, because no details of its running in those early days or other reminiscences have been handed down to us. Furthermore it carried only first and second class passengers, and not many of those. Its full load of seven vehicles leaving Paddington was conveyed only as far as Swindon, for there two coaches were detached, one for Cheltenham and one for Weymouth. When it was first put on in 1862 the main part of the train – three vehicles – went to Torquay, and as far as Churston, then known as Brixham Road, and there was a through carriage for Plymouth, which was attached to a slow train at Newton Abbot. The seventh coach, fifth from the engine leaving Paddington, was for Exeter; but so light was the patronage at times that it was not run every day.

Light though the load was, especially west of Swindon, much difficulty was found in keeping time, and from 1865 each year saw a progressive deceleration. In 1868 it was taken off altogether. But with war on the Continent bringing a surge of prosperity to this country the 'Dutchman' was re-instated, and in 1871 accelerated to an extent surpassing the inaugural best of 1862. Moreover in its new form it was a purely West of England express, and the full load was taken through to Newton Abbot. To Exeter its timing was the fastest yet, in 4¼ hours from London, inclusive of stops at Swindon, Bath, Bristol and Taunton, for which the timetable allowed a total of 22 minutes, leaving a running average speed over the 194 miles of exactly 50 mph. The successive stages were as follows:

Paddington to Swindon, 77·3 miles, 53·3 mph
Swindon to Bath, 29·6 miles, 46·8 mph
Bath to Bristol, 11·5 miles, 38·4 mph
Bristol to Taunton, 44·8 miles, 52·7 mph
Taunton to Exeter, 30·8 miles, 47·4 mph

The above timings substantiated the claim that 'The Flying Dutchman' was then the world's fastest train.

Nearly half the total allowance for station stops was spent at Swindon, and of this there is a story to be told. The catering contractors who ran the refreshment rooms at the station there had a clause in their agreement requiring that every passenger train passing through must be stopped for at least ten minutes to enable passengers to obtain refreshment; and a pretty mad dash it was at times. Apart from that enforced stop however the spectacular London–Swindon run at 53·3 mph seems to have been interpreted rather liberally. It is a definite, if very gradual rise all the way, and the prevailing wind would generally be adverse; and whatever the timetable might say, the drivers had their own way of working the train. From all accounts it seems that the sharp booking of 87 minutes from Paddington to Swindon was hardly ever kept, and the arrivals for the refreshment stop were regularly about 3 minutes late. I have seen it suggested that as no buns, sandwiches or other enticements were offered to the enginemen they took no particular interest in getting to Swindon on time; but actually it would have been more than any station official's life was worth to try and curtail the refreshment stop below the advertised 10 minutes. The fact was that the succeeding point-to-point allowance of 38 minutes for the 29·6 miles on to Bath, including two steep descending gradients, was quite easy, and one could regain those two or three minutes without extending the engine.

The Flying Dutchman in the last days of the broad gauge passing Ealing. Note 'mixed gauge' track, and early form of tall signal, with arm working in a slot in the post.

Whatever the pangs of hunger might be felt on reaching Swindon one can imagine it must have been something of a relief to climb down from those broad gauge carriages for a brief respite, for even the first-class compartments were less than 8 ft wide across, and the 'seconds' were less than 6 ft. The bodies were 10 ft 6 in wide, and in the 'seconds' seating six-aside, the man in the middle did not see much of the passing scene! The clerestory roofs provided some additional lighting for those so deeped ensconced within. The composite carriages run on The Flying Dutchman had three compartments for second class, and two for first, with a luggage compartment in between. As the time approached for the final conversion of the broad gauge tracks to standard gauge a number of new carriages were built at Swindon with narrow bodies, but carried on broad gauge frames and running on broad gauge bogies. They were designed so that they could be converted in the quickest possible time. They were longer and heavier than the old 40 ft long wide-bodied carriages and did not make the job of hauling them any easier. It is, moreover, not generally realised that the standard

3

Broad gauge engine of the Flying Dutchman, Emperor, *at Exeter, St David's station.*

broad gauge express locomotives of the 4-2-2 type, so revered by Great Western enthusiasts, had remained virtually unchanged in their design for more than 40 years. At the time of the conversion of the gauge in May 1892 twenty three of them remained, and then they all went to Swindon for a mass execution!

Although I am not nearly old enough to have seen one of them in the flesh I find it easy enough to understand the veneration in which they were held by the railway enthusiasts of the day, and indeed by the locomotive men of the Great Western Railway. I have a copy of one of the most beautifully and accurately reproduced of the 'F. Moore' paintings, showing the engine *Great Western* in her final form, with a cab, and the superb polished brass splasher over the driving wheel extending downwards to well below the footplate level. Those famous engines were unusual in carrying no running numbers, and it is not surprising that with only their names to identify them they became imbued with personalities rarely attained by other locomotives. Until the year 1887 they were attached to only two running sheds, twelve of them at Westbourne Park, about a mile outside Paddington and the remainder at Bristol. Except for one turn the latter stud worked only over the Exeter road to and from Newton Abbot, while in the ordinary course the London engines did not go beyond Bristol. In 1887 an additional West of England express was put on, appropriately named the 'Jubilee', this conveyed third class passengers, and in consequence was timed at a slower speed than the 'exclusive' Dutchman, and its afternoon counterpart, the 'Zulu'. The introduction of the Jubilee led to the stationing of three of the famous 8 ft 4-2-2s at Newton Abbot, for the first time in history.

To modern eyes these broad gauge engines would have had a rather antique appearance from the height of the chimney; but although the boiler was large for the day the width apart of the driving wheels on the 7 ft gauge enabled the boiler to be set low, between the wheels, whereas on the standard gauge a boiler of such size would have had to be pitched much higher. It is interesting to recall that the final version of the broad gauge express locomotive boiler had a total heating surface of just over 2000 sq ft, while the standard gauge 4-2-2s that took up the same work after conversion of the gauge had less than 1500 sq ft. Because of their squat appearance the

The 'narrow', or standard gauge Flying Dutchman passing through Uphill cutting near Weston-super-Mare, hauled by one of the Dean 7 ft 8 in in 4-2-2 locomotives.

broad gauge 8 ft 4-2-2 express engines had a deceptively massive look from the front end, and without a reference to actual dimensions one was left wondering how those tall chimneys cleared the bridges and the tunnels! In those last years of the broad gauge there was a gentleman of the name of Malan who took many fine photographs, and he was given a footplate pass to ride the Flying Dutchman from Newton Abbot to Bristol and back. Apart from the roughness of the riding, and the incessant vibration, which he noticed probably more from unfamiliarity with locomotives than that the *Iron Duke* and *Rover* were actually rough by footplate standards, the most lasting impression seemed to be how often he thought the funnel would be knocked off when passing under a bridge!

After the conversion of the gauge the addition of the new 'Cornishman', running non-stop to Exeter, completely stripped the old 11.45 am Flying Dutchman of all its glamour, though the corresponding eastbound train leaving Plymouth at 8.30 am and also known as the Dutchman came very much into the limelight in 1903. It had been quickened by a non-stop run from Plymouth to Newton Abbot in 1899, and leaving Bristol at 12 noon ran up to Paddington in 2 hours 40 minutes, with stops at Bath and Swindon. Then, in 1903, in keeping with the tremendously enterprising policy of the new century there came a sensational acceleration. Using the newly completed Badminton line the up Dutchman thenceforward ran non-stop to Paddington in the level two hours, an average speed of $58\frac{3}{4}$ mph to arrive in London forty minutes earlier than previously, leaving a new train at 12.5 pm from Bristol to run via Bath in the previous times of the Dutchman. For a time, amid the excitement of the Bristol-London runs, regardless of the speed the train had already made up from the West, the old nickname fell somewhat into disuse, while in the following year, 1904, the alteration of the departure time of the down train from the historic 11.45 am which had prevailed unbrokenly - save for the 1867-9 lapse - for more than 40 years, to 12.25 pm was a further break with the old traditions.

A still greater break was to come in 1906, when the shorter route from London to the West of England was opened, by the completion of the 'cut-off' line across South Somerset from Castle Cary to Cogload Junction, five miles on the London side of Taunton. The principal expresses were transferred to this route, including the up Dutchman. Although this change gave an arrival in London 25 minutes earlier even than the 'flying' run of 1903, the city of Bristol lost its two-hour crack express, and for a time had to put up with its relatively slow 12.5 pm making several stops. The travelling habit was necessarily growing however, and with the up Dutchman conveying no more than six coaches on its two-hour flight to London and already well loaded on its arrival from the West, passengers joining at

Bristol could well have found difficulty in finding seats. It was indeed not long before a new 12 noon express, starting from Bristol, was put on to provide for the growing traffic.

After conversion of the gauge haulage of the Dutchman, and indeed all other West of England expresses on the Great Western, was entrusted to William Dean's beautiful 7 ft 8 in 4-2-2 singles, and it is fortunate beyond measure that a full-sized replica of one of the most celebrated of all the 80 engines of the class has now been constructed, and is on display at Windsor. This is engine No. 3041 *The Queen*, which in 1897 was used to haul the Royal train conveying Queen Victoria from Windsor to Paddington, for the Diamond Jubilee celebrations. Although it is not operational everything about the replica is absolutely right, and as for the 'finish', it is regal to the last degree, though in truth not greatly superior to the way in which the original engines of 85 or 90 years ago set out to haul The Flying Dutchman or any other of the Great Western expresses of the day. So far as the replica is concerned I feel that photographs of such a glorious creation can speak more than pages of description. Many of the old broad gauge names were used on the new engines, and a pleasing touch was that one of them, No. 3009, was named *Flying Dutchman*, a title that had not been used in broad gauge days.

The new century was nevertheless bringing a new look to Great Western express passenger engines. In 1900 the rather angular-shaped 'Atbara' class engines took the road, followed in 1903 by the famous 'Cities'. It was one of these latter, the *City of Bristol* that worked the up Dutchman, when the two-hour non-stop run from Bristol to Paddington was inaugurated, and it continued doing so daily for some weeks afterwards. It was not on the Dutchman itself however that the City class engines won their lasting fame. In July 1903 His Majesty King George V, when Prince of Wales, paid a visit to the West Country, and three saloons for the Royal party were attached to the first portion of the Cornishman. Only two coaches were run for ordinary passengers, but as 'a good run' had been asked for in high quarters, a compartment was reserved for two influential 'railway-acs', as they were then called: the Rev W. J. Scott, and Charles Rous-Marten, a technical journalist of international fame. The *City of Bath* engine was put on to the job, and her crew obliged with 'a good run' in very truth. With the modest load, totalling about 130 tons behind the tender, they passed Exeter, 193·6 miles from Paddington, via the Bristol avoiding line, in 172¼ minutes, having averaged 67·4 mph from the start; and by running the curving and severely graded 52 miles on to Plymouth in 61 minutes made a record time of 233¼ minutes from Paddington.

At the time of this run the recently inaugurated two-hour sprint of the up Dutchman from Bristol to Paddington was considered to be really 'something', even though the semi-Royal train of July 1903 passed abreast of Temple Meads station, on the avoiding line, in a little less than 1¾ hours from London. This latter was considered to be a very special once-in-a-way achievement. It was a feeling, nevertheless, that did not last for long, because the year 1904 saw the climax of the exciting competition with the London and South Western Railway in connection with the Ocean liner traffic from Plymouth. The rival company took the passengers, and the Great Western the mails. Before the contest was over the engines that had won their spurs in working The Flying Dutchman had made speed records that lasted for thirty years. The Dean 4-2-2 singles *Wilkinson*, *Duchess of Albany* and *Sir Richard Grenville*, together with the cities, *Exeter* and *Gloucester* all built up the tradition of breathless haste, until, on 9 May 1904 the *City of Truro* became the first locomotive anywhere in the world to be accurately recorded, by Charles Rous-Marten, at 100 mph (or perhaps a fraction over); while later in the same journey the 4-2-2 single *Duke of Connaught* took the train from Bristol (Pylle Hill Junction) to Paddington in 99¾ minutes.

But I must return to the Dutchman itself, of which, after 1904, only the eastbound run remained in recognisable form; and by that time Mr Churchward's large standard engines were coming upon the scene. And there was an important change in the working. In broad gauge days the famous 8 ft 4-2-2 engines did not work beyond Newton Abbot. The ugly 4-4-0 saddle tank engines of the South Devon Railway took over, and the tradition of an engine-change at Newton Abbot continued into the earliest standard gauge days. The beautiful Dean 4-2-2 single-wheelers would not have been much use on the fearful inclines of the South Devon line. But the 4-4-0s of the 'Atbara' and 'City' classes worked through to Plymouth, and the stops at Newton Abbot became purely for traffic purposes rather than engine changing, and often the addition of extra coaches from the Torquay line. With large 4-6-0 locomotives available for its haulage the up Dutchman became a progressively heavier train. It originated at the one-time South Devon Railway terminus at the Millbay station in Plymouth at 8.35 am, climbed laboriously up to the through station at North Road, and then ran non-stop to Newton Abbot.

Meanwhile with the introduction of the large 10-wheeled locomotives, 'Atlantics' as well as 4-6-0s, and the three 4-cylinder compounds imported from France, through engine working between London and Plymouth became the rule, rather than the exception. But in the early 1900s while there were an increasing number of the rather gaunt, high stepping, new outside-cylinder locomotives to be seen outside the sheds at the Laira, as the Dutchman got away from Plymouth on its eastbound run, there were still plenty of glittering polished brass domes among the ranks of engines being prepared for the road. Many of the newcomers were at first unnamed; but then gradually they blossomed forth with titles from the Waverley novels, Ladies of history and fiction, and later, to emphasise the impeccable character and sterling qualities of the new engines, Saints and Stars! The parts of them that could be burnished were 'got up' as brilliantly as ever were the great domes of old, while the traffic department finding there was by that time power, and to spare, did not neglect to pile on the coaches behind them.

Far behind were the days when the up Dutchman was limited to six coaches on its fast run from Bristol to Paddington. It now left Plymouth

The Lightning, *standard gauge express locomotive used on the Flying Dutchman, seen here in the engine yard at Exeter.*

with at least that number, while at Newton Abbot it not only attached a substantial section from the Torquay line but two slip coach portions. The main part of the train would be running non-stop over the 142·9 miles from Taunton to Paddington, via the new route, but slip coaches were detached at both Westbury and Reading, giving an excellent service up from the West Country. The new route, as well as providing a notably quicker service, gave a pleasant change in scenery, from the Athelney marshes, and the eastern ridges of the Mendip hills, to the northern slopes of Salisbury Plain, the Vale of Pewsey, and then over Savernake Forest to the Kennet Valley. If one cared to look out of the right hand window to watch the detaching of the slip coach at Westbury, then looking from the rear there was the superb prospect of the White Horse, on the steep slopes of Bratton Down. The Great Western named one of the Dean 4-2-2 singles *White Horse*, but that was in honour of the most ancient of them all, the symbolical figure on the flank of the downs by Uffington, seen from the original route of The Flying Dutchman. The post-1906 eastbound train passed within sight of a second White Horse in the Vale of Pewsey; but this second one, seen to the north of the line after passing the one-time junction of Patney is comparatively modern, having been cut in the downland turf as recently as 1812. The one on Bratton Down is believed to have been first cut about a thousand years ago!

In the years between the two world wars, when the locomotive department of the Great Western was 'hitting the headlines' with the achievements of its new 'Castle' and 'King' class 4-6-0s the up Dutchman had become a very heavy train. It was the return working for the engine that had gone down the previous day on the Cornish Riviera Express, and was manned by the most elite of top-link drivers and firemen. By the year 1938 the Dutchman was allowed no more than 145 minutes to cover the 142·9 miles from Taunton to Paddington, and the Reading slip coach was due to arrive in 108 minutes, (106·9 miles from Taunton). When the train was restored to a semblance of its pre-war speed, in 1947, the Westbury slip coach was not re-instated, but a stop was made there instead, though the slip-coach at Reading was restored. The total scheduled running time from Taunton to Paddington was 168 minutes, and it was on that timing that the competing engines from other regions were tested in the locomotive interchange trials made by the newly-established Railway Executive, after nationalisation of the British Railways, in 1948. It was incidental rather than intentional that such visiting celebrities as the LNER streamlined 'A4' Pacifics, the Stanier 'Duchess' class Pacifics of the LMS, and the remarkable air-smoothed 'Merchant Navy' class of the Southern should have been called upon to work a train with such historic associations as the up Dutchman; and as strangers

The Flying Dutchman too heavy for one engine. One of the Dean 7 ft 8 in 4-2-2s piloted by a 2-2-2 No. 1124 at Paddington.

to the route much of the running they made was not representative of the best they could do.

Some years after the trauma of the trials themselves, when the controversy over the official report published later had died down, I had two runs on this famous train with Great Western engines that between them surpassed anything done in the heat of the competition in 1948. The first was with the last but one of all the 'Castle' class engines to be built, No. 7036 *Taunton Castle*, and the circumstances were unusual, right from the start. Laira shed normally had a 'King' class engine for the Dutchman, because it was one of their hardest turns; but on the previous day I had ridden down from Paddington on the footplate of the *Taunton Castle* and she was in such superb form that the London driver and fireman, who would be taking the Dutchman next morning, asked for her again, instead of a 'King', even though they were warned that the load would be fourteen coaches from Newton Abbot. What no one down at Plymouth knew that morning was that there would be yet another coach to be added at Taunton; and, when having made a splendid run up from Newton they drew in, the locomotive foreman at Taunton had a second engine ready to couple on to assist, because he felt that 'fifteen' would be more than a 'Castle' could manage. But the London driver and firemen had such confidence in the *Taunton Castle* that they disdained any help, and went on their way with the enor-

11

mous load of 535 tons. If one recalls that when, in 1903, the up Dutchman was accelerated to a two-hour non-stop run from Bristol to Paddington the load varied between 150 and 175 tons the task set to the *Taunton Castle* will be better appreciated; and they ran ahead of time all the way to Paddington!

Despite the consistently heavy load of this train a total of nine minutes was cut from the time schedule of this train by 1953, and I had the privilege of a footplate pass to see how it was done, with engine No. 6023 *King Edward II*, hauling a load of 500 tons as far as Reading, where we detached a two-coach slip portion. By then we had gained seven minutes on the *new* schedule, with a lovely engine and an expert Plymouth crew. There was plenty of fast running, and while we bowled smoothly along I thought of that visitor of more than sixty years earlier who was so affected by the severe vibration of the old broad gauge engine, and had to hang on tight at anything of a curve. On the *King Edward II* so far as speed was concerned the high-spot came in the descent of the Wellington bank, just after the line has passed, in the Whiteball Tunnel, from Devon into Somerset. As usual when riding on Great Western locomotives I was standing in the left hand corner of the cab, and with the engine riding so smoothly that I had no need to touch the cab-side for support, we reached and sustained a top speed of 92 mph. This was indeed a thrilling memory of the Dutchman in its last years of steam haulage: *The Flying Dutchman* indeed!

2

THE NORFOLK COAST EXPRESS

In the general upsurge in growth of population in Great Britain in the Victorian era there were many examples of what could be called 'new towns'. Some were purely industrial, like the one where my father's business was for many years, Barrow-in-Furness; others like Blackpool were created purely for pleasure, but on the northern coast of Norfolk there was one, the origins of which were more subtle , perhaps to use a Victorian word, more genteel. This was Cromer, which a writer in one of the earliest volumes of *The Railway Magazine* called 'The goal of the Great Eastern crack express'. The railway to it had not been opened until 1876, and then it was only a local branch line; at that time it was no more than a pretty village, perched on the top of the cliffs in the heart of what is sometimes called 'Poppyland'. But it so happened that a journalist who contributed to *The Daily Telegraph* discovered it, and started writing of its rural charms. What finally put Cromer on the map was when he broke into verse with 'The Garden of Sleep'. Set to music it became the most popular ballad of the day, and it is related how soulful tenors told how:

> 'On the grass of the cliff,
> At the edge of the steep
> God planted a garden,
> The Garden of sleep.'

By that time the little East Norfolk Railway had been absorbed into the Great Eastern, and that company, with characteristic enterprise, began to develop the holiday potential of the coast of which the poets sang. The outcome was that in the summer of 1897, a special Cromer express was put on, leaving London, Liverpool Street at 1.30 pm and running the 131 miles to North Walsham non-stop in 160 minutes. This station is only 8¼ miles short of Cromer, and the stop was made to provide a connection to the developing little resort of Mundesley, to which a branch line was then being constructed. Cromer itself was reached at 4.25 pm at an overall average speed of 47½ mph. There was a corresponding train that left Cromer at 1 pm and ran at the same speed non-stop from North Walsham to Liverpool Street. They ran only from July to September, and from their first introduction were in every way the show trains of the Great Eastern Railway. It was remarkable that on a railway serving such well-established and populous centres as Colchester, Cambridge, Ipswich and Norwich that such preferential treatment should have been given to 'The Garden of Sleep', quite apart from the Royal Mail Service to the Continent, via Harwich. Even when first put on it was no lightweight either. Its minimum formation consisted of six 6-wheeled coaches, three bogie 8-wheelers, and a four wheeled luggage van, weighing with passengers and luggage about 180 tons. In that very first summer however its popularity was already such that it sometimes loaded to no less than 17 vehicles, at that time all non-corridor.

The Locomotive Department of the Great Eastern Railway was then in the charge of James Holden, and by 1897 he had done much to replace many of the old, heterogeneous designs that had originated from the constitutent companies with new standard types, and had between 1886 and 1897 built no fewer than 110 of a good, workmanlike 2-4-0 design, with 7 ft diameter coupled wheels. But he built also twenty further engines having the same machinery and design of boiler, but with only a single pair of driving wheels, thus of the 2-2-2 type. The second batch of these engines built in 1892 had boilers carrying a higher steam pressure of 160 lb per sq in, against 140 in the earlier batch. Now one would have thought that with relatively heavy trains, to be worked over a route that included many stiff gradients, a locomotive of the 2-4-0 type, with greater weight available for adhesion, would be preferable to a 2-2-2. But this was evidently not thought to be so on the Great Eastern, because after use of a 2-4-0 on the inaugural trip of the London–North Walsham non-stop run, six of the 2-2-2s with the higher boiler pressure were specially allocated to the job, and had it to themselves for the first summer of its operation.

There was another factor to be accounted for. The tenders fitted to the Holden express locomotives carried no more than 2640 gallons of water, and this would not have been nearly enough for a non-stop run of 130 miles. The longest that had been made prior to the introduction of the Cromer expresses had been the 69 mile run of the Continental boat trains from Liverpool Street to Parkeston Quay, Harwich. So it was necessary to install water troughs, and this was done at two locations, one on the London side of Ipswich tunnel, and the second near Tivetshall, about 100 miles from Liverpool Street. While this might have been thought an expensive solution for the benefit of no more than one train in each direction, and moreover running for only three months in the year, and the fitting of water scoops

Engine of the type used on the Cromer Express when first introduced. Great Eastern 2-2-2 No. 1000, built at Stratford Works in 1893.

on the tenders of the engines specially allocated to the Cromer trains, it later became a general facility that was of value on trains whereon the locomotives worked through from London to Norwich, or Yarmouth. It avoided the need for taking water at one of the intermediate stations and saved the time thus involved.

When the Cromer trains were first put on the six crack 2-2-2 express locomotives set aside for the duty were divided between Ipswich and Norwich sheds, and this arrangement, and the method of manning them remained unchanged during the entire life of the Norfolk Coast Express, as it was later named, and through four generations of locomotives. In more recent times the practice of enginemen working what are called 'lodging turns' in which they had to spend a night, or nights away from their home station became unpopular to the extent of leading to at least one strike in protest; but at the time the Cromer expresses were first put on it was considered a prestige duty, at any rate so far as Ipswich and Norwich sheds were concerned. Each of the six 'star' engines had their own crews, and no other, and they worked the train every third week. On Mondays, Wednesdays and Fridays the duties were as below, and reversed on the following three days.

IPSWICH ENGINE AND MEN	NORWICH ENGINE AND MEN
10 am Ipswich to Liverpool Street	9.5 am Norwich to Cromer
1.30 pm Liverpool Street to Cromer	1 pm Cromer to Liverpool Street
5.30 pm Cromer to Norwich	5.30 pm Liverpool Street to Ipswich
Lodge at Norwich	Lodge at Ipswich

It was a long day for the men, but the mileage was only 230·8. The timings remained unchanged until the end of the 1914 summer season. The Norfolk Coast Express was not restored to its North Walsham non-stop run after the first world war.

The booked running times of the train, which remained unchanged during the eighteen summer seasons that the North Walsham non-stop run was in operation were as follows:

Distance Miles		Time (Down) min	Av. Speed mph	Time (Up) min	Av. Speed mph
0·0	Liverpool Street	0	—	159	30·0
4·0	Stratford	9	26·6	151	51·5
10·0	Chadwell Heath	16	51·5	144	61·2
20·2	Shenfield	29	47·1	134	51·9
29·7	Chelmsford	39	57·0	123	53·4
38·6	Witham	49	53·4	113	52·5
51·7	Colchester	64	52·5	98	46·7
59·5	Manningtree	73	52·0	88	46·0
68·7	Ipswich	83	55·1	76	59·5
80·6	Stowmarket	97	51·0	64	69·0
82·9	Haughley	100	46·0	62	55·6
100·5	Tivetshall	120	52·8	43	42·6
114·0	Trowse	134	57·9	24	16·0
114·8	Wensum Junction	137	16·0	21	43·7
130·1	North Walsham	158	43·7	0	—

In studying the foregoing times it must also be borne in mind that there were permanent speed restrictions – to 20 mph at Stratford, 30 mph at Chelmsford, 40 mph at Colchester, 25 mph at Ipswich, 15 mph through Trowse and over the swingbridge at Wensum Junction, and finally 35 mph at Wroxham, where single line working began. Furthermore, the Chadwell Heath to Shenfield section included the formidable Brentwood bank, where speed usually fell to less than 30 mph, while it needed a vigorous acceleration from that 25 mph through Ipswich to make an average of 51 mph onwards to Stowmarket, all gradually uphill. The only stretch where one could go hard without any interruption was indeed between Ipswich and Trowse, and even then there were gradients to be surmounted. It was anything but a straightforward run, and remarkable that it should have been worked by engines of the 2-2-2 and 4-2-2 types in its early days.

No less surprising were the loads that were sometimes conveyed. When Mr Holden's large 4-2-2 engines with 18 in by 26 in cylinders had taken the place of his earlier 2-2-2s, and the middle section of the train consisting of 8-wheeled bogie coaches had included a dining car, the maximum loads in the summers of 1899 and 1900 sometimes totalled up to more than 270 tons, made up of twelve 6-wheelers, four bogie corridor 8-wheelers and a four-wheeled fruit van. To the select band of enginemen to whom the working of the train was entrusted it was a point of honour to keep time, no matter how severe the loading, or the running circumstances; and no matter what transpired no driver would dream of asking for an assistant engine. Other Great Eastern trains might be double-headed, but never the special Cromer express! The engine livery was gorgeous in itself, so much so as to lead one dedicated enthusiast to suggest that it was really a bit gaudy. The basic colour was a rich 'Royal blue' lined out in red, but there was plenty of extra adornment in polished brass and copper work, and the 2-2-2 engines stationed at Ipswich and Norwich were the first Great Eastern locomotives to carry the Company's coat of arms on their driving wheel splashers. This practice was continued on the large 4-2-2s that succeeded them in 1898.

As the turn of the century drew near the Great Eastern Railway had perforce to think of still bigger trains, especially in the height of the holiday season. At that age in railway development it was hardly fair that while a

One of the Claud Hamilton class 4-4-0s which had a notable record of performance on the Norfolk Coast Express. This one, No. 1802, is seen on the Cambridge line near Audley End.

few passengers paying the standard third class fare should be accommodated in relatively palatial bogie corridor carriages with access to a restaurant car, the majority had to be packed like sardines into little jogging non-corridor six-wheelers. It was not only third class passengers who were denied the comforts of corridor stock. At its maximum loading the Cromer express had two all-first class six-wheelers in its formation, and one six-wheeled composite, and a six-wheeled composite brake van. The Cromer expresses were however fortunate in having *any* corridor coaches in their normal rake. The Continental boat trains between Liverpool Street and Harwich were made up entirely of six-wheelers, and until 1898 the only trains that had any restaurant car accommodation were the North Country Continentals running between Harwich and York. But with larger carriages being built at Stratford Works and the call for increased luxury on long distance trains it was clearly necessary to plan for larger locomotives. The only trouble was that the Great Eastern, unlike the major railways going north from London, had a long distance passenger traffic that was markedly seasonal, making its major demands upon locomotive tractive power for only a few months in the year.

However advantageous from the advertising and publicity aspects the principal express passenger services, particularly those confined to the summer holiday season, represented a source of revenue that was a very small proportion of the total traffic receipts of the Great Eastern Railway. It carried great quantities of agricultural produce from all parts of East Anglia; it brought coal from the South Yorkshire and Nottingham pits, fish from Yarmouth and Lowestoft, while its short distance commuter traffic in East London was prodigious. Among other railways it had the homely nickname of 'Sweedy'. Yet for all that bigger passenger engines were needed, and James Holden having the very talented designer F. V. Russell on his staff at Stratford, set him to work out the design and details of a 4-4-0 that should have the same size of driving wheels as the single-wheeler. In using this latter description I am always reminded of the puzzlement it once caused to a perspicacious sub-editor dealing with one of my earlier books, who could not understand how there could be locomotives with only a single wheel! With an almost lifelong familiarity with the term that signified a locomotive with a single pair of driving wheels one is inclined to forget how odd it could sound to a non-technical mind.

Russell's new engine was completed at Stratford Works on St Patrick's Day, March 17 1900, and was numbered 1900 in honour of the new century. Like the 'singles' it had 7 ft diameter driving wheels but larger cylinders, and a considerably larger boiler. It was named *Claud Hamilton* in honour of the Chairman of the Company, and was the first of a large and very successful class. The running number allocated to the locomotive was a handsome gesture to the new century, but it gave a misleading impression of the total stock. At that time the Company owned only about a thousand locomotives all told, and as if to make amends for this deception when further engines of the 'Claud Hamilton' class were built they were numbered in reverse order, downwards from 1899. Numerology apart they were extremely successful. With larger cylinders than the 4-2-2s and a higher boiler pressure they were capable of very hard work, and while the 'singles' when extended to their utmost were able to run the special Cromer expresses to time, with loads up to 270 tons, the 'Claud Hamilton' class 4-4-0s did equally well with up to 400 tons.

All the same it would seem that the new engines were accepted with some reluctance by the top link men at both Ipswich and Norwich. The *élite* crews at both sheds had developed a positively loving affection for the big 4-2-2 singles, and with the 'Claud Hamiltons' of the 1890–1899 series arriving while the summer non-stop running to North Walsham was in progress the existing links were left largely unchanged. It was only in the following summer, when another eight new engines were sent to be divided between Norwich and Ipswich that the single-wheelers were finally displaced and transferred elsewhere. Even then one gathered that it needed some persuasion to get the senior Ipswich driver, 'Chuffy' Cage, to give up his 'single' No. 12 and take instead a new 'Claud Hamilton' No. 1881. It was not long however before he and the other drivers in the Cromer link were doing exceedingly fine work with their new engines. For a time some of them, like their predecessors of the 2-2-2 and 4-2-2 types, were oil fired; but this practice was discontinued in the early 1900s when the price of the oil rose over the economic limit for railway operation in that era.

The 'Claud Hamilton' class engines were very strong and capable of getting away with a big load, but they were not notably free running, as compared with some of their contemporaries on other railways, and they rarely attained maximum speeds of much over 70 mph. It was not necessary, nor indeed desirable on the Great Eastern Railway. In their pioneer days the constituent companies had mostly been short of capital, and the lines had been built as cheaply as possible, following the lie of the land with frequent changes of gradient to avoid expensive earthworks in the form of deep cuttings and high embankments; but worse than that was the rather scant attention given to the formation of the roadbed. The component parts of the permanent way, the rails themselves, and the sleepers were sound enough, and of the standard excellent quality general on the railways of Great Britain by the early 1900s; but the foundations were not so substantial nor the drainage so effective as on some other railways, and this led to

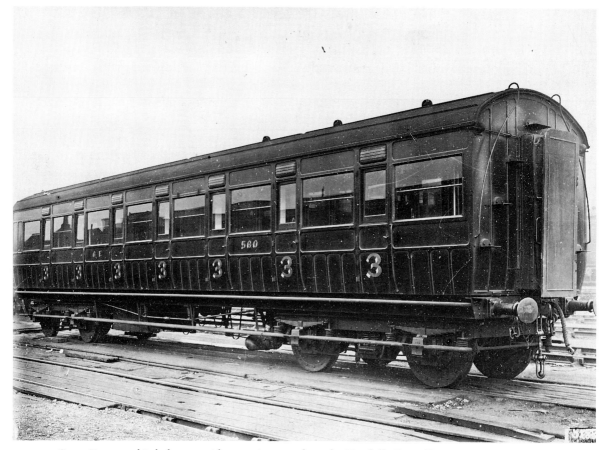

Great Eastern third class corridor carriage used on the Norfolk Coast Express.

rough and unsteady riding at times, though the 'Claud Hamilton' engines were inherently good in themselves.

The number of permanent speed restrictions on the line to Cromer has already been mentioned. The engines rode so well, and recovered so quickly from a lurch due to bad track that the more experienced drivers certainly turned a blind eye to the official limits laid down in certain places, especially where they could be reasonably sure that no one was looking! They would not, for example, exceed the 25 mph imposed at Ipswich, where some senior official might be about, and still less the 15 mph over the Wensum swing bridge on the outskirts of Norwich. But it was another matter altogether at places like Chelmsford and Colchester. A railwayman from another department riding on the footplate for the first time has recalled how he was nearly shot sideways out of the cab when they went through Colchester at

Interior of the first class dining car: note the fine table-linen and cutlery, and anti-macassars on the leather padded seats.

nearly 60 mph instead of the prescribed 40, though apparently a passage through Chelmsford at a full 60, instead of the ultra-cautious limit of 30 mph (!) was not so bad.

Extension of the facilities provided by the special summer 'Cromer Express' began in 1898, when the branch line from North Walsham to Mundesley was opened; but the later development that led to the change in name of the train came in 1906, when the so-called 'Cromer spur line' was opened, giving access to the coastal resorts of West Runton and Sheringham. With the through carriages added for both Mundesley and Sheringham, and the former extended along the coast to Overstrand – 'The Garden of Sleep' – the name of the train became 'The Norfolk Coast Express'. This was appropriately followed in the 1907 summer season by the provision of entirely new corridor stock for the whole train, giving all passengers access to the restaurant cars. The new trains which had a basic make-up of twelve coaches, provided a finely uniform external appearance, in contrast to the mixture previously presented, of flat roofed six-wheelers, some elliptical roofed bogie stock, and a clerestory roofed dining car to which no more than a few of the passengers could reach. The make-up of the new trains, all of bogie, elliptical-roofed corridor stock was as follows:

> Brake van and third class
> Two all-third class coaches
> Third class restaurant car
> Kitchen car
> First class restaurant car
> First class coach
> Brake van
>
> All the above for Cromer. Then:
> Composite coach, part first, part third
> Brake van and third class
>
> For West Runton and Sheringham
> And finally:
> Composite coach, part first, part third
> Brake van and third class
>
> For Mundesley and Overstrand

The tare weight of the standard twelve coaches was 312 tons, but as previously mentioned, with extras added bringing the load sometimes up to fifteen, the total tonnage to be hauled by the locomotives was sometimes nearly 400 tons. Lunch, I may add, in either first or third class car was half-a-crown, with children at half price!

The route of The Norfolk Coast Express is not one of the most striking scenically on the British railways; but in any case the charm of the counties Essex and Suffolk is not 'worn on their sleeves', as the saying goes. As a lover of John Constable's art I can well appreciate that the delicate beauty of the scenes he so brilliantly portrayed is scarcely to be noticed from an express train passing nearby at 60 mph. There are moments, as when passing beside the estuary of the Stour at Manningtree where one's imagination is roused by the nearness of the sea, while the perambulation of the Norwich avoiding line and the crossing of the swing bridge give a chance to see the splendid spire of Norwich Cathedral. North of Stowmarket, the divergence of the line to the west at Haughley Junction, taken by the North Country Continental boat express reminds me of the nearness of a place that strangely gave its name to a Great Western locomotive. Except for the pioneer unit of the class that worked The Norfolk Coast Express for so many years the Great Eastern did not name its engines; and just as well some might add, for when a systematised form of nomenclature is adopted and a class runs to more than one hundred, there can be some oddities.

Well, the Great Western having had its quota of 'Courts' and 'Abbeys', and currently in process of building 'Castles', then required a patronymic for a new class of fast mixed traffic 4-6-0s; and having had their fill of the upper echelon of stately homes with a series of 'Courts' lighted next upon 'Halls'. Now these locomotives were very successful, and their total soon extended far beyond the first century. The topographical records of the West Country and Wales were scoured for more names, and eventually the search extended to North East Yorkshire and the Lake District. I had always been mildly amused at these far-ranging titles, and wondered if the 'spotters' who delighted in ticking off in their notebooks, as seen, some of these remote residences had any idea where they actually were; and then, in the course of some ramblings near Bury St Edmunds, I came across Hengrave Hall. It rang a bell in one niche of my multi-tracked mind, and when I got home I confirmed that there was indeed a Great Western engine named thus, No. 5970. How Swindon latched on to Hengrave Hall I cannot say for certain, although the connection may have originated thus. Despite its vast production of steam locomotives Swindon was still an essentially country town, and many Great Western men taking a leaf out of the book of their great Chief Mechanical Engineer, G. J. Churchward, were keen gardeners and horticulturalists; and when the Drawing Office was seeking desperately round for more 'Halls' some fruit grower amongst them may have recalled that the greengage was 'invented' at Hengrave Hall. It was quite accidental, and would not have occurred if the owner of the property, a man named Gage had not lost the label of one of the plum trees he had imported from France. The fruit when it came was of a fine green colour, and his gardeners for want of any other name called it a green Gage after their master.

The end of the line for the main section of the Norfolk Coast Express once moved that great locomotive historian, E. L. Ahrons, to one of his many witticisms. 'The Cromer district,' he wrote, 'is one of England's beauty spots, where a peaceful holiday may be spent with advantage. The Great Eastern station stands somewhat outside the town, and is perched upon the top of a hill, to which only a psalmist or a member of an Alpine club could do justice. The beauties of its situation – for it really commands a very fine view – appeal with special force to the weary traveller who wishes to catch a train there on a hot day, with somewhat limited time for the process. I suppose its position could not be helped, since the structural make-up of the scenery absolutely precluded any suitable gradient for a descent into the town, so that the Great Eastern must often have cast longing eyes on the low-lying station of its Midland and Great Northern rivals, whose line reaches Cromer along the coast from the West.' Today however all is changed. Trains from the Norwich direction take the Cromer spur on which the Sheringham through coaches from the Norfolk Coast Express used to travel, and they get to the bottom of the hill and make a near 'U' turn to the right to terminate in the one-time M & G N station. The old Great Eastern station on the hill top is now no more.

The last phase in the history of The Norfolk Coast Express, when haulage was taken over by the new superheated 4-6-0s of the '1500' class lasted for only two years; for although these engines were first introduced in 1912 the six allocated to the Cromer link were not completed at Stratford until the early months of 1913, and the train itself did not run again after the summer season of 1914. The introduction of the new engines was marked by tragedy, less than a fortnight after the service had begun, when the up train came into collision with a light engine at Colchester. It has always been a matter of surprise to me as to why the express engine, No. 1506, came to suffer so severely. The light engine, a standard Holden mixed traffic 2-4-0 had been halted some distance ahead of the station, prior to shunting back, and had been forgotten by the signalman. Its driver, when he saw the signals lowered for the express, sent his fireman back to give warning, and started away ahead. But the express came through, crashed into him and its engine turned over on its right hand side. Although it should have been obeying the 40 mph speed restriction through Colchester station, and although the light engine was moving away, the crash was of such severity that the express engine was a 'write-off' and its driver and fireman were both killed. A guard travelling in the front van was also killed, but there were no casualties among the many passengers travelling in the train.

The '1500' class 4-6-0s were excellent engines. In appearance they looked like an elongated version of the later varieties of the 'Claud Hamiltons', with all features of the outward design style faithfully reproduced. But technically they represented a big advance in engineering practice, with boilers incorporating a superheater, a larger firegate, and piston valves vertically above the cylinders instead of the traditional Stratford arrangement of slide valves underneath the cylinders. They represented not only a notable increase in nominal tractive power, but greater thermal efficiency and reduced coal consumption by use of superheated steam. But although finely proportioned and impressive locomotives they were actually not so large as they might appear. The very large cab helped to create this illusion. In any case engine designing at Stratford had always to be done with a watchful eye on the weight. Great Eastern track imposed severe limitations upon the loads that could be carried; and while at about the same time the Crewe drawing office was designing for the London and North Western Railway a 4-6-0 that would have an adhesion weight of 59 tons, the most Stratford could put on to the three coupled axles of the '1500' class was 44 tons. But within certain limitations they did splendid work from the outset.

On the Norfolk Coast Express the big summer loads that had taxed the capacity of the 'Claud Hamilton' 4-4-0s – and their firemen! – to their limit were tackled with relative ease, and although no acceleration of the service was planned, beyond indeed that which had remained unchanged since 1897, there was far more margin in reserve. Nevertheless those large cabs, that looked so commodious and comfortable were not an altogether un-mixed blessing, especially to a third man riding on the footplate. I had a short ride from Colchester to Ipswich on one of them, in later years, and inside the cab the splasher over the rear pair of coupled wheels was covered

Post-1918 successor to the Norfolk Coast Express: the Cromer Express of 1922 climbing the Brentwood bank, hauled by one of the 4-6-0 locomotives.

by a large tool box; and to keep out of the fireman's way I had to sit on this with my legs dangling in the direct line of the fire! Great Eastern men had become used to those long cabs on the 'Claud Hamiltons'; but in later years when the old railway had become a part of the London and North Eastern system, and larger engines were designed for use in East Anglia, some of the '1500' class 4-6-0s, surplus to requirements were transferred to Aberdeen for use on the former Great North of Scotland line up to Elgin.

This also was a route over which there were severe limitations upon axle loading. The ex-Great Eastern engines were ideal, in providing some badly needed additional tractive power; but on the footplate the Scottish engine-men were at first quite at sea. They were used to small, very compact 4-4-0s, on which the fireman could take a charge of coal from the tender, and in a single movement swing round and deliver it through the firehole door. On the '1500' class the firedoor was a long way ahead, and the firemen had to take two or three steps forward in order to reach it. The engines became nicknamed the 'Hikers' in consequence. This yarn is however taking the story very many years ahead of the great days of the Norfolk Coast Express. It was never revived after the first war. The London–North Walsham non-stop run was operated for a time by certain week-end relief trains in the height of the summer, but today, in what is sometimes called 'The age of the train' poor Cromer gets no more than a few crumbs from the rich man's (Norwich's) table, in the form of 'second class only' multiple unit diesel sets. The fastest service from London now takes 3 hours 16 minutes compared to the 2 hours 55 minutes of the Norfolk Coast Express prevailing from 1897 to 1914. Oh dear!

3

THE SOUTHERN BELLE

November the first, 1908: a day of golden late autumn sunshine, and beneath the elegant, still-new glass roof of the enlarged Victoria station stands a train claimed by the London Brighton and South Coast Railway as the most luxurious in the world – 'The Southern Belle'. It is due to leave on its inaugural run, non-stop to Brighton at eleven o'clock. For some years previously Pullman cars have been run on the Brighton expresses, and on Sundays there was a whole train of them; but this was the first occasion that a daily service had been initiated, weekdays and Sundays alike. And what a train! There were seven cars only in the beautiful dark brown and cream livery of the Pullman Car Company, all twelve-wheelers, and although first class only the return fare from London to Brighton, 102 miles of luxurious travel was, believe it or not, just twelve shillings. Handsome though the train was outside, with each car bearing an individual name, like some gracious ship, the interiors would be breathtaking to those now used to the spartan uniformity of the HSTS.

When the London and North Western Railway were building a new Royal Train King Edward VII was asked how he would like the interior of his private saloon decorated, and he replied simply 'Make it like a yacht'. The same elegant treatment might well have been applied to the cars of The Southern Belle, all of which were different from each other. At opposite ends of the train were two cars, named the *Verona* and the *Albert*, which had brake compartments, and like the rest of the train the seating was quite unlike first class. It consisted entirely of armchairs, casually arranged, but nevertheless seating 31 passengers in each car. The cabinet work was in so-called wainscot oak and holly, in the style of the French Renaissance period, and the chair and sofa coverings were in a fine mohair velvet of a light coffee colour. The carpets and blinds were in shades of green. In the middle of the train was the buffet car, named *Grosvenor*, which had seating for 25. Whether they were allowed to travel in it for the entire journey I do not know, but the decor was certainly attractive enough to make one linger.

Brighton express locomotive power before the Southern Belle: a Stroudley 2-2-2 Hurstmonceaux in the celebrated yellow livery.

This car was decorated in the Adam style with woodwork in Spanish mahogany, rich inlaid with satinwood. The easy chairs and settees were upholstered in green morocco leather, while the pile carpets were in shades of soft green, with a 'fleur-de-lys' pattern. The blinds, which could be drawn for the final homeward run at 5·45 pm from Brighton, were of green damask silk. Two of the parlour cars, the *Bessborough* and the *Princess Helen*, each seating 33 passengers, were also decorated in the Adam style, with colour scheme and appointments similar to the buffet car *Grosvenor*; it is rather amusing nevertheless to find in more than one of the rather fulsome contemporary descriptions of these cars that the decorative style is referred to as the "Adams", in the plural. I suppose that to a railway orientated mind the name of the former locomotive engineer of the neighbouring London and South Western Railway would register more readily than that of the exquisite artistry of Robert Adam, in architecture as well as interior decoration.

The other two cars of the original Southern Belle of 1908, the *Cleopatra* and the *Belgravia*, were parlour cars decorated in the style of Michele Angelo Pergolesi, a devoted admirer, collaborator, and follower of the style of Robert Adam. In these two Pullmans the wood was of East Indian satinwood, with quartered panels inlaid with grey sycamore, boxwood, greenwood and tulipwood. The easy chairs and settees were upholstered in a closely mohair velvet, of 'fleur-de-lys' design in shades of blue, with a

28

delicate tracery of gold showing through the velvet pile. The deep pile carpets were in shades of deep rose. One might feel some regret that the journey time of this lovely train lasted only one hour, though one can be fairly sure that few of its patrons paid much attention to the incidentals of the journey. One is reminded of one such, when the first passenger alarm system was installed, pulling the communication cord and stopping the train. When the guard arrived to find out what the matter was this super-first class passenger merely asked for a whisky and soda! Before leaving for Brighton even the most non-railway minded of those earliest passengers on The Southern Belle could scarcely fail to notice the splendid appearance of the new Victoria station.

A traveller at the latter part of the nineteenth century, sickened by the delays and frustrations at the Victoria of old, might well rub his eyes in sheer disbelief if he had come back ten years later to sample The Southern Belle and witnessed the transformation that had taken place. The old station had certainly been the very personification of railway muddle and ineptitude. In 'Brighton' eyes it always had to play second fiddle to London Bridge, where the headquarters of the Company were, and which handled by far the greater proportion of the London commuter traffic. But with the increasing vogue of taking seaside holidays and the relative nearness of the fashionable and aristocratic districts of Belgravia and Mayfair there was every justification in having Victoria as a far more commodious and efficient terminus than it had ever been. After all, even the most opulent members of society still travelled by train in 1908. It is perhaps not generally known that the London Brighton and South Coast Railway did not own Victoria Station. It was the property of the Victoria Station and Pimlico Company, which had been incorporated in 1858, to build not only a station and its approach lines, but the viaduct over the River Thames to carry the line to Battersea Park. This company had leased half the station to the Brighton Railway, and the other half, from 1861 jointly to the London Chatham and Dover, and strangely enough to the Great Western. It proved a very profitable investment, and for very many years it paid a dividend of 9 per cent on its ordinary shares.

The reconstruction of the Brighton side of the station, which had been completed early in 1908, was on the most lavish scale. It not only more than doubled the floor area of the old station, but included a scientifically laid out arrangement of tracks and platforms that increased the efficiency of traffic operation out of all recognition. The main line platforms were made long enough to accommodate two full-length main line express trains, one behind the other, but with intermediate point connections so that the one nearest to the buffer stops could leave without interfering with one at the outer end, which might then be loading. There is no doubt that main line electrification was prominently in the minds of the Brighton Railway management, and it was on the advice of their celebrated Consulting Electrical Engineer, Sir Philip Dawson, that they adopted the relatively-high-tension alternating current system of traction for their first installation, on the South London line, with overhead wire current collection. This, it was considered, was more suitable for main line work than the third or fourth rail direct current systems then being installed elsewhere. And so The Southern Belle went out of Victoria and across the Thames 'under the wires', and continued so as far as Balham Junction, where the electrified South London diverged eastward to run through Peckham Rye, and so round to London Bridge.

The next stage of the journey across Tooting Common was a favourite haunt of the moving train photographers of the pre-1914 era, before the electrification and all the paraphernalia of overhead wires and their supports was carried southwards from Balham to Croydon. While naturally the expert workers sought to capture the morning run of The Southern Belle, with its full complement of seven Pullman cars, the plates of those days needed careful development. At that hour the sun would be shining directly on the front of the engine, with the wheels all in shadow.

One of the smallest engines to haul the Southern Belle: one of the 'B4' class 4-4-0s by R. J. Billinton here seen at Clapham Junction, on a South Coast express.

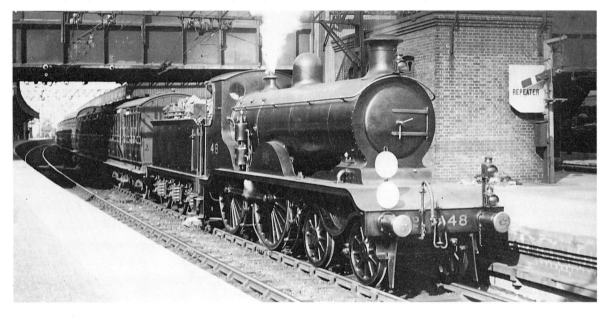

The doyen of moving train photographers, F. E. Mackay, brought this particular technique to perfection, in the many shots he secured of this lovely train, at a place relatively near to his home in Battersea. By afternoon, of course, the lighting was perfect for down trains, and the 3.10 pm Southern Belle, often reduced to no more than four cars on this run, came in a procession of other trains hauled by a galaxy of earlier Brighton locomotive types, ranging from B4 'Scotchmen', 'Grasshoppers', 'Gladstones' and the occasional 'single wheeler'. The striking 'yellow' livery that had endeared them to locomotive enthusiasts had by that time been superseded by the more practical, yet highly distinctive amber, and of course equally well burnished up by the cleaners.

If a passenger had time to stroll up and have a look at the engine before starting he could well be intrigued by the array of visual indicators carried on the lamp irons over the buffer beam. These signified the route that was to be taken, and when the The Southern Belle was inaugurated the code was a great deal more complicated than it was subsequently made. Some of the trains carried square white boards with two horizontal black stripes, but in combination with these were white discs, discs with a black cross, and discs with two small black diamonds. Combinations of all these were sometimes displayed, and how anyone along the line could identify where a particular train was supposed to go baffles the imagination, particularly as there was no easy way of reproducing those signs at night.

Not long after The Southern Belle had started running however a much simpler code was introduced, using only two types of disc, plain white, and white with a black cross and these were replaced after dark by white and green lamps. As there were six places on the front of an engine where lamps or discs could be fixed, by ringing the changes one could produce a large number of route indications. There were in fact fifty-two in all. To the uninitiated however the carrying of lamps as well as discs in the day time could be regarded as confusing, because on some locomotives lamps were hung on every available bracket. There are photographs of The Southern Belle with the official daytime code with a disc with a black cross (the hot-cross bun!) over a plain white disc on the two-tier lamp iron over the left hand buffer (looking at the front of the engine), and every other lamp iron occupied by an unlighted lamp. Presumably they were carried there for convenience, because those lamps did not form any part of the headcode. Other photographs showed some of the lamps missing while still more, particularly of the 4-6-2 tanks, showed no lamps at all on the front of the engine. The artist of the Locomotive Publishing Company, whose oil paintings were signed F. Moore, slipped up once over this, when he produced a splendid picture of The Southern Belle in Victoria Station, ready to start, on what was obviously a gloomy winter's day outside. It carried the correct disc code, and a lamp on every available lamp iron; but he showed all those lamps as lighted!

From a junction south of Purley, with the picturesque name of Stoat's Nest, the line as far as Redhill was jointly owned with the South Eastern Railway. It ran through an immensely deep, and steep sided cutting in the chalk of the North Downs, leading to the Merstham tunnel. But the trouble was the trains of one joint owner always seemed to get in the way of one belonging to the other, and eventually things got so bad that the Brighton decided to have a line entirely their own from Stoat's Nest to a point south of Redhill, where they would be clear of the joint ownership. Diverging to the right, the new line ran immediately alongside the old, but on a steeper rising gradient, because just short of Star Lane intermediate signal box it crossed over, giving briefly a quite breathtaking glimpse of the old line, lying so dramatically deep in its own cutting. Even the higher altitude of the new line could not avoid a fairly long tunnel under the crest of the North Downs; but once the summit was topped the train soon began to develop some real speed. Abreast of Redhill it was over 'sixty' for the first time in its journey, and by Horley it would be seventy miles per hour, or more.

Before leaving the neighbourhood of the new avoiding line however, and its references to Stoat's Nest Junction, one cannot pass further down the line without recalling the picturesque names that the Brighton Railway adopted for some of its main line signal boxes. There was one location nearer London that had the delightful name of *Jolly Sailor*, and not much farther to the south was *Windmill Bridge*. The latter lasted until the days of colour-light signals, but in much earlier days *Jolly Sailor* became the prosaic Norwood Junction. Then, near Haywards Heath there was *Folly Hill*, and in the immediate approach to Brighton itself *Lover's Walk*. But the gem of the whole collection was at St Leonards, where the coast line from Brighton converged with the South Eastern line that had come south through Tunbridge Wells. This point was romantically named *Bo-Peep Junction*.

Reverting once more to the trains themselves, the lineside photographers, and the occasional enthusiast who went for the ride just to log the running times and speeds, had no cause to complain of lack of variety in the loco-motives that hauled The Southern Belle. Photographs reproduced in *The Railway Magazine* during the first four years that the train ran show no less than five different classes of express passenger engine on the job. The original Marsh non-superheater 'Atlantics' opened the ball, but very soon the superheated 4-4-2 tank engines of the 'I3' class took turns, and at times the older, but powerful 'B4' class 4-4-0s, of R. J. Billinton, (the 'Scotchmen') worked the train, even with the maximum load of seven Pullmans. Then came the superheater Atlantic tender engines of the '421' class, and finally Earle Marsh's two masterpieces, the 4-6-2 superheater tank engines *Abergavenny* and *Bessborough*. At one time all Brighton passenger engines were named, right down to the humblest 0-6-0 tank; but Earle Marsh did away with all that, and in his time only a handful of main line express engines retained names. The first of the new 4-6-2 tanks of 1912 revived a title carried by one of the old Stroudley 2-2-2s, named in honour of the Marquis of Abergavenny, a former Chairman of the Board, while Lord Bessborough was the reigning Chairman.

Despite these varying ages, and details of design all these different engines appeared to haul The Southern Belle with complete success. The 'B4' 'Scotchmen' would probably have been extended more nearly to their limit than the others, as will be appreciated from the following comparison of the basic dimensions of all five classes. They all had coupled wheels of roughly the same diameter, and the piston stroke was the same at 26 inches. Earle Marsh took advantage of superheating to reduce the boiler pressure, but it is remarkable that no advantage was taken of the higher steaming capacity of the 4-6-2 tank boiler to increase the tractive effort above that of the 'I3' 4-4-2.

SOUTHERN BELLE LOCOMOTIVES

Type	4-4-0	4-4-2	4-4-2T*	4-4-2*	4-6-2T*
Cylinder dia in	19	18½	21	21	21
Boiler Pressure lb per sq in	170	200	160	170	160
Tractive Effort lb	17000	18930	19630	20750	19630

* Superheater engines

From an early date in the working of the train the engine on the 11 am down from Victoria was on the return leg of an interesting round trip. It left Brighton on the 8.45 am up, non-stop to London Bridge, a train that conveyed a high proportion of first-class passengers and was generally known as the 'Stockbrokers' Express'. After arrival at London Bridge the engine went 'light engine', tender first, round the South London line in time to take The Southern Belle back to Brighton. In the early days of the service patronage of the intermediate runs at 1.20 pm up from Brighton, and 3.10 pm returning was often not heavy, and the train was reduced to no more than four cars.

Having rejoined the old line at Earlswood the train, or rather those running it, came under the effects of the marvellous uniformity of gradient engineered by its builder, J. U. Rastrick, who despite carrying the line through hilly country and surmounting three hill ranges so contrived it that the gradient is 1 in 264 throughout the rest of the way to Brighton – either up or down – except for one or two short lengths of still easier inclination. So from our 70 to 75 mph maximum at Horley The Southern Belle climbed to Balcombe Tunnel and then, descending, crossed the great viaduct over the valley of the Sussex Ouse, with its thirty-seven brick arches, 92 ft above the valley below. Sweeping over it at 65 to 70 mph one could be aware of little more than its ornamental stone balustrades, and a fleeting glimpse of the Italianate pavilions, thought to be a contribution by the architect David Mocatta, that mark its beginning and end on each side of the line. But viewed from a distance it is an immensely satisfying man-made contribution to the beautiful Sussex landscape.

The speed reaches its maximum, sometimes nearly 80 mph below Haywards Heath, near Keymer Junction where the line to Lewes and Eastbourne diverges sharply to the left, and by this time the distinctive line of the South Downs is prominent ahead. The line is climbing again to its last summit; but before attaining it there is a long tunnel to be passed through, Clayton. As a very junior schoolboy I had been intrigued by a chance remark by one of my teachers that on the Brighton line there was 'a tunnel long enough to commit a murder in!' This indeed was Clayton, the longest on the Brighton line, 2266 yards to be exact, and its northern end is distinguished by an ornate castellated portal. Travellers by ordinary trains would have no chance of getting more than a fleeting sight of one of its tall octagonal flanking towers, with their ornamental crenellated tops. The actual bore at the entrance is gothic shaped, very much enlarged outward to the face of the brickwork, but what made the tunnel entrance unique was the existence of a cottage, overlooking the railway, and ensconced between the two tall towers. The line is still rising at 1 in 264 throughout the tunnel, and at the summit point, which comes exactly at the southern portal, the speed of the train would not have been much more than 50 mph. After that it is downhill all the way into Brighton.

With the speed rising rapidly again the line leads through beautiful country, of richly wooded coombes and glimpses of the fascinating chalky crests of the South Downs, and that inevitable brightening of the atmosphere as the coast is neared. Near Patcham, if one knew just where to look out for them, there were two closely adjacent windmills on the ridge, nicknamed Jack and Jill; but then came the short bore of Patcham Tunnel, and the brakes were going on for the final approach to Brighton. On some trains a stop was made at Preston Park station, 1¼ miles short of the terminus to detach through carriages for Hove and Worthing, which would be conveyed

One of the large Atlantic engines, introduced by D. Earle Marsh.

The Southern Belle just after Grouping, amid the hill country of the South Downs near Patcham. The engine, Earle Marsh 4-6-2 tank No. 325, formerly named Abergavenny, *has been repainted in the Southern green livery.*

round the Preston spur line, avoiding Brighton station altogether; and then the complications begin in earnest. The happily named Lovers' Walk signal box was passed on the right. This was one of the old Saxby and Farmer type, with the cabin and the locking frame carried high up on stilts, but with the train finally slowing down, attention is drawn to the left hand side of the line, where the Brighton locomotive works were ranged immediately alongside. There was not much to be seen from a passing train however as the factory premises are enclosed by a high wall.

On arrival at Brighton, if one was not in an immediate hurry to leave for the sea front, or the attractions of the famous Pavilion, it was worth while walking back to the outer end of the platform for a look at what were a most unusual, and I believe unique group of signals. Just beyond the confluence of the Lewes branch with the main line, and beside the high wall of the Locomotive Works building, there was a gantry spanning all the tracks, but this was just the penultimate group, leading to the final array at the very entrance to the platforms. It was a little odd to find signals there in any case, because one could justifiably imagine that by that stage in the journey the train was 'there' – home and dry! But that was not all. Five of these lofty semaphores had a 'distant' arm below them, in the ordinary way suggesting that these were the preliminary warnings of yet another signal box ahead. Actually it was a very special use, quite outside the ordinary British code of semaphore signalling indications. The platforms at Brighton Central, like those at Victoria were very long, and it was possible to berth two short trains one behind the other. The home signal arms at the entrance when lowered gave leave to enter, but under caution; if the distant arm also was lowered the line was clear right up to the buffer stops.

Among the many restrictions upon passenger travel of any kind imposed during the first world war, let alone anything suggestive of luxury, The Southern Belle was taken off, and when it was restored afterwards it was but a pale shade of its old self. At first there was little demand for first class Pullman travel, and with few if any third class cars available the accommodation was augmented by adding several ordinary third class coaches, non-corridor at that. Very often in those immediate post-war years one saw the spectacle of a train calling itself The Southern Belle with its third class carriages packed, but with merely a handful of first class passengers in the Pullmans. Very quickly however more third class Pullmans were introduced, and by the summer of 1922 the train was all Pullman again, often loading quite heavily. A normal week-end formation was one of nine cars, but only two of them first class. The appearance of the train was certainly improved from that of 1920-1, but none of the third class cars had a brake compartment in which heavy luggage could be stowed, and it was necessary to run

The pullman car Belgravia, *Southern Belle 1908.*

an ordinary brake van, next to the engine on the down journey. Although there were then seven of the large 'Baltic' tank engines available, the Marsh 'Atlantics', both superheated and otherwise were used frequently, and appeared to do just as well as the six-coupled engines.

In a different age however The Southern Belle never regained its old character; and with Grouping and the disappearance of the characteristic Brighton engine livery it was only another step towards the replacement of the old stalwarts, and eventually to electrification. It is good to recall however that while the 'Baltic' tanks were rebuilt as tender engines and moved elsewhere the 'Atlantics' continued to do good work on the Brighton line. They hauled the Newhaven boat trains, while others of the class were stationed at Bognor. I found one of these latter in great form with a heavy week-end load on the 6.20 pm down from Victoria as late as June 1934 when despite a load of 375 tons, nearly 100 tons heavier than the pre-war train, we ran fully up to Southern Belle standards until turning westwards off the Brighton main line at Three Bridges.

4

THE WEST COAST CORRIDOR

One of the most intriguing fields of enquiry for those who delve into railway lore is to try and trace the origin of some of the nicknames that were in common use for many years among railwaymen but which were never published officially, and were little known by the travelling public. 'The Flying Dutchman' was a case in point, but a far less obvious one was that of the West Coast Corridor, or simply 'The Corridor', for it was not even the first British all-corridor train. That distinction went to the Great Western 11.25 am from Paddington to Birkenhead, which began running on 7 March 1892. Long before that, however, long before the new corridor carriages and dining cars were introduced, the West Coast train at 2 pm from Euston to Glasgow and Edinburgh, run jointly by the London and North Western and Caledonian Railways, had become an institution. The Glasgow portion became all-corridor on 1 July 1892, and the Edinburgh section was similarly uplifted a month later. The original composition of the northbound train was of ten vehicles, six for Glasgow, including the dining cars, two for Edinburgh and two for Aberdeen. The dining cars were of the clerestory roofed type, but the rest were of the Wolverton designed 45 ft long bogie flat-roofed type. The term 'flat-roof' was used to distinguish them the later 57 ft carriages with high elliptical roofs. Those of the earlier vehicles were not actually flat, but were much 'flatter' than the later ones.

To the railway enthusiasts of the day, however, the train, more than in its accommodation, became famous through its engine: yes, engine, in the singular! Because before it became all-corridor it was worked between Euston and Crewe exclusively by the Webb 3-cylinder compound No. 1304 *Jeanie Deans*. It was a good name for the engine of one of the most famous Anglo-Scottish expresses. The three-cylinder compounds may not have been the most successful of Webb's engineering achievement, but he came nearest to a resounding success in the class of ten locomotives of which *Jeanie Deans* was a member. Yet in some ways, as well as in her rather exclusive duties *Jeanie Deans* was the odd one out. The London and North Western Railway had always been traditional in its engine naming, in that most of the titles were handed down from older engines as they became life-expired and had to be replaced. But by the mid-1880s traffic was increasing to such an extent that the capital stock was having to be constantly increased, and new engines were being built at Crewe in far greater numbers than the older ones were being scrapped, and many new names had to be found. It was unthinkable in that era that any London and North Western passenger engine should be unnamed.

The ten new three cylinder compounds, with larger boilers, and 7 ft diameter driving wheels were named after ships of the White Star Line fleet of steamships sailing from Liverpool, in connection with which the L & NWR ran many special boat trains to and from Euston for the American traffic. Then, while these engines were still under construction at Crewe, Webb was invited to send an engine to the Edinburgh Exhibition of 1890. Obviously he would send one of his latest, but none of the names already chosen would be really appropriate for Edinburgh - *Teutonic, Adriatic, Coptic, Ionic* and so on. At that time the Waverley Novels of Sir Walter Scott were in the forefront of popular fiction, and so what better name for the engine going to the Edinburgh Exhibition than the heroine of *The Heart of Midlothian* - Jeanie Deans? During her sojourn at the Exhibition she carried a special number, 3105; this was not her allocated running number for traffic purposes, but her number in order of new construction at Crewe. The three thousandth locomotive turned out at that works had appeared in July 1887, *Jeanie Deans* came about two years later. After the exhibition she took her normal number 1304, and was allocated to Camden shed. She took up regular working on the 2 pm Scottish express in January 1891, even before it had become all-corridor, and she worked it without a break, Euston to Crewe and back, 316 miles a day, until 1899, except for the few occasions when she was under repair.

North Western engines of that era were rostered regularly for extensive monthly mileages, and the engine of the 'Corridor' was not due back into Euston, on the corresponding southbound express until 10.45 pm. As on many similar duties the engine was double-manned, with the two regular crews working the train on alternate days. But the remarkable thing about this particular duty was that one of the two drivers of *Jeanie Deans*, David Button, was on the job for twenty-five years. At the latter end of this remarkable innings the working of the Corridor was shared with another top-link Camden partnership, and they and their regular engines alternated between the 2 pm and 12.10 pm departures from Euston, in each case to Crewe and back in the day. *Jeanie Deans* was superseded in 1899 by one of the Webb four-cylinder compound 4-4-0s No. 1911 *Centurion*; but not this engine, nor either of the succeeding four-cylinder compound 4-4-0s *Albemarle* and *Royal Oak* was Driver Button's engine for as long as he had *Jeanie Deans*, because in 1904 he was given one of the new 'Precursors' No. 659 *Dreadnought* to be succeeded two years later by a 4-6-0 of the 'Experiment' class, No. 1987 *Glendower*. This latter engine became veritably the 'pride of the line', and was photographed on the 'Corridor' more often than most engines. It was during her spell of duty, in 1908, that the magnificent new twelve-wheeled coaching stock was introduced in the Glasgow and Edinburgh sections, and the train became one of the most luxurious to be found anywhere in the world.

The two trains built for the Corridor service, leaving Euston and Glasgow at 2 pm each weekday were unlike any others in the ordinary passenger workings of the London and North Western, and Caledonian Railways. The unusual design of the carriages had however been anticipated a year earlier in the stock built for the American Specials running between Euston and Liverpool. At that time the cream of the American traffic passed

A 'portrait' of the first West Coast corridor train, at Wolverton carriage works, headed by the famous Webb three-cylinder compound locomotive No. 1304 Jeanie Deans.

through Liverpool, and the coaches were constructed something along American lines in having entrances only at the ends. The American Specials had a full brake van at each end of the train, but the new stock built for the West Coast 'Corridor' trains did not have so much luggage space. The standard formation of the northbound train was:

Brake third: 5 compartments, 40 seats
Composite: 16 thirds, 27 firsts   Glasgow
Dining Car: 21 thirds, 15 firsts   Portion
Brake third: 5 compartments, 40 seats
Dining Car: 21 thirds, 15 firsts   Edinburgh
Composite: 24 thirds, 24 firsts   Section
Brake third: 4 compartments, 32 seats
Brake composite: 16 thirds, 12 firsts for Aberdeen

All the foregoing were of the magnificent twelve-wheeled stock, with end doors only, though the dining cars in both Glasgow and Edinburgh sections differed from the rest of the twelve wheeled cars in the train in having clerestory roofs, in contrast to the high elliptical roofs of the rest of the

The Corridor composed of the fine 12-wheeled stock getting into its stride near Harrow, hauled by Precursor class 4-4-0 No. 1309 Shamrock.

eight-coach set. Leaving Euston the train also conveyed a through portion for Whitehaven, which was detached at Preston, and a through carriage for Knutsford. These were of ordinary LNWR eight wheeled bogie corridor stock, and not of the special twelve-wheeled type.

When I first travelled by the 'Corridor' my parents lived at Barrow-in-Furness; and while the coaches in the Whitehaven section, in which I rode for much of the journey were certainly very smooth-riding and comfortable it was with a feeling of positive opulence that one went forward to the dining car in the Edinburgh portion for lunch, soon after leaving Euston. For the riding of those massive twelve wheelers, through three of which one had to walk to reach the dining car, was something quite 'out of this world' for that time. Truth to tell, I cannot recall having travelled in any coaches, anywhere in the world that were better, even after the passage of more than fifty years since they ran in the 'Midday Scot' of LMS days. They were massively as well as elegantly built: 65 ft 6 in over the bodies, and weighing no less than 40 tons each. Although the LNWR still provided second class on some of its express trains the Corridor was first and third only, and the latter, travelling at the basic fare of one penny a mile, had some most luxurious accommodation. The seats were trimmed in crimson and black velvet, the floors covered with bordered cork linoleum, and the walls were framed with teak, having the upper and lower panels in oak. Each compartment had two wide windows on the outside, and the framing between them was quite narrow, so as not to obtrude upon the outlook.

Although belonging to the West Coast joint stock, jointly owned by the London and North Western and Caledonian Railways, these beautiful coaches were painted in the LNW colours, with white upper panels, and dark chocolate brown bodies. The roofs also were painted white when new, but they did not stay like that for long, and when I saw the train in pre-grouping days the roofs were usually looking light grey. Elsewhere these coaches were always immaculate. They carried the special coat of arms of the West Coast Joint Stock, which consisted of a lion rampant, above sprays of rose and thistle. The painting style of Caledonian carriages was almost indistinguishable from that of the North Western in monochrome photographs; but actually the bodies were painted a deep purple. It always amused me when the nationalised British Railways were experimenting with new styles for coaching stock that one essay was a rather feeble imitation of the North Western style, and some publicist gave it the unspeakable title of 'plum and spilt milk'! To those of us who were old enough to remember what the true North Western coach colours were like it was rather pathetic.

From what I have written about the third class compartments of the Corridor it can be imagined that the firsts were something really special;

The beautiful 12-wheeled West Coast Joint Stock introduced on the service in 1908.

and they certainly were. Three seats were provided on each side of the compartment, with folding arm-rests for division, and trimmed fixed elbows at the sides. The seats were trimmed with figured green Blenheim moquette. Over the seats were self-contained luggage racks, with brackets and cord netting for parcels. The windows had adjustable blinds, of figured brown and gold tapestry, fixed in mahogany woods, while in addition there were green figured merino curtains, with fringes, which could be drawn across the windows, instead of drawing the blinds down. This gave the compartments a pleasant cool appearance in hot sunny weather. Like the 'thirds', the first class compartment also had lino covered floors but with a loose rug in addition, laid down the centre. But one much appreciated feature, which I personally have missed in more recent coaching stock of the compartment type, were the pictures of interesting places served by the London and North Western and Caledonian Railways. They were mounted above the seats, and beneath the luggage racks, and the fine photographs thus displayed were an added incentive to anyone who had the urge to travel further.

From what I have already written about the coaches it will be appreciated that the Corridor, from 1908 onwards, was no light weight to haul about. The minimum load leaving Euston was of eight 12-wheelers, with one

8-wheeler each for Whitehaven and Knutsford on the tail; but when I saw it, and from many photographs, there was usually an extra 8-wheeler in the Aberdeen section, and two coaches for Whitehaven. This would mean at least 400 tons tare. In consideration of this the timing south of Crewe was easier than that of many other North Western expresses. A stop was made at Willesden Junction to take up passengers from the north-western suburbs of London, and then the 77.2 miles to Rugby had to be run in 87 minutes. The succeeding 75.5 miles to Crewe were allowed 89 minutes, respective average speeds of 53.2 and 50.8 mph. The Knutsford coach was detached at Crewe, and the Aberdeen and Whitehaven sections at Preston, leaving a minimum of seven 12-wheelers, or a gross load of about 300 tons to be taken over Shap, and then by the Caledonian over Beattock summit.

From introduction of the new twelve-wheeled stock in 1908 the 4-6-0 locomotives of the 'Experiment' class were normally employed south of Crewe, and almost invariably north thereof. From Euston *Glendower* was one of the favourite engines, but certain later engines of the class named after English counties, namely *Bedfordshire* and *Westmorland* were both reported as doing fine work with this heavy train. Some hard work was needed in the North Country. The 90 miles from Preston to Carlisle were booked to be covered in 104 minutes, and then, after a level start of 27 miles, to Carnforth, there came the ascent to Shap, in which there is a vertical rise of 885 ft in 31½ miles. The time allowed for this distance was 42 minutes, and it used to be almost a point of honour with the drivers to keep this schedule, rather than take things a little easier uphill and regain what had been lost by a fast run down from Shap Summit to Carlisle. There was certainly some margin for recovery on this final downhill section, for which 32 minutes was allowed for 31½ miles. Those luxurious twelve-wheelers rode as smoothly on the curvaceous lengths of the mountain country as they did in the green shires of Southern England; and if a driver had some leeway to make up the passengers would not feel any ill-effects from a spurt up to 80 or 85 mph, even round some of those curves. One of the 'Experiment' class 4-6-0 locomotives was timed at 93 mph between Penrith and Carlisle.

That mountain section, between Lancaster and Carlisle, was a lovely run on a summer evening. The train left Preston at 6.24 pm and after a level run at 60 mph across the North Lancashire plain one dipped down to the shores of Morecambe Bay. Although always known as the West Coast Route this was the only glimpse of salt water in the entire 299 miles between London and Carlisle. It was an appealing glimpse nevertheless, because across the miles of gleaming yellow sands were piled range upon range of the Lakeland hills : nothing very bold or dramatic, but ample to entice anyone with a love of wild upland country to explore more deeply into that region. The broad vista from Hest Bank always brings back boyhood memories to me, for was not my own home out there to the west, on the very fringes of that delightful country! But the Corridor itself, sweeping through Carnforth plunged northwards into an area of tumbled hill ranges until, with the steepening of the gradient and the slackening of the pace, it passed through Oxenholme, the junction for the branch line to Windermere. Then, as the exhaust beat from the engine became louder, and speed for the first time dropped below 40 mph a wide panorama of majestic upland country opened out to the west. Hereabouts the line is climbing high on a shoulder of Hay Fell, and while today the modern electric trains go dashing up at 80 and 85 mph the measured progress of the Corridor gave time to enjoy the scene, which extends far beyond the trough in which Windermere lake lies hidden, to the knobbly profiles of the Langdale Pikes.

The smooth rounded summits of the fells that seem to encompass the railway on every side at Grayrigg are in striking contrast to the far-off Lakeland heights just glimpsed; but now the Corridor is quickening its pace again, as the line dips gently down into the Lune gorge, and begins a nearly-level five mile run to Tebay. The mountain solitude of this part of the line has now gone for ever, because the M5 motorway has been constructed higher up the slopes on the left hand side of the railway, and the trains themselves match, and surpass, the haste of the modern highway. Where the Corridor of old would have been running at 60 to 65 mph when it took water from the Dillicar troughs, the 'Electric Scots' of today are often doing 100 mph! Taking water at those troughs was a much photographed spectacle in the days of the London and North Western Railway, to record which brought some of the few moving-train camera experts from the South of England; but not for the Corridor, because it was not due to pass Tebay until 7.26 pm and by that time, even in summer, the gorge would be deep in the shadows of evening.

Tebay was a busy railway outpost in those days and it remained so until the very end of steam traction. Lying at the foot of the Shap Incline it had a shed housing a considerable number of engines, the sole function of which was to give rear-end banking assistance to heavy trains up the 5½ miles of severe gradient to Shap Summit. With passenger trains there was no rigid rule about the loads that could be taken without assistance. It was left to the judgment of the driver. Sometimes when the load was manageable on the easier gradients south of Carnforth, but too heavy for the mountain section a stop would be made at Oxenholme for a pilot to couple on ahead of the train engine, and in such cases the pilot would continue through to Carlisle, to be available to assist another heavy southbound train up to

Shap. The northbound Corridor rarely needed assistance, and it ran through Tebay at about 60 mph ready to 'charge' the Shap Incline. In contrast to the country farther south the line here climbed over a bleak open moorland, which could nevertheless look most appealing when the last rays of the setting sun gave a particular glow to the heather.

The fast run down to Carlisle could sometimes give enthusiasts of the stop-watch some exciting data, but to most 'railwayacs', as they were known in the early 1900s, there was the eager anticipation of the engine-change at Carlisle, and the replacement of the black North Western by one of the magnificent blue Caledonians, even though by that time in the evening it was usually too dark for that splendid colour and its impeccable finish to be fully appreciated. According to the public timetable there would be precious little time for a through passenger to nip out briefly on the station platform to watch the engine changing, for the public timetable showed a wait of no more than two minutes. The working book however allowed five minutes, though of course if the North Western had brought the train a minute or so early, and the engine-change was very smart there was nothing to stop the train being despatched again at the public time, without waiting for 8.13 pm. And here, at Carlisle, the traveller was presented with

The Corridor on the Caledonian, southbound near Rutherglen, hauled by the big 4-6-0 No. 907 that was damaged beyond repair in the terrible Quintinshill disaster of 1915.

a locomotive working tradition that lasted even longer than that of *Jeanie Deans*.

In 1903 J.F. McIntosh, Locomotive Superintendent of the Caledonian Railway, built two enormous 4-6-0 express locomotives, with the intention of avoiding the need of assistant engines on the Beattock Bank, which was as steep as Shap, but twice as long. The two engines, Nos. 49 and 50, took their turn on the Corridor before the new stock of 1908 was introduced, and did very well; but the locomotive authorities at St Rollox felt that an even larger boiler was desirable, and in 1906 five further 4-6-0s were built, of which the first, No. 903 was named *Cardean*, after the Perthshire estate of Edward Cox, the Deputy Chairman of the Company. As soon as she had been 'run-in', after construction, *Cardean* was assigned to the Corridor, and like *Jeanie Deans*, in both directions. She took the 2 pm from Glasgow down to Carlisle, and then returned on the 8.13 pm; and apart from the few occasions when she was stopped for repairs, she was on that job, and no other, for ten years. Even more remarkable perhaps was that during that time she had only one regular driver, David Gibson, of Polmadie shed. There was no double-manning with *Cardean*. The journey time in both directions of running was little more than two hours, with about three hours on shed at Carlisle; and this could be comfortably accomplished during the ten hour day that was then the norm for enginemen.

During this ten-year spell *Cardean* became almost as much an institution as the Corridor train itself. When working south from Glasgow she was photographed at many parts of the line, though the favourite places used by English enthusiasts who journeyed to Carlisle were on the open sections south of the Floriston woods, or north of Gretna. The late afternoon sun would have been getting low enough in the sky to cast shadows across the track at the more picturesque locations, though one of these enthusiasts ventured far enough into the wilds to secure a memorable picture of her descending the Beattock Bank, which was made the subject of one of the most beautiful of the 'F. Moore' coloured postcards, and which could then be brought for one penny! In the years before 'daylight saving' it was natural that the down Corridor, leaving Carlisle at 8.13 pm was not photographed. Thus it was that one feature of the train's working was perhaps not generally known. North of Carstairs, after the Edinburgh section had been detached, the Glasgow portion took the Holytown route, avoiding Motherwell, and this required use of a different semaphore headcode from the familiar form for the Glasgow–Carlisle line via Motherwell, sometimes humorously referred to as 'the bow tie'. The code for the Holytown route was different in that the right hand arm of the semaphore was inclined downwards, and it was photographed on at least one occasion.

A photographer from Gateshead, R.J. Purves, whom I came to know well in later years in connection with signalling work on the North Eastern, had a field day at Carlisle not long before the first world war, and he got the engine of the down Corridor during her turn-round time on Kingmoor shed. It was one of the very few occasions when *Cardean* was not on the job, but one of the earlier McIntosh 4-6-0s was there and looking very splendid, with the semaphore headcode already set for the northbound journey. This engine, and her sister No. 50, were unique on the Caledonian Railway, in having the Company's impressive coat of arms encompassed by huge sprays of laurel leaves. Though the tenders of the 'Cardean' class were equally large the surrounding decoration round that coat of arms was more modest. It is remarkable that *Cardean*, in taking over haulage of the Corridor at Carlisle, partnered no few than four generations of London and North Western locomotives, and all of these in turn had notable records. It was a record for the class rather than of individual engines, for only one, the *Sir Gilbert Claughton* of 1913, had anything of an individual spell, and then for no more than a few months.

The 'Experiment' class 4-6-0s, which were in possession south of Carlisle when *Cardean* first took over, were to some extent superseded from 1911 when the superheater 4-4-0s of the 'George the Fifth' began working north-ward from Crewe. These engines did some outstanding work on the mountain sections, though in bad weather conditions they suffered from limited adhesion weight, and were a prey to slipping. The superheated version of the 'Experiment' class, the 'Prince of Wales' class, again put up some very fine performances, but the ultimate answer to the problems of the mountain section, with ever increasing loads was the 'Claughton' class, with four-cylinders, a larger boiler and firebox, and tractive power that enabled loads of the line-maximum of 420 tons tare, to be taken northbound over Shap without any assistance. After its initial running trials the pioneer engine of this class, engine No. 2222 *Sir Gilbert Claughton*, worked regularly on the northbound Corridor leaving Crewe at 5.19 pm. In this case it was only a one-way run on this most famous of West Coast trains. It passed the southbound Corridor somewhere between Wigan and Preston, and the en-gine and crew of the down train had a fairly long stop-over in Carlisle, working south on the 1 am 'sleeper', non-stop to Crewe.

The northbound Corridor was still running to its pre-war timings in the earlier summer of 1916 when I first travelled on it, as far as Preston, in the Whitehaven portion; but after that its departure time from Euston became progressively earlier, to maintain a reasonable time of arrival in Glasgow in spite of much decelerated running and a maximum permissible speed of 60 mph. The stop at Willesden was cut out and its time of 101 minutes for the

Engine for the Northbound Corridor being prepared at Kingsmoor sheds, Carlisle, 4-6-0 No. 49, with the distinctive semaphore head-code in front of the chimney.

82.6 miles from Euston to Rugby was only one minute slower than the previous time, which of course included the extra needed for slowing down and regaining speed after the stop. I travelled by the train in April 1920, and noted a sound performance by the second of the 'Claughton' class engines, the *Sir Robert Turnbull*, by that time seven years old, with a heavy train of 460 tons. Later that same year a new star of the first magnitude took up working on the Corridor; this was the first post-war 'Claughton', which was set aside as the London and North Western Railway's mobile War Memorial. It was specially numbered 1914, named *Patriot* and had a specially large nameplate, with the following inscription below the name: 'In memory of the fallen L & NWR employees 1914-1918'. *Patriot* worked on the Corridor from Euston to Crewe and back for several months in the winter of 1920-1.

With the incorporation of the L & NWR into the London Midland and Scottish system however all began to change, and with Midland principles of management and operation taking preference, the loads that were allowed to be hauled by individual engines were much reduced. As a result, to the disgust of North Western locomotive men the Corridor had to be

49

double headed every day, between Euston and Crewe. In the North also there were changes. The Aberdeen and Whitehaven coaches were detached at Crewe and the main part of the train stopped at Lancaster instead of Preston, and with the reduced load not often exceeding the new top limit of 360 tons the train often ran through from Crewe to Carlisle without a pilot. In Scotland the workings were also much changed, while of course the beautiful twelve-wheeled coaches had to be repainted in Midland red. Their riding was as good as ever, but the interiors began to look a bit 'tatty'.

The major development, which gave the final *coup* to the old order on the West Coast route, was the almost simultaneous introduction of the new 'Royal Scot' class of three cylinder 4-6-0 locomotives and the naming of the trains themselves. The morning Anglo-Scottish express at 10 am from Euston was named 'The Royal Scot', and the Corridor became 'The Midday Scot'. On the latter all the old engine workings were changed. Three of the new engines were stationed at Rugby, and worked the train from Euston to Crewe, while in the north one engine worked right through to Glasgow, with Crewe and Polmadie men on alternative days, lodging overnight. The Rugby men with the engines *Grenadier Guardsman*, *Royal Fusilier* and *Sherwood Forester* did adequate, if not very inspiring work; but north of Crewe, with a through run of 244 miles, and the Shap and Beattock summits to surmount there were problems. As time went on the new engines proved to be heavier coal burners than was anticipated, and runs that began well deteriorated as the journey progressed as drivers worried whether they would have enough coal to get home. This trouble was eventually cured by the fitting of a different type of piston valve, and the story is continued in a later chapter. At this stage, with the old faithful Corridor train now emblazoned 'The Midday Scot' this chapter can well be ended.

5

THE CORNISH RIVIERA EXPRESS

In the earlier chapters of this book I have been writing of famous trains whose heyday was in pre-war years, some indeed that hardly survived at all in their original form afterwards. But in coming to the Cornish Riviera Express, although it was launched with a considerable flourish of trumpets in that same earlier period it did not blossom out into its full maturity until after its revival, and re-instatement at full pre-war speed in the autumn of 1921. In the resurgence of pioneer spirit on the Great Western Railway following the final abolition of the broad gauge in 1892 the making of lengthy non-stop runs was a prestige feature of the new service. The run of the down 'Cornishman' was in due course extended over its first 194 miles, from Paddington to Exeter, and then in 1904, following the introduction of locomotives like the 'Atbara' and 'City' class 4-4-0s that could take the fearsome gradients of the West Country as much in their stride as the long stretches of level running east of Newton Abbot, the non-stop run was extended to Plymouth, 245 miles from London.

Pride in this train, and in its world-record length of daily non-stop led to an unusual announcement in *The Railway Magazine*. On the last page of its issue for July 1904 there were banner headlines:

THREE GUINEAS FOR A NAME FOR A TRAIN

Then followed a whole page of instructions, explaining how every reader had an equal opportunity of obtaining the three guineas, and how James Inglis, the General Manager of the Great Western Railway would judge the entries and award the prize. One of the most amusing statements in this lengthy verbage read : 'Nor is the prize of three Guineas the only advantage the successful Competitors will obtain. His name will become known (and will be handed down to future generations of railway officers and *railway-acs*) as the originator of the title of "......" for the 10.10 am ex Paddington.' In the meantime *The Railway Magazine* referred to it as 'The 3.T.F.'

51

(Three towns flyer), these being Stonehouse, Plymouth and Devonport; but the actual competition ended in something of a flop. Out of 1286 entries Inglis chose 'The Riviera Express', and the prize money was divided between two competitors whose names were never heard of again. But the title was never used. It was interesting that one or two of the suggestions that were discarded at the time were afterwards adopted in much later years, such as 'Cornish Riviera Limited' and 'Royal Duchy Express'. One is really rather surprised at the actual choice, because in those days 'Riviera' was almost universally applied to the lands of the Mediterranean. The later qualification 'Cornish Riviera' was a very logical solution.

Despite all the publicity very little detail of its running at first got into the railway press. In its early days, running via Bristol, its load was no more than six coaches; and after 1906 when it was transferred to the new route and had twenty minutes cut from its running time, few if any of the stopwatching railwayacs of the day seemed to travel by it. The Rev. W.J. Scott had a ride in it in the winter of 1909-10, with an unspecified four-cylinder 4-6-0 of the 'Knight' series; but my friend the late A.V. Goodyear when doing the field work for a scholarly article in *The Railway Magazine* in March 1912 entitled 'Heavy Express Work between Paddington and Exeter' gathered all his data from runs on the 11.50 am 'Torquay Diner', and the 3.30 pm from Paddington, both of which stopped, rather than slipping coaches at Exeter. On Scott's journey the load was one of nine coaches when leaving Paddington, with one each slipped at Westbury, Taunton and Exeter, representing actual loads of 300, 270, 240, and 205 tons on the four successive stages.

As a very junior schoolboy in 1913, waiting at Reading West station for the late afternoon auto-train to take me home to Mortimer, I used to see the up Cornish Riviera Express come through. It was a very grand train in my eyes, with a highly polished engine, but never with many coaches. Not until after the war, however, and the pre-war schedule had been restored did the train really begin to come with the limelight of railway publicity, under the invigorating leadership of the newly appointed General Manager of the Great Western Railway, Felix J.C. Pole. As a spectacle at that time the train and its locomotives were not impressive. The famous chocolate and cream coach livery of broad gauge days had been changed to tuscan red, albeit plentifully adorned with black and gold lining out; but in 1921 the locomotives were still in the plain unlined green of wartime, with all the brass and copperwork painted over. It was my first winter in London, studying for an engineering degree at Imperial College, and on my free Saturday mornings I often made my way to Paddington to see the Cornish Riviera Express go off. Despite the drab colouring of the engine and coaches

The first eastbound Cornish Riviera express leaving Penzance, on 1 July 1904, hauled by the 4-4-0 engine No. 3450 Swansea (*Bulldog class*).

it was a great sight, never less than twelve coaches, in eight distinct sections. Weymouth had two coaches, slipped at Westbury; Minehead and Ilfracombe one each, slipped at Taunton, and Torquay one, slipped at Exeter. There was one coach allocated to Plymouth passengers, while through coaches for Falmouth and St Ives were detached at the stops at Truro and St Erth. Only four coaches including the dining car remained on arrival at Penzance.

The Great Western had never followed the practice of the London and North Western Railway in providing corridor connection from slip coaches to the rest of the train, and thus it was only passengers travelling to Plymouth and beyond who enjoyed the pleasure of taking lunch en route. The coaching stock was uniformly of the 70 ft type except for the through carriage for Ilfracombe. On the London and South Western line from Barnstaple some of the curves are so sharp that the sideways displacement of the middle of a 70 ft coach would cause it to foul some of the lineside structures, and so the longest that could be run were the 57 ft type. Most of the other coaches on the Cornish Riviera Express leaving Paddington in 1921 were of the so-called 'Toplight' variety, because they had hammered glass toplights above the windows. This type of Great Western coach dated from around 1912. The dining cars were very interesting. They were the very first examples of Swindon's departure from the clerestory roofed type of coach used in the latter years of the broad gauge, and developed into the fine corridor stock used on the crack trains in the early days of all-standard gauge. But for the inauguration of the Plymouth non-stop trains of 1904 an entirely new type of restaurant car was introduced having a high elliptical roof, and an extreme width of 9 ft 6 in. They looked rather odd in a train otherwise uniformly of the clerestory roofed stock and were nicknamed the 'Dreadnoughts', but they were, of course, the forerunners of the future standard.

When the 'Toplight' 70 ft coaches were introduced the earlier 68 ft restaurant cars of 1904 were included in the new set trains. They had to provide for lunching, or serving teas in only six out of the eleven ordinary coaches in the train leaving Paddington, and the seating accommodation for 18 first-class passengers and 32 'thirds' was adequate. It was usual to serve at least two sittings of lunch, and at busy times sometimes three were necessary. Lunch on the train was an enjoyable prelude to a holiday in the West Country for many passengers. Luxurious travel, such as that provided on the West Coast Corridor train, was no part of Great Western practice. The coaches were comfortable, and rode smoothly, but there was a striking comparison in pure physical features between a 70 ft 'toplight' weighing 33 tons and seating 80 third-class passengers, and a West Coast 65 ft 6 in composite, seating 16 third and 26 first-class passengers, and weighing 40 tons! The essential job on the Great Western holiday routes was to carry as many people as possible with the minimum of weight to be hauled by one engine.

In 1921 the West of England trains from Paddington were hauled exclusively by the four-cylinder 4-6-0s of the 'Star' class designed by G.J. Churchward and first built at Swindon in 1907, after the engine machinery had been tried out on a prototype, the *North Star* built in 1906 as an 'Atlantic'. By the summer of 1914 there were 61 of them in service, including the prototype, which in 1909 had been converted to the 4-6-0 type. The construction of this class of locomotives had been spread over eight years, but in 1921 it was evident that the earliest of them, dating back to 1907, were still considered equal in every respect to the later ones, and some of the finest runs on the Cornish Riviera Express in its first months of restoration

*The Cornish Riviera Express leaving Paddington hauled by the 4-6-0 locomotive
No. 4050* Princess Alice.

were made by engines of the very first batch, the *Lode Star* and the *Red
Star*. Both engines would of course have been to Swindon for general repairs
several times in the intervening years, and each time they would almost
certainly come out with a different boiler from that they carried previously.
Repairs to boilers usually took longer than the time needed by the frames
and the machinery, and for that reason the stock of boilers was usually
maintained at a few more than than the total number of locomotives. In
any case the boiler used on the 'Star' class was a standard also used on the
two-cylinder 'Saint' class 4-6-0s and on the 2-8-0 heavy mineral class.

The problem presented in the working of the westbound Cornish Riviera
Express was severe, not only in respect of the length of run to be made
non-stop but also because of the increasing labour of surmounting the West

Castle class 4-6-0 No. 4032 Queen Alexandra, *at Penzance, having worked the Cornish Riviera westwards from Plymouth.*

Country gradients. It is true that the trailing load was successively reduced by the detaching of slip portions and that in 1921 the gross load behind the tender, leaving Paddington of 425 tons, was reduced to 355 tons from Westbury, 295 tons from Taunton and 260 tons beyond Exeter. But that was not all. Although the 'Star' class locomotives were efficient, and probably burned less coal in relation to the work done than any other express passenger locomotive in Great Britain at the time, the labour of handling that coal was considerable. By the time the train passed Exeter substantial inroads would have been made upon the supply carried on the tender; and although the total of 6 tons would have been more than adequate for the $225\frac{1}{2}$ mile non-stop run, the coal space at the rear end of the tenders had a flat bottom, and supplies tended to stay there rather than trim obligingly forward as the fireman used up that which was nearest to hand. And so, as the journey progressed some labour was involved in raking supplies forward, in addition to actually shovelling into the firebox.

The Cornish Riviera Express was worked by London and Plymouth men on alternate days, and with healthy competition between the two sheds, Old Oak Common and Laira, some extremely good work was done. Drivers and fireman treated this tough assignment as a challenge to their skill, so much that the Traffic Department took advantage of it to add a few extra coaches; it was not unusual for the westbound train to be loaded up to fourteen coaches when leaving Paddington, with one extra in the Torquay slip portion and another extra in the section that went through to Penzance. This was the maximum that could be handled by one engine. If more than eight coaches remained after detaching the slip portion at Exeter it was necessary to stop at Newton Abbot to take an assistant engine over the very severe gradients of the South Devon line. While this was essential to avoid any risk of stalling on the banks it unfortunately occupied precious time. It is at this stage that the enquiring traveller might well ask how the extra-ordinary alignment and exceptional gradients came about, recalling the care and skill Brunel lavished in producing so many straight and level lines elsewhere. Unlike the Great Western itself however, the South Devon Rail-way, which began as an independent company, did not have the immense financial backing enjoyed by the GWR, and the importance of carrying railway communication westward from Exeter to Plymouth was small by comparison. So to economise on construction costs, and to minimise opera-tional expense afterwards Brunel decided on two lines of approach, both of which proved disastrous.

The traffic was not expected to be heavy, and the original authorisation was for a line with only a single line of rails; and Brunel with the intention of avoiding entirely the use of ordinary locomotives adopted the system of 'atmospheric' propulsion, as referred in the chapter on 'The Flying Dutch-man'. With the light trains anticipated it was thought that gradients would have been of no consequence, and in the hilly country west of Newton Abbot, Brunel went ahead regardless of hill and dale, including such slopes as 1 in 40, and even 1 in 36. These would slow down a well-loaded family car on a modern highway, let alone a juggernaut. But worse than the gradients were the curves. To minimise constructional costs by avoiding earthworks the line was carried on so curvaceous an alignment in this tumbled hilly country than even on the downhill stretches 50 mph was about the maximum that could be run safely. When the 'atmospheric' had proved a total failure and recourse had to be made to steam locomotives, after toiling uphill there was no chance of making up a little time by speeding downhill. The Cornish Riviera Express of the early 1920s was allowed 45 minutes to cover the 32 miles from Newton Abbot to Plymouth, and with the maximum permissable load of eight coaches I have known one of the 'Star' class engines brought down to 11 mph in fighting its way up one of the worst inclines.

However toilsome it could be for the enginemen it was a lovely ride for the passengers, through a glorious unspoiled countryside, on the one side with glimpses of the heights of Dartmoor, and on the other of lands stretching away to the South Hams. At Brent, in the early 1920s, heavy down expresses that had been doubleheaded from Newton Abbot usually stopped a second time to detach their pilots, so that they could return quickly, light engine, and be available to assist a second train. In July 1925 I photographed the big 2-6-2 tank engine No. 3121 twice within three hours, first assisting the 11.28 am from Newton Abbot (5.30 am from Paddington via Bristol) and then on the summer 11 am from Paddington to Penzance. In both cases it coupled off at Brent. When two such stops were made, as on one journey when I was travelling on the Cornish Riviera Express, and an engine of the 'Queen' series had one coach over the maximum permissible load, the time spent standing at Newton Abbot and Brent, and that involved in slowing down and gaining speed afterwards eventually made us about ten minutes late in arriving at Plymouth, though on a wet day if an attempt had been made to take that overload up those exceptional gradients, a bout of wheel-slip could easily have led to complete stalling in open country, and the loss of time would have been far more serious.

It was not until the introduction of the very much more powerful engines of the 'King' class, in 1927, that the maximum load for an unassisted engine was increased on the South Devon line. Even then it was not in exact relation to the tractive power of the locomotives as can be seen from these comparative figures:

Engine Class	Tractive power tons	Maximum load tons	Ratio: load to trac. power
'Star'	12·4	288	23·2
'Castle'	14·1	288	20·4
'King'	18·0	360	20·0

Although the 'Castle' was a more powerful engine than a 'Star' the increase was not considered enough to justify increasing the load. One extra coach of the heaviest kind used on the Cornish trains would have brought the tonnage up to 326, and this was thought to be too much. The 'Castle' introduced in 1923 was a very successful engine, and enabled the maximum load trains to be handled more efficiently. But having arrived at Plymouth, usually nonstop from Paddington, the next problem in working the Cornish Riviera Express was the difficult line in Cornwall itself, because another 80 miles remained before the terminus was reached at Penzance.

In steam days, and almost invariably between the two world wars, engines were changed at Plymouth. The very large and heavy 'King' class

Heavy traffic at Paddington: No. 1 platform just before the departure of the Cornish Riviera Express. The Weymouth coaches, to be slipped at Westbury, are at the rear of the train.

engines were not allowed to cross Brunel's 'Royal Albert Bridge' across the Tamar at Saltash; and in Cornwall on the steeply graded, and incessantly curved main line there was only one place where any real express speed could be permitted – a short length of 'straight' east of St Germans. This was so short however as to be of no value with a heavily loaded steam locomotive. Engines like the 'Star' and 'Castle' class had no opportunity to develop their outstanding abilities as high speed express units, and the most useful types in Cornwall were those with two cylinders and the Stephenson link motion form of valve gear. When I first went to Cornwall, in 1924, the 2-6-0 mixed traffic engines were used almost to the exclusion of all other types, and they were followed some years later by the 4-6-0s of the 'Hall' and 'Grange' classes, but with boilers the same as those of the 'Stars'.

59

Locomotives apart however the Cornish main line had a character all its own; and if one was not weary of travel by the time the train left Plymouth, and merely impatient to get to journeys end, the run through Cornwall was one of continuing and varied delight.

No Englishman worthy of the name can fail to be thrilled by the sight of ships of the Royal Navy, and even before the line has entered Cornwall, a viaduct abreast and high above Devonport Dockyard provides sights well calculated to stir the blood; and then comes the crossing, at dead slow speed, of one of Brunel's masterpieces, the Royal Albert Bridge. It has been said of Brunel that everything he did was either a colossal success, or an equally colossal failure, and in crossing the Royal Albert Bridge into Cornwall one can forget the fiasco of the 'atmospheric' system of propulsion, and rejoice that so magnificent an example of his work spans the River Tamar at Saltash, and that with careful and unremitting maintenance it remains as sound as when he built it, 125 years ago. There is no need to hang out of the window to appreciate its elegant proportions, because once into Cornwall the line swings round in almost a complete right angle to the left, and provides a superb backward view of it. Soon however the line swings westward from the Tamar estuary to follow the north bank of the Lynher River. The one-time single-tracked main line of the Cornwall Railway ran closer to the shore in Brunel's days, and this brings recollection of

At the head end: on left engine No. 4078 Pembroke Castle *heading the third portion of the Cornish Riviera Express, while on right engine No. 4018* Knight of the Grand Cross *is on the second part, in June 1926.*

another of the great romances of early West Country railway building, the timber trestle viaducts.

As with the South Devon, so with the Cornwall Railway, which from its inception was equally closely associated with the Great Western, there was far from any superabundance of cash available, and even in following the lie of the land for much of the route there were many deep valleys to be crossed. For these Brunel used a picturesque, superbly engineered design of timber trestle construction, which showed not only his genius in initiation of novel methods, but his foresight in providing for the efficient maintenance of them for many years subsequently. By the time I first travelled to Cornwall all those on the main line had been replaced by massive stone viaducts; but their replacement was primarily due to the need to widen the line for double track, and the need eventually to carry heavier locomotives. But the Cornwall Railway itself originally continued from Truro to a terminus at Falmouth, and on what later became no more than a branch line, all eight of these splendid timber viaducts remained, and I travelled over them on a number of occasions. The final stage of the run of the Cornish Riviera Express was made over what was once yet another separate company, the West Cornwall Railway.

The doubling of the line, and the replacement of the timber viaducts took place mostly before the end of the nineteenth century, and thus before the days of the Cornish Riviera Express; but one notable section remained until 1908, and was thus used by the train when it was running to its accelerated timing, and arriving at Penzance at 5 pm. A decision had been taken to build a deviation line further inland from the stretch across the creeks of the Lynher River between Saltash and St Germans, which would eliminate the need for two out of the six. Three of the original viaducts took the line across tidal waters, and Brunel could not use his normal practice of building stone piers, from the tops of which the radiating trestles spread out. Instead he drove timber piles down into the mud of the river beds, in one case extending to 70 ft below high water mark before reaching a solid foundation. These piles were extended vertically upward to form the main and only support for the horizontal bridge girders, also, of course, entirely in timber; and it must have been a stirring sight to see the Cornish Riviera Express, hauled by one of Churchward's 'Bulldog' class 4-4-0s with six of the huge 'Dreadnought' type elliptical corridor coaches crossing the Forder or the Nottar Viaducts, 67 ft above high watermark, on a gallery supported on what looked like the slenderest of stilts. The inland deviation was completed in 1908, and included fine new stone viaducts at Forder, Grove and St Germans, and thereafter 4-6-0 locomotives of the 'Saint' and 'Star' classes could run in Cornwall, also from 1923, the 'Castles'.

When the train was re-introduced in 1921 it ran non-stop between Plymouth and Truro, and when I first travelled on it the timing for the 54¾ mile run was 81 minutes. This average speed of only 40½ mph was an adequate commentary upon the difficulties of the line. I have a log of the eastbound run on which a two-cylinder 4-6-0 engine, the *Lady of Shalott* took 79¼ minutes, with a train of seven coaches, and even on the downhill section from Doublebois to the Defiance halt, just before Saltash, the average speed was no more than 48 mph. In the later 1920s the growing popularity of Newquay led to the regular inclusion of an additional through carriage and the insertion of a stop at Par to detach it. By that time the 'King' class engines were on the job, and not only had the once exceptional fourteen-coach train leaving Paddington become the regular load, but seven minutes had been cut from the London–Plymouth time, reducing it from 247 minutes to the level four hours, and requiring a start to stop average speed of 56·4 mph.

For a sightseer, whatever his or her interests, the ride through Cornwall had something for everybody. To an engineer, crossing the present viaducts, the stone piers that supported Brunel's trestles were still alongside; the China Clay workings around St Austell, are intriguing seen from afar looking like so many tents of the Gods, while the tin mining country beyond Truro arouses memories of Trevithick. For those with other interests there is the sparse run of Restormel Castle, perched upon its height, and looking down upon some of the loveliest inland scenery in Cornwall, followed by the grey old town of Lostwithiel, with its lofty church spire surmounting a very beautiful octagonal lantern tower. Then, after leaving Par there is a brief sight of the open sea, and a golf course on the cliff edge such as to tempt the veriest tyros of the game!

Railway enthusiasts will no doubt be interested to see the place after which one of the most famous of all Great Western engines is named, the 'City of Truro', and I am sure they would not be disappointed at the gracious panorama that opens out as they cross the lengthy viaduct, at one time the longest of all the historic timber trestle viaducts. Then having parted with the Falmouth coach, the train goes on through the mining country, and makes a brief stop at Gwinear Road to set down passengers for Helston and the Lizard. Lastly to St Erth, the station whose platforms are lined with palm trees, where the St Ives coach is detached, and finally, with only four of the original fourteen coaches left, across the narrow isthmus to the south coast once more, for the breathtaking *denouement* of the entire journey, the wonderful sight of St Michael's Mount with its fairytale castle, rising majestically from the waters of Mounts Bay. A few minutes later the train draws into Penzance.

6

THE FLYING SCOTSMAN

In 1919 as a schoolboy still in my early teens I stood enthralled on Selby station and watched as, at ten minute intervals, the two sections of the morning Scottish express passed through. The first was the 9.50 am relief and the second, the time-honoured 10 am, the train that for 57 years had left London at that time for Edinburgh and which was originally described in the time-tables as the 'Special Scotch Express'. As always there was rivalry between Kings Cross and Euston for the Anglo-Scottish passenger business, and from its inception in 1862 the 10 am from Kings Cross carried first and second-class passengers only. The rival train from Euston, which ran to slower timings carried all three classes. Then, in 1872, when the Midland Railway decided to convey third-class passengers on all its trains the Great Northern did the same, with the exception of the Special Scotch Express; but to give their patrons something extra for their money, they and their partners the North Eastern accelerated that train by a full hour between London and Edinburgh, cutting the time to 9½ hours. Again, in 1876, when the Midland were about to open the far-famed Settle and Carlisle line, and were in a position to accelerate their Anglo-Scottish service, the East Coast partners cut a further half-hour off the time of the Special Scotch Express.

The Midland running from St Pancras, and beset with well established rivals to both east and west, had to fight hard for traffic, and it did so by progressive acceleration of service, and some skilful advertising of the scenic charms of its route to Scotland. On the West Coast route, the dominating personality was Richard Moon, the formidable Chairman of the London and North Western Railway. He was opposed to all proposals for service acceleration, as being liable to increase operating and maintenance costs, and so disturb the established profitability of the company. So long as the Kings Cross route was the only competitor, not conveying third-class passengers on the best trains, all was well; but the entry of the Midland into the competitive field changed the situation for both Kings Cross and Euston,

63

and two moves of major consequence sparked off the first 'Race to the North'. The first of these was the decision of the East Coast, in November 1887, to admit third-class passengers to the Special Scotch Express, and this was followed in June 1888, by acceleration of the West Coast train by a full hour, to run on equality with the East Coast, both taking nine hours from London to Edinburgh. How things worked out in the heat of competition can be appreciated from the two fastest runs made in August of that exciting year.

Route	Distance Miles	Total time mins	Average Speeds mph	Average Running Speed mph
East Coast	392·7	447	52·7	57·7
West Coast	399·8	458	52·3	56·2

The final column in this table of comparisons shows the average speed when the time of stoppages en route is deducted, and these included not only the relative brief halts to change engines, but also the 25 minute luncheon stops, at York, and at Preston.

Great Northern Atlantics were the standard engines on the Flying Scotsman in pre-Pacific days: seen here is No. 4414 in LNER colours at Grantham.

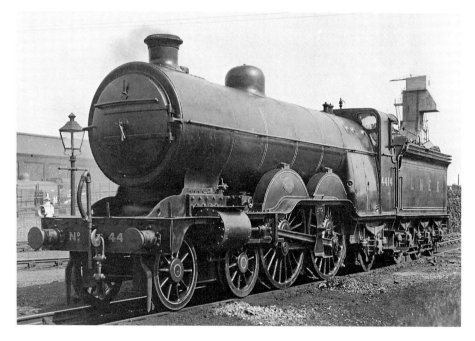

It is probable that the name *Flying Scotsman*, or more likely then *Flying Scotchman*, originated at this time, though quite unofficially, and applied indiscriminately to both competitors! In his *History of the Great Northern Railway*, published in 1898, W.J. Grinling refers to the two Flying Scotchmen, being the 10 am departures from Kings Cross and Edinburgh, and the book included a reproduction of a photograph titled 'The Up Scotchman', taken almost head-on from the open-lattice footbridge at Sandy station; but judging from the high-lighting and the direction of the shadows it could not have been the 10 am up from Edinburgh, because that train was not due to pass Sandy until around 5.20 pm, and by that time the shadows from the various buildings, including the signal box, would be lengthening, and across the tracks. Reverting to the running times however, after the excitement, on both sides it was felt that the competition had gone far enough, and for the winter service of 1888–9 the East Coast and West Coast companies agreed on minimum times of 8¼ hours from London to Edinburgh by East Coast and 8½ hours, by West Coast, having consideration to the rather longer distance to be covered, and the more severe gradients of the West Coast.

The up Flying Scotsman, non-stop from Edinburgh passing Grantham, headed by 'A1' class Gresley 4-6-2 No. 4475 Flying Fox.

When competition in amenities began to replace the competition in speed, and the beautiful twelve-wheeled bogie clerestory corridor stock replaced the old six wheelers the greatly increased loads soon brought to an end the inflexible rule of Patrick Stirling's day, 'one train, one engine'. Indeed that much loved old Scots engineer had made it impossible for his express locomotives to be double-headed, by omitting to carry the brake connection pipe through to the front buffer beam! But in the early 1900s the new 'Atlantic' engines of H.A. Ivatt were tackling any load the Traffic Department liked to ask of them; and when war came in 1914, and restrictions upon travel facilities led to the cancellation of many express train services, those that remained, still taken by one 'Atlantic' engine, became heavier than anything previously dreamed of. Whereas the daytime Anglo-Scottish expresses of the 1900–1914 period rarely loaded to more than 300 tons,

March 1938: Class 'A3' 4-6-2 No. 2507 Singapore *has just backed on, at Newcastle, to take the train forward to Edinburgh.*

trains of 500 tons and more were taken out of Kings Cross from 1916, albeit at slower scheduled speeds. Still the morning express for Edinburgh left at 10 am and when the Government rules for the rationalisation of passenger travel were introduced, it became the *only* train by which one could travel from London to Edinburgh in the daytime. Bookings were not permitted by either of the one-time competitive routes from Euston and St Pancras.

The seeds of a new competition between the East and West Coast routes to Scotland were sown in 1922 when the first two engines of the 'Pacific' type for the Great Northern Railway were built at the Doncaster Plant, and the second of them, No. 1471, was at first stationed at Kings Cross, and worked daily to Grantham on the 10 am express. A fine photograph of this new engine so engaged was published in *The Railway Magazine* and the train was described as the '10 am Down East Coast Restaurant Car Express' – not a whisper of 'The Flying Scotsman'. At the beginning of 1923 came the Grouping of the British railways, and the entire East Coast Route from London to Aberdeen, formerly consisting of the Great Northern, North Eastern and North British Railways, became united in the new London and North Eastern Railway; and with the former Great Northern locomotive chief Herbert Nigel Gresley appointed as Chief Mechanical Engineer of the new group a continuation of Doncaster practice was to be expected. A further ten engines of the 'Pacific' type were built during the year 1923. It was when one of these new engines No. 1472 was being 'dolled-up' in readiness for display at the great British Empire Exhibition, at Wembley in 1924 that the name 'Flying Scotsman' was applied officially, and then only to a locomotive and not to any particular train. In fact the engine chosen for exhibition was normally stationed at Doncaster, and did not take any part in the working of Anglo-Scottish expresses.

It was when some new coaching stock was introduced in the autumn of 1924 that the name 'Flying Scotsman' was used officially for the 10 am expresses from Kings Cross and Edinburgh. More significant however than the use of the famous name was the incorporation of technical features that were new to the East Coast Anglo-Scottish service. First, and most out-wardly apparent was the use of a triplet articulated dining car set, in which the first and third-class saloons had between them a kitchen car. Before succeeding H.A. Ivatt as Locomotive Engineer of the Great Northern Rail-way, Gresley had been Carriage and Wagon Engineer, and he had done a considerable amount in developing the principle of coach articulation, in flexibly coupling two coach bodies, and supporting the point of junction on a single bogie. Thus, in an articulated 'twin', only three bogies would be needed, instead of four in the case of two separate coaches. In the triplet restaurant car sets for the Flying Scotsman a total of only four bogies was needed, and the weight of the assembly thereby much reduced. Moreover, the set rode very smoothly. This was not the first time an articulated dining car set had been used on the Kings Cross route because in 1921 a *quintuple* set was introduced on the London–Leeds service, with complete success, and on this, like the new Anglo-Scottish triplet sets of 1924, the cooking was all-electric. But a feature of the ordinary coaches that attracted considerable attention from passengers was the *decor*.

In earlier chapters of this book, particularly when writing of The Southern Belle, I have referred to the tendency developing in twentieth century rolling stock to make the interior decoration more and more ornate; but with the new LNER Anglo-Scottish stock this tendency was entirely reversed. The prevailing note throughout the trains was simplicity. The walls of the first-class restaurant cars were lined with large naturally coloured mahogany panels, and the usual net racks and hat pegs were of the plainest possible design. The seats in the first-class compartments were of the armchair type, comfortably upholstered in green morocco leather, fitted with specially constructed cushions. The floors were covered with green indiarubber over felt, which deadened sound, and seemed very soft when walked upon. The third-class compartments were upholstered in crimson and black plush. Externally, the characteristic varnished teak finish was applied, though these trains marked the final end of the turn-of-century clerestory roofed coaches that were always so admired. Gresley himself, when Carriage and Wagon Engineer of the Great Northern Railway changed to elliptical roofs and pronounced bow-ends for new coaches built in the early 1900s, and this style was continued in 1924. As yet there was no increase in speed. A minimum time of 8¼ hours between Kings Cross and Edinburgh was faithfully observed, and paralleled by the West Coast route, but competition between the two old rivals began to take another form in 1927.

With family motoring still in its infancy, and the main highways undeveloped, tourist traffic on the railways in the summer holiday season had grown to the extent that the principal express trains from London could be confined to purely Scottish passengers; and after some preliminary skirmishes in 1927 with the LMS running their 10 am train non-stop from Euston to Carnforth, and then stopping only for a locomotive change, while the 9.50 am relief to The Flying Scotsman was run non-stop from Kings Cross to Newcastle, the stage was set for the epoch-marking development on the East Coast route for running The Flying Scotsman itself non-stop over the 392·7 miles between Kings Cross and Edinburgh. It was a bold and spectacular venture, but one that was not undertaken without a great deal of preliminary engineering work. In that first season of 1928 the overall time remained at 8¼ hours, thus involving an average speed of no more than

47·7 mph. This in itself would not have demanded unduly strenuous work from the powerful Gresley 'Pacific' locomotives, even with loads that some- times reached nearly 500 tons; but there were two factors that had to be provided for, namely the adequacy of the coal supply, and the hours in which the enginemen would be on duty.

As originally built and running up to the year 1927 the Gresley 'Pacific' engines were requiring at least 50 lb of coal per mile in heavy express duty and this would have meant a total of 9 tons on the run from London to Edinburgh. The original tenders carried no more than 8 tons, but a very important alteration to the valve gear of the locomotives had greatly im- proved their performance, reducing their coal consumption to less than 40 lb per mile on duties such as these. But the question of manning remained and Gresley introduced the novel idea of having a tender with a corridor through which one engine crew could relieve the other at the half-way point of the journey, about a dozen miles north of York. It meant, of course, carrying two crews instead of one, and in designing these special corridor tenders, the coal carrying capacity was increased from 8 to 9 tons. In 1928 when the non-stop London–Edinburgh run was first introduced it was essential that the only engines to be fitted with corridor tenders were those having the improved valve gear. The Wembley Exhibition engine No. 4472 *Flying Scotsman* was naturally one of these, and a second London-based engine No. 4476 *Royal Lancer* was available as a standby, though naturally the *Flying Scotsman* itself was used as often as possible. The Edinburgh engines fitted with corridor tenders, and used on the 'non-stop' were No. 2569 *Gladiateur*, 2573 *Harvester* and 2580 *Shotover*, though the manning over the northern part of the journey was shared, on different occasions, between enginemen from Gateshead and Haymarket (Edinburgh) sheds.

The enthusiasts who studied the finer point of locomotive performance were very much inclined to dismiss the working of the non-stop Flying Scotsman as something not worth the lengthy journey involved. Certainly they would not be able to observe any examples of maximum power output – nothing to compare, for example, with what was demanded from the same class of locomotive on the sharply timed, and heavily loaded expresses between London and the cities of the West Riding. But the running of the 'non-stop', as it was always known among the London enginemen was a test of their skill in another direction. On other trains to which far less publicity had been focussed, if at some point in the journey adverse signals compelled a dead stop a driver could 'open out' his engine, run faster than usual, and make up the lost time. From the very inception of the summer working of The Flying Scotsman it had been impressed upon all concerned that the journey should be made non-stop; and this instruction applied not only to the train crews but to every traffic man, and every signalman along the line – 392¾ miles of it.

On the open line this would not be too difficult, but the East Coast route to Scotland led through some busy and complicated traffic centres, notably Doncaster, York and Newcastle, and at holiday times there was always a great deal of cross movement. At holiday times one could hardly expect the mass of excursion trains to be run with the precision of the 'non-stop', and although the 'paths' of these trains were always carefully plotted out beforehand late running was often inevitable. Then it was up to the 'man on the ground' to decide how other trains could be further delayed in order to give the 'non-stop' a clear run through. All this was long before the days of

A famous Edinburgh 'A3', No. 2795 Call Boy *passing Retford, on the southbound 'non-stop' in 1934.*

large panel signal boxes, when the men responsible for traffic regulation had the outstanding advantage of an immense illuminated diagram of all the tracks in the surrounding area of a large centre with the positions of approaching trains pinpointed by indication lights. When the 'non-stop' was first introduced all the signalling was by semaphore arms, mechanically actuated, and at a big centre like York regulation was the responsibility of the Assistant Station Master, who was constantly in touch with half a dozen or more signal boxes, entirely by telephone. I have had the privilege of seeing one of those remarkable men at work, on a hectic Saturday morning just before a Bank Holiday, and I marvelled at the almost uncanny grasp he had, entirely in his mind's eye, of the constantly changing traffic position.

The vital part to be played by the enginemen of the 'non-stop' was to approach each of the major centres precisely on time. It would have been fatal to have run with a minute or two in hand, to offset the chance of delays. I shall always remember the remark of one of the top-link Kings Cross men after a successful run, with the northbound train. 'It was touch and go at York,' he said. 'If I'd been half-a-minute early I'd have been stopped.' In 1932, after four successful summer seasons, the overall time from London to Edinburgh was quickened by three-quarters of an hour, and the average speed required was stepped up to 52·4 mph. There was no difficulty in this from the locomotive point of view, but once again the timetabling required accurate observation. The running speeds over the successive stages would appear to be uneven, but these were essential to fit in with other trains. The booked timings were thus:

Section	Distance Miles	Booked Average Speed mph	Booked Time Minutes	Time Minutes Actual
Kings Cross–Peterborough	76·4	58·0	79	78¼
Peterborough–Grantham	29·1	49·9	35	35
Grantham–Doncaster	50·5	54·1	56	55½
Doncaster–York	32·2	49·6	39	40½
York–Newcastle	80·1	53·4	91	89
Newcastle–Berwick	66·9	50·2	80	75¾
Berwick–Edinburgh	57·5	49·3	70	73¼

Running times of an actual run on which I travelled are given in the last column of the above table. The London driver passed Doncaster 1¼ minutes ahead of time and then eased down, so as not to be early at York. The Edinburgh man who took over, at Tollerton 9¾ miles north of York, was 4 minutes early by Durham, but eased down very much and passed through the Newcastle area only 1½ minutes early. The engine was in good fettle however and we made some good speed onwards to Berwick, passing there 5¾ minutes early. Traffic was not heavy on that part of the line, but although we had passed into Scotland in such good style there was no point in running further ahead of time. I was privileged to go through the corridor tender north of Newcastle and spend some time on the footplate and I saw then that everything was going very smoothly with plenty of coal left, and the engine as quiet as a sewing machine. We arrived in Edinburgh 2½ minutes early.

For the summer season of 1935, when as in the years from 1932 the train would once again be running to the 7½ hour non-stop timing, some beautiful restaurant cars were introduced and the style of internal decoration reverted to the ornate. The first-class were furnished in the French style of a drawing room of the Louis XIV period, in pale pink and white. But my most vivid recollection of travel in these cars is not of the 'non-stop' summer running but of a winter's afternoon in the February of 1936. In the previous autumn the spotlight of attention on the East Coast route had been switched from the Flying Scotsman to the new high-speed streamlined Silver Jubilee, which is described in a later chapter of this book; but interest in the performance of the breathtaking silver painted streamlined 'Pacific' engines was diversified on Saturdays. The Jubilee did not run on that day, and the London engine that had taken the streamliner north on the Friday returned from Newcastle to Kings Cross on the Flying Scotsman, on the following afternoon. It was always a very heavy and well patronised train, never less than fifteen coaches; moreover, the train involved much harder running than in the period of the non-stop because, although the arrival time in Kings Cross was the same, intermediate stops had to be made at Berwick-upon-Tweed, Newcastle, Darlington, York and Grantham. In one respect things were not so exacting because engines were changed at Newcastle.

I was collecting data on the working of the streamlined engines for some articles in the technical press, and was privileged to spend sometime on the footplate. For most of the way southbound from Newcastle we were running in blizzard conditions, but it had little or no effect on our speed; but it was when going through the corridor tender for the last time, after we had left Grantham, that the extraordinary contrast on such a day between travelling conditions in the train and on the engine were borne home to me. In the dining car it was tea time; against a background of soft shaded lights, in that elegant saloon the white-coated stewards hurried to and fro bringing piles of hot toast. Passengers shrank from the windows where ice had packed up outside and snow spluttered against the panes. Then after making my way through the narrow passage of the corridor tender I entered an

'A4s' on the Flying Scotsman: one of the blue streamliners, No. 4489 Dominion of Canada *at Stoke summit, 100 miles from Kings Cross. The photograph has caught a moment when the Canadian presentation bell is actually being tolled.*

eerie dusk, lit only by the glare of the fire. The driver was perched on the left hand side of the cab, constantly looking out: brasswork glinting in the firelight: pressure gauge needles pulsating: the engine riding very 'hard' but steady. The cab glasses were almost blocked with packed up ice, but the queer streamlined front hurled the exhaust steam high and clear, and despite the weather every signal stood out clear and brilliant. The fireman silhouetted against the dazzling arc of light braced himself against every swing of the engine, stoking, adjusting the injectors, occasionally looking out too. And below Little Bytham the speed rose to just over ninety miles an hour.

In 1935 however, and again in 1937, the prestige of The Flying Scotsman had been to some extent stolen by the brilliant début, first of the Silver Jubilee and then of the Coronation streamlined trains. But for the summer traffic of 1938 new trains composed of the traditional teak bodied stock were to be introduced that were to embody a number of important technical advances; these, such as air-conditioning throughout, though deeply inter-esting from the engineering viewpoint, were not such as to 'hit the headlines' of popular publicity, and after all the 'razmataz' of Coronation year the introduction of the new trains was likely to pass almost unnoticed, parti-cularly in view of the worsening international situation on the continent of Europe. My friend the late E.G. Marsden then held the office that would now be termed Press Officer, but which on the LNER was titled Information Agent. The year was the fiftieth anniversary of the first 'Race to the North', and he conceived the idea of displaying the new Flying Scotsman against a replica of the old one. The Stirling 8 ft bogie 4-2-2 engine No. 1 was in the old Railway Museum at York and to have it, and perhaps to run it, in conjunction with one of the latest Gresley streamlined 'Pacifics' seemed a good way of emphasising the developments of fifty years on the East Coast route. There was only one man who could endorse such a proposal, and that was Gresley himself.

Marsden told me how, not without an attack of 'butterflies in the tummy', he sought an interview, in order to put the suggestion, 'because' he added 'if the Great Man is not amused, one had to be sure of a quick line of retreat!' But Gresley was delighted. Not only did he arrange for the old Stirling engine to be taken into Doncaster Plant, given a thorough overhaul, and put into full working condition, but enough six-wheeled coaching stock of 1888 vintage to make up a seven-car train was located, completely refur-bished and adorned with the old coat of arms of the East Coast Joint Stock. Then on the day the new Flying Scotsman train had its Press Run the guests of the LNER were taken from Kings Cross to Stevenage in the 1888 vintage train, hauled in gallant style by the Stirling 4-2-2 engine, and there they transferred to the new train for a very fast run to Grantham. That delightful exposition certainly started something, because in subsequent weeks the vintage train was used for many special excursions. In the meantime the new trains, with all their additional amenities, had taken up regular service, and had become the subject of some controversy among certain erudite connoisseurs of express train operation.

It was after the period of non-stop running during the summer was ended, and the train was carrying its minimum winter load of fourteen coaches, that the critics began to weigh in. The rake included not only the usual full restaurant car accommodation for first and third class, but a very attrac-tively styled buffet car. The decor throughout was very attractive, and in addition to the air conditioning all the windows were double glazed. This made for a considerable increase in the weight to be hauled. The previous train, of fifteen coaches, including the triplet-articulated dining car set had a tare weight of 482 tons. The new train of fourteen vehicles, which because of the inclusion of the buffet car provided less seating, weighed 503 tons. It set a severe task to the streamlined 'Pacifics' and some of the critics felt it was too much, seeing how fast and demanding the scheduled running times had become; but in the winter of 1938 with slightly reduced loads the Flying Scotsman had a marvellous record of punctuality. I examined the working results during the first three weeks of December. The average load on seventeen noted occasions was 480 tons tare, or about 510 tons with passengers and luggage, and on no occasion was there a single minute to be booked against the engine. In fact, in recovering time lost by signal and permanent way checks an aggregate of 110 minutes was *gained*, or an average of 6½ minutes a trip. Nine different engines and ten different crews were involved, and far from heavier loads overpowering the locomotives one of the finest runs of all was made on a day when a tonnage of 560 was conveyed.

The summer of 1939 however was no time for flights of fascinating railway publicity, and with the onset of war in September the Flying Scotsman, like all other famous British express trains was lumped into the pool of greatly decelerated service. The summer service of 1938, and the early part of the winter that followed, saw its swan song; for when the time came after the war for the 'non-stop' to be revived, it was titled The Capitals Limited, and from 1953 The Elizabethan. The latter, accelerated ultimately to a brilliant 6½ hour non-stop run, provided a magnificent steam finale on the East Coast route, still worked by the incomparable Gresley streamlined 'Pacifics'; but it was not the Flying Scotsman.

7

THE IRISH MAIL

In days gone by communication with Ireland was always of major importance, and well before the introduction of railways construction of the Holyhead Road (now the A5) and the beautiful suspension bridge over the Menai Strait was considered to be one of the greatest works of Thomas Telford, first President of the Institution of Civil Engineers, and sometimes jokingly referred to as 'The Colossus of Roads'! After the opening of the bridge the average time taken to convey the mails from London to Dublin was 50 hours. When the Chester and Holyhead railway was completed, but while the final link across the Menai Strait had to be made by coach, the Irish Mail train service was inaugurated, on 1 August 1848. It was the first train in Great Britain, if not the whole world to have an official name, though this was not displayed on the carriage roof boards until the summer of 1927. It was not until two years after the Irish Mail had started running that Robert Stephenson's great Britannia Tubular Bridge was complete, and the whole journey from London to Holyhead was made by train.

From its inauguration the service was run in conditions virtually dictated by the Post Office. The convenience of passengers was quite a minor consideration. Moreover there was the deuce to pay if there was any late running. When the contract was renewed in 1860, jointly between the Post Office, the London and North Western Railway, and the City of Dublin Steam Packet Company, which operated the mail boats, the total journey time between London and Dublin was fixed at 11 hours, and believe it or not, the contract included a penalty clause that imposed a fine of £1.14s (£1.70p) for every minute by which the contract time was exceeded! The London and North Western Railway had the task of maintaining an overall average speed of 42 mph between Euston and Holyhead, and this was better than might otherwise be imagined. There were intermediate stops to be made at Rugby, Crewe and Chester, at all of which a large amount of mail had to be handled, and at Holyhead itself there was a further complication in that the mail packets sailed from the outer end of the Admiralty Pier. At that extremity the structure was not able to take the axle loading of even the modest little express engines of the day, and the mail had to stop at the entrance to the pier to change engines, for something even smaller, to complete the last stage of the run.

This clumsy arrangement prevailed so long as the City of Dublin Steam Packet Company had the contract for the conveyance of the mail by sea, even after the London and North Western Railway had built their magnificent inner harbour, with facilities for the trains to run alongside the steamers and the transfer of mails and passengers to take place in sheltered, largely undercover conditions. In the early years of the twentieth century, when the fine 4-4-0 and 4-6-0 locomotives of George Whale's designs worked the mail trains, the run out to the end of the Admiralty Pier was made by one of the so-called 'Special' saddle tank 0-6-0 engines. It was an incongruous sight to see one of these tiny little things, with its driver and fireman out in the open without any protection of a cab, puffing its way out on to the pier, with a heavy corridor dining car train. Several times prior to the outbreak of war in 1914 the London and North Western Railway had attempted to secure the contract for carrying the mail across the sea; but sentiment in Ireland was always 'touchy' in this respect, and on one occasion when the English railway's contract bid was favourable and

The down Irish Mail leaving the Britannia Tubular bridge, in LNWR days, hauled by 2-4-0 engine No. 1519 Duchess *and 4-6-0 No. 257* Plynlimmon (Prince of Wales *class).*

was actually accepted by the Post Office such a storm was raised in Dublin that the L & NWR was asked to withdraw. And so, until 1920, mails and passengers changed from train to boat at the end of the exposed Admiralty Pier!

Quite apart from its official name the Irish Mail can claim three other 'firsts' in railway history, and in this connection it should be added that from very early days there was a day as well as a night service over which the Post Office exercised just as stringent a control of scheduling and time-keeping. The first of the three innovations was concerned purely with railway operating. In the late 1850s a draughtsman in Crewe Works, John Bland by name, made some preliminary sketches of an apparatus by which locomotives could take up water without stopping, from a trough laid between the rails. The great locomotive engineer John Ramsbottom quickly appreciated the value of such a device, at a time when longer non-stop runs were being demanded; and under his direction the idea was quickly developed, trial apparatus made, and by the time the exacting Post Office contract of 1860 was concluded the first water troughs in the world had been installed near Aber, a wayside station on the North Wales coast between Llanfairfechan and Bangor. The Irish Mail was then able to run non-stop over the 84 miles between Chester and Holyhead.

The other two 'firsts' were for the comfort of passengers. The timing of the outward bound night mail, dictated by the Post Office, was not particularly attractive to passengers, because it involved the change from train to boat at three o'clock in the morning. The more leisured and wealthy passengers took the day mail, and it was for their comfort that luncheon baskets were introduced in 1876, to be purchased while the train was at Chester. They subsequently became popular on a number of other railways, even after the introduction of dining cars. Very many years later I remember my mother deciding to have luncheon baskets as an alternative to a restaurant meal on one of our holiday journeys; but the baskets themselves, I recall, were so enormous as to be an embarrassment in a carriage with many other passengers. In the first-class compartments of the Irish Mail in late Victorian days I should imagine however that our own problem would not have arisen. The luncheon baskets on sale at Chester were of two kinds:

The 'Aristocratic', containing:	The 'Democratic', containing:
One pint of claret or half-pint sherry	Cold meat or pie
Chicken, ham, or tongue	Bread and cheese
Butter, cheese, bread, condiments	Pint bottle ale or stout
(Price five shillings)	(Price half-a-crown)

The last of the innovations first introduced on the Irish Mail was Webb's soda-acetate foot-warmers provided in cold weather. They cooled down quickly however with the salt crystals solidifying, and at each stopping station porters used to enter the carriages to shake them up, and regenerate the heat. The comments aroused, between passengers hitherto maintaining the frigid silence of convention between strangers, is said to have originated the modern figurative expression, 'breaking the ice' – yet another 'first' for the Irish Mail!

Both day and night mails included a travelling post office carriage, with apparatus for picking up and setting down mails at full speed. This practice became very popular in years before the first world war, and many quite small towns on railways all over the country had lineside standards and nets where mails could be collected and set down. But the supervisor in charge of the travelling post office on the down night Irish Mail had a duty that was unique. In days before wireless telegraphy came into general use the 'King's Time' was sent from London to Dublin every night, and ten minutes or so before the departure of the mail train from Euston a messenger used to arrive from Post Office Headquarters at St Martins-le-Grand with a watch, carried in a leather pouch and this was taken all the way to Dublin, so that the Post Office Officials there knew the correct time. After the establishment of the Irish Free State the tradition was continued, but in an abbreviated form. In the 1930s, when I was occasionally travelling by the night Irish Mail I saw the old ritual being performed at Euston, and was once shown the watch itself – a magnificent, if wholly utilitarian timepiece. At that time it was carried only as far as Holyhead.

In the later years of the first world war when passenger train speeds all over Great Britain were generally much decelerated, the timings of the night mails, particularly between Chester and Holyhead were kept quite smart, including a run over this section of 84½ miles in 93 minutes. The loads also were at times extremely heavy. The largest engines then in use were the 4-6-0s of the 'Prince of Wales' class, but for traffic working they were grouped with the very efficient superheater 4-4-0s of the 'George the Fifth' class, and required to take a tare load of 400 tons before a pilot engine could be claimed. Just before the war the London and North Western Railway had built a new series of the 4-6-0 engines all of which, with one exception, had been named after poets and men of letters, and quite a number of these engines were at one time engaged on the Chester and Holyhead line. The Irish Mails, both day and night changed engines at Crewe, but Holyhead itself was a fairly large shed, and units stationed there alternated with Crewe engines. Unlike the situation that prevailed on the Scotch Corridor trains, as referred to in Chapter 4, the express locomotives at Holyhead, and Crewe were nearly all common user. Quite a variety of poets were to be seen on the Irish Mails in the war years, *Lord Byron*, *Robert Louis Stevenson*, and *Sir W.S. Gilbert*, being noted at different times.

While not strictly coming within the title of Irish Mail it must be recorded that prior to the first world war there were two other services from London to Dublin in each direction, one by day and the other by night. On both of these the L & NWR steamers made the sea crossing, and departure was from the palatial inner harbour station. The day express leaving Euston at 1.20 pm was cancelled early in the war, but it was not until 1918 that any appreciable deceleration of the mail trains took place either by day or night. At one time there had been no fewer than four runs made non-stop over the 105¾ miles between Crewe and Holyhead, with the fastest in 122 minutes; but in the restoration of fast running after the war none of the Irish mail trains passed Chester without stopping, except on occasions of very heavy traffic when there were relief portions, apart from those including the travelling post office carriages. The mail portion of both the day and night trains consisted of one post office sorting carriage, and a stowage van. There were times however when the outgoing mail to Ireland was very heavy between Euston and Crewe, and more than could be dealt with by the crew of a single sorting van. Then advantage was taken of the running of the West Coast Postal Special, 15 minutes ahead of the night Irish Mail. Bags were collected at speed by the 'Special', sorted, and appropriately bagged up in one of the TPO carriages then set down at one of the lineside nets to be collected a quarter of an hour later by the Irish Mail, ready sorted, and needing only to be stacked in the storage van.

During a family holiday in North Wales in 1921 I was able to see something of the working of the day Irish Mails, both of which passed each other near Colwyn Bay around 1 pm. A favourite place for observation was near Llandudno Junction, where the trains were running slower than normal for the speed restriction through the tubular bridge at Conway and the curve through Conway station. Towards the end of the summer season the loads were very heavy but it was not often that either train was double headed. There was a lineside vantage point from which the mail bag exchanging operation could be watched, and as a locomotive enthusiast I was fascinated in the variety of locomotives seen working those two trains. Despite their great power the largest L & NWR express locomotives of the 4-6-0 'Claughton' class were not used, because on account of their length there was some difficulty in turning them at Holyhead. Reliance had to be placed on the inside cylinder 4-6-0s of the 'Prince of Wales' class, and on 4-4-0s. When double heading was needed one often saw some interesting combinations because a variety of older classes was used for assisting.

The up Irish Mail, in the shadow of Penmaenmawr mountain, hauled by Renown class 4-4-0 No. 1968 Cumberland *and 4-6-0 No. 233* Suvla Bay.

Between Chester and Llandudno Junction the line following the North Wales coast was little removed from dead level, except at the modest 'hump' between Abergele and Colwyn Bay where the line was carried over the Penmaenrhos headland; and to keep time meant steady continuous running at around 60 mph. The fastest running of the journey usually took place on the Isle of Anglesey, where the gradients were more markedly undulating. The timing of the down day mail was eased to 103 minutes from Chester to Holyhead in the last year of the war, and with this concession considerably heavier loads than the standard 400 tons were often taken without assistance, and often with notable gains on schedule time. With catholicity in taste, and an almost complete absence of system in its engine naming one often saw some odd associations of names on double-headed trains and three combinations that I have known may be quoted. *Colossus* and *Sir W.S. Gilbert*; *Prince Leopold* and *Charles Wolfe*; *Duchess* and *Plynlimmon*. The train engines in all these combinations were 4-6-0s of the 'Prince of Wales'; of the leaders *Colossus* was a four-cylinder Webb compound 4-4-0 of the 'Jubilee' class, while both of the others were of the spritely little

Travelling post office van, as used on the Irish Mail.

2-4-0 'Precedent' class of 1874 vintage. But I have also seen trains almost as heavy as the foregoing taken without assistance, by the 'Prince of Wales' class 4-6-0s *Lord Byron*, *Admiral Jellicoe*, and one of the post-war built series, not then named, No. 67.

I was never one for spending long vigils at the lineside recording the names and number of the engines that passed; but I was trigger-happy enough with an old folding Brownie camera, from which I still have the more than indifferent results I then secured. The notes of the trains I snapped over sixty years ago are enough to whet the appetite of those who would have been day-long train spotters, and at various times during that holiday on the up day Irish Mail alone I photographed a 'George the Fifth' 4-4-0 solo, the *Thomas Houghton*; a 'Precursor' 4-4-0, the *Phalaris*, piloting another 'George', the *Staghound*; and then, a great sight, two 'Prince of Wales' 4-6-0s *Victor Hugo* leading, and *Lord Byron* next to the train. The up Mail was often heaviest at mid-week, because it then conveyed through carriages from Holyhead to Manchester, which were detached at Chester. Curiously enough these three carriages were always marshalled next to the engines, ahead of the post office vehicles, and were thus cut off from the rest of the passenger part of the train. Travellers to Manchester therefore had no access to the dining cars, because one could not pass through the postal vans.

The grouping of the British railways, in 1923, and the inclusion of the London and North Western within the vast new London Midland and Scottish system did not have any immediate change in the working of the Irish Mails; but when the new 'Royal Scot' class locomotives were introduced in 1927 there was a considerable reorganisation of the locomotive rostering, and for the first time Holyhead engines and men began working through to Euston, on a 'double-home' basis. Though not so long as some of the through workings assigned to the new 'Royal Scot' class locomotives the run of 264 miles between Euston and Holyhead was by far the longest ever regularly worked by engines of the former L & NWR and a small batch of 'Claughton' class four-cylinder 4-6-0s was stationed at Holyhead specially for the job. From that time onwards none but Holyhead men worked regularly on the Irish Mails. The day trains had some fairly sharp timings over the West Coast main line, including one of 83 minutes start to stop over the 77·2 miles from Willesden Junction to Rugby. But the immediate post-war timing of 103 minutes from Chester to Holyhead was not greatly accelerated, becoming first 100 minutes, and then 98 in the last years before the second world war. Except in the height of the summer however the down train attached a heavy tail of through coaches from Manchester at Chester, and often went forward with a load of well over 500 tons.

Although the long through run of 264 miles between Euston and Holyhead was considerably greater than anything envisaged at the time the engines were first introduced, in 1913, the 'Claughton' class had no difficulty in keeping time with loads up to 420 tons, and in the last years of the L & NWR when engines were still being changed at Crewe there is a record of one of them taking a load of 480 tons from Chester to Holyhead in 98 minutes. I have vivid memories of a journey by the up night mail in the late 1920s, on a raw January night. This was not in the cosy pleasance of a sleeping car, but following a wait on Crewe platform at two o'clock in the morning! I cannot now recall how I came to be changing trains at that unearthly hour, but when a smartly polished-up 'Claughton' brought the train in from Chester several minutes early I was glad to find a warm and comfortable compartment. The up Night Mail then ran non-stop from Crewe to Euston, at the not very exciting average speed of 51·2 mph; but with a fair load of just 400 tons I was interested to see how the engine would perform on this long duty, and I stayed awake for some time logging the running times. It was soon evident that the engine was in top form, and by Rugby we were getting well ahead of time. After that the effort began to be relaxed a little, and so did I. Falling asleep at last, I awoke to find us running into Euston exactly on time – 5.50 am on a January morning – and fortunately there were plenty of taxis waiting.

In the later 1930s railway business of one kind or another took me to Ireland many times, and while the night mail was not the most comfortable way of travelling time was never on my side in those days, and the early arrival of the mail steamer at Dun Laoghaire made the connections I needed when travelling beyond Dublin. I well remember a hectic day when I had an engine pass to ride the 'Limited Mail' of the Great Northern from Dublin to Belfast, returning by the corresponding train returning south at 5.40 pm from Great Victoria Street. In between arrival and departure in Belfast I had some signalling business to attend to up on the north coast at Coleraine and a lunch with my railway friends in Portrush. The Great Northern and its enginemen did me proud, and I was exhilarated rather than jaded, when I transferred from the footplate to the train for the last stage of the run, from Dublin down to the pier station at Dun Laoghaire. Incidentally in the 1938 *Bradshaw*, it was still named 'Kingstown'. Being a good sailor I always enjoyed the sea passage, but on that particular trip I must admit that at first I was more interested in the excellent dining saloon menu than any features of navigation. By nine o'clock that evening, despite the convivial lunch at Portrush, I was ravenous!

Although this is a book about trains one cannot write of the Irish Mail without some reference to the splendid 'express' steamers that made the crossing between Holyhead and Dun Laoghaire in 2 hours 55 minutes. The contract time required a speed of 25 knots, and made them among the fastest merchant ships afloat, and required turbines of no less than 16,000 horsepower. Moreover it was a tradition of the Irish Sea that the mail steamers *Cambria*, *Hibernia* and *Scotia* steamed at full speed regardless of the weather, even in dense fog. Other shipping knew the times they were due and kept out of the way! The journey by the inward bound mail that I shall always remember more vividly than any other was in the 'jumpy' days of 1939, weeks only before the outbreak of war. I had been to Cork riding on the beautiful new 4-6-0 of the Great Southern Railways, *Maeve*, and had returned on the 'English Mail'. This train like its counterpart on the Great Northern had a through section for Dun Laoghaire, but I had been riding on the footplate, and after a trip not without steaming troubles I was indescribably dirty. On arrival in Dublin I had to go back and find a place in the train, which had been crowded from the time we left Cork; but in Dublin we found crowds of additional passengers waiting, all anxious to get back to England in view of the ominous news from the Continent, and not very keen, in those jammed corridors, to make room for a dirty fellow in overalls, who might just have been on the run after blowing up a bank!

Political scares apart the eastbound night mail was a much more conven- ient service to the passenger than its west-bound counterpart, and with the boat docking at Holyhead just after midnight one could turn in at once. I usually indulged myself to the privacy and comfort of a sleeper, though I must admit railway interest kept me awake until we were well on our way. The up Night Mail was always a very heavy train, never in my travelling experience loaded to less than 500 tons on leaving Holyhead, and, after the 'Royal Scot' class 4-6-0 locomotives had taken over from the 'Claughtons', not piloted. The train then leaving Holyhead at 12.13 am was allowed 97 minutes for the run of 84·4 miles to Chester, and I usually logged the running as far as Llandudno Junction, this being one of the few occasions when I used a stop-watch while dressed in pyjamas. By Colwyn Bay, unless the running was unusually interesting I had 'nodded off'. I would wake with

The Irish Mail by sea, at 25 knots (!): the RMS Hibernia *at speed.*

The down Irish Mail hauled by a Royal Scot class 4-6-0 No. 6116 Irish Guardsman emerging from the Conway Tubular bridge, beneath the battlements of Conway Castle.

a start when we had drawn to a stop at Chester, but after that my next conscious moment would be when the steward brought an early morning cup of tea, and we were nearing Euston. One could, of course, stay in the car for some time after the actual arrival of the train.

I was always interested in the actual engines stationed at Holyhead and working on the mail trains. In London and North Western days, when all the express passenger engines, both old and new, were named it was only in a very few cases that any regard was paid to personal associations in the allocation of engines to individual sheds and duties, and the same attitude prevailed after the introduction of the 'Royal Scot' class 4-6-0s. Certainly the first fifty engines were confined to the West Coast main line, with most of them on duties that took them at different times almost anywhere between Euston and Glasgow. But when another twenty were added to the stud, and some became available for use elsewhere the same indiscriminate way of allocation prevailed, and although there were four bearing the names of famous Irish regiments, only one of these, No. 6120 *Royal Inniskilling Fusilier* became stationed at Holyhead and worked on the Irish Mails, though I have seen two of those with Welsh titles on the job, the *Welsh Guardsman*, and the *Royal Welch Fusilier*. One of the oddest combinations I ever saw when travelling down to Crewe one morning was the use of the *Gordon Highlander*: a Scottish named engine, with a Welsh driver (one of the several Jonesses from Holyhead), travelling through England, on the Irish Mail!

But all in all, despite my deep involvement with the train in later years and the fascinating quirks of history like foot-warmers, luncheon baskets, and the GPO watch, it would seem that boyhood impressions are the most lasting; and in that summer of 1921 travelling home from Llandudno, with vivid recollections of that most appealing stretch of line through Conway, and beneath the headlands of Penmaenbach and Penmaenmawr, I was to be treated to one last impression of the Irish Mail. We were travelling in a train bound for Manchester, and having had one or two intermediate stops to make we were travelling between Flint and Chester on the relief line, at about 60 mph. Then, somewhere near Sandycroft, going great guns and on the very next track to us came the Irish Mail. Never before had I been so near to a big engine going hard. It must have been going about 5 to 10 mph faster than we were, and the noise of its exhaust and machinery close at hand was terrific. It was a 'Prince of Wales' class 4-6-0, one of the many built since the war that had not been named, and as a locomotive enthusiast I am ashamed to say that I cannot remember the number. The long train passed steadily by: TPO vans, ordinary carriages, the dining cars, 'London (Euston) and Holyhead'. My boyish cup of happiness was full.

8

THE ATLANTIC COAST EXPRESS

From its very inception, in January 1923, the Southern Railway began to get a bad press. It is true that much of its rolling stock used on main line trains was non-corridor, and not particularly opulent, even in the first class, and except for a few trains the speeds were indifferent; but taken all round the three constituent companies were all doing a reasonably good job. It was not until July 1923 however, that the new top-level management team was announced, and even then without any clue as to the new General Manager. All three constituents had chief officers of outstanding ability and record of achievement, and all three had been knighted for their services. Senior of them was Sir William Forbes, of the Brighton, of which line he had been General Manager since 1899. Beside him was Sir Percy Tempest, primarily a civil engineer, who had indeed been Chief Engineer of the South Eastern and Chatham since 1899. On that line he succeeded Sir Francis Dent as General Manager in 1920, while continuing to hold the office of Chief Engineer. Youngest of the three was Sir Herbert Walker, of the London and South Western Railway who, compared to the others, was a relative new-comer to railways south of the Thames for until his appointment on the L & SWR in 1912, the first twenty-seven years of his railway service had been on the London and North Western.

Until the end of 1923 these three senior executive officers acted jointly; but then with Forbes and Tempest retiring Sir Herbert Walker got the job, and it was not long before the press, and such of the travelling public as dared to criticise realised that they had to deal with a tartar! Some relatives of mine were living in Eastbourne at the time, and a deputation of season ticket holders waited upon Sir Herbert to lay before him the inadequacy of the service to and from London and the unsatisfactory condition of the rolling stock. He swept aside their complaints, and threw in one of his own, namely that the state of the carriages was entirely due to the filthy habits of the passengers! After that, of course, in the eyes of the popular press the Southern could do nothing right. The Beaverbrook papers formed the spearhead of the attack; but after some stormy months the nettle was grasped by the appointment of J.B. Elliot, hitherto Assistant Editor of the *Evening Standard*, as Assistant to Sir Herbert Walker for publicity, and later for advertising also. Elliot moreover was a nephew of Lord Beaverbrook, and as well as being a first rate newspaper man he had a natural flair for publicity. Within a remarkably short time he had put the Southern in the very front rank.

His first step was to bestow names upon the principal express passenger locomotives of the company. It was announced as a Board decision. It may have been, but Elliot was behind it. In any case he was given the job of breaking the news to R.E.L. Maunsell, the Chief Mechanical Engineer. In 1925 he and his staff were bringing out a new and greatly improved version of Robert Urie's 'N15' class 4-6-0, which had been the premier locomotive design of the London and South Western Railway and had been engaged principally on the West of England service; but it was intended that the new engines should have a wider field of activity, including the Continental Boat Expresses to Folkestone and Dover. In a flash of inspiration however, having regard to the close association of the old L & SWR with the West Country, Elliot recommended naming the new engines after characters, and places in the legend of King Arthur, but when the idea was put to Maunsell, the Chief Mechanical Engineer with a touch of his native Irish wit replied: 'Tell Sir Herbert Walker I have no objection, but I warn you it won't make any difference to the working of the engine!' As a piece of publicity it was a stroke of genius: a marvellous counterblast to the glittering named engines of the Great Western, and the public loved it. *King Arthur, Queen Guinevere, Camelot, Tintagel, Sir Galahad, Sir Bedivere* – they breathed the very spirit of the West Country, especially to the partisans, when some of the names, like *Lyonesse*, were poached un-ashamedly from Great Western territory!

The next step was to glamorise the principal express train to the West of England. The eleven o'clock from Waterloo had been the basic service for more than twenty years, expanded in pre-war summers into three sections, 10.50 am to Plymouth, 11 am to Padstow, and 11.10 am to Ilfracombe. This succession of fast expresses was not very practical, because delays to the first of the three were inevitably passed back to the later ones; and when in 1924 the service was restored to something like its pre-war speed the Bude and Padstow section ran at 10 am and the Plymouth and Ilfracombe portions at 11 am. In the winter months the post-war 11 am carried through portions for no less than eight destinations, one coach only each for Sidmouth, Exmouth, Exeter (the restaurant car), Bude, Padstow and Plymouth, and two each for Ilfracombe and Torrington. The last named destination

89

*The Atlantic Coast Express passing Surbiton at 60 mph hauled by engine No. 776
Sir Galagars of the King Arthur class.*

occasionally led to the entire train being described as a 'Torrington
Express', though one fancies that not a few onlookers would be unable to
pin-point Torrington on the map! Then, in the summer of 1926, in opposition to the 'Cornish Riviera Express' of the Great Western the 11 am was
named the 'Atlantic Coast Express', even though only half its destinations
were on, or near to the north coast.

By the autumn of 1926 the prestige of the Southern Railway was increasing by leaps and bounds. The new 'King Arthur' class locomotives were
winning golden opinions from all who had to use them; the Atlantic Coast
Express had been successfully launched, and in the late summer of that year
Eastleigh Works startled the railway engineering world by completing the
most powerful express passenger locomotive yet to take the road in Great
Britain, the *Lord Nelson*. The claim of omnipotence was soon substantiated
by some spectacular performance on a special test run from Waterloo to
Exeter. The Southern 'star' was very much in the ascendant. During the
winter months the Atlantic Coast Express usually took a load of twelve

The Atlantic Coast Express near Yeovil: a fourteen coach load hauled by engine No. 740 Merlin, one of ex LSWR 'N15' series, assimilated into the King Arthur class.

coaches out of Waterloo. In addition to the destinations previously mentioned there was a through carriage for Seaton, which was detached at Salisbury. There was an additional stop at Sidmouth Junction, where the carriages for Sidmouth and Exmouth were detached, the latter, en route providing a service to Budleigh Salterton. At Exeter the train was divided, the first portion going forward to Barnstaple, Torrington and Ilfracombe, and the second serving Plymouth, Bude and Padstow.

As on the Great Western run to the West of England all the fast running was performed east of Exeter. The legacy that the Southern inherited from the London and South Western Railway was indeed a fortunate one so far as track alignment was concerned, particularly in respect of the section west of Salisbury, which ran through a very hilly and beautiful countryside. George Stephenson's famous pupil, Joseph Locke, was the engineer, and despite the difficulty of the terrain he laid out a track so straight that on the westbound journey there were no speed restrictions anywhere between Salisbury and the approach to Exeter. Eastbound, it was only when the trains were almost in sight of Salisbury, on the curve through Wilton, that any reduction below full speed was required. During the summer months, when some trains were booked to run non-stop over the 88 miles from Salisbury to Exeter, the fastest timing was 98 minutes; but this booked average speed of 54 mph did not give any real impression of the speeds that were necessary to keep time over that very hilly road.

I logged a run on one of the summer non-stops on which the fluctuations in speed, without any signal or other incidental checks were: 58½, 45½, 83½, 66, 82, 48½, 82, 70, 75, 48, 68, 32½, 82, 19, 83½, 70½, and 88 mph. The actual average from start to stop was 55¾ mph. The engine was the *Maid of Astolat*, hauling an eleven coach train of 380 tons, and going full tilt downhill on the favourable stretches the shorter inclines could be rushed at minimum speeds of 45 to 48 mph; but it was another matter when we got to Crewkerne and had to climb the longer bank up to Hewish Crossing, and speed fell to 32½ mph. We soon regained some fine speed on the long descent past Axminster, where we were doing over 80 mph for 5 miles on end, but then came the worst bank of all, up to Honiton Tunnel, 7 miles of it, at an almost Highland-Scottish inclination of 1 in 70. There the speed fell to 19 mph. It was followed by a glorious dash for Exeter, on which speed finally touched 88 mph at Broad Clyst. On a run like this the face of a locomotive enthusiast would be well-nigh glued to the window to sight and clock the whizzing mileposts; but not all railway enthusiasts are addicts of the stop watch, and they, together with many other passengers would have been enjoying the beauty of the countryside. One is barely through the London 'stockbroker belt' before that beauty is richly unfolding before us.

While we are climbing swiftly over the heathlands on Surrey's western border, and then doing a mile-a-minute plus over the fine straight levels that extend almost to Basingstoke it is a good opportunity to say something of the train itself. Railway amalgamation, when such strongly individualistic constituents as those fused into the Southern are involved, is bound to bring moments of stress, particularly when decisions have to be made about the future liveries of locomotives and coaching stock. On the Southern, the South Eastern and Chatham had not changed its locomotive style from the austere battleship grey of wartime and choice for the future had lain between the chocolate brown of the Brighton and the olive green of the South Western, and both companies had taken to painting their coaches in the same colours. Choice of the South-Western green for the enlarged company was a happy selection, because it gave the trains a distinctive appearance in joint stations, contrasting notably with the red of the LMS, the chocolate and cream of the Great Western and the varnished teak of the LNER. The Southern locomotives matched the coaches.

On the first stage of the westward run of the Atlantic Coast Express after the steady near-uniform speed in the first hour out of London the journey was usually enliven by two peaks of high speed west of Basingstoke, first at Andover, where I once clocked a 'Lord Nelson' class 4-6-0 at 91 mph, and then on the final descent from Amesbury Junction to Salisbury, again often well over 80 mph. For a short time the practice was adopted of working one engine through from London to Exeter, with a change of crew at Salisbury; but after a time the older practice of changing engines was resumed, with the London men returning with their own engines, and the train worked forward by Salisbury or Exmouth Junction men. In the 1930s while the train was usually hauled down from Waterloo by 'Lord Nelson' class engines, stationed at Nine Elms (Battersea) between Salisbury and Exeter the engine was almost invariably a 'King Arthur', from which one could expect some exhilarating performance.

Publicity for Southern Railway activities, under the skilful hand of J.B. Elliot took some interesting and slightly unusual forms. With a view to catching the eye of what might be called 'the upper crust' of holiday travellers he brought into partnership a skilled journalist and an artist of rare quality, E.P. Leigh-Bennett and Leonard Richmond. Between them they produced two sumptuously illustrated books, which were sold for the incredibly low prices of one shilling (5p), and half a crown (12½p) respectively. Leigh-Bennett was very far removed from the usual idea of a popular publicity journalist. In the first of their books *Devon and Cornish Days* he begins:

'I have just been down to look at a possible place for you this summer; and this is what I found.

'I had got on quite friendly terms with the Atlantic Coast Express, and with its cheery guard, and its padded Dining Car. We spent most of the day together. Someone brought me a cup of tea at Okehampton, and then a pipe and I gazed upon Cornwall rolling up from the south-west: a pleasant contemplation.

'The scene opened out suddenly at Wadebridge; for thence the river Camel really begins to assert itself and become maritime in manner. Pale fawn sand and clumps of green glistening seaweed on its widening banks – that arch glance of the sea. Besides, a tang of salt came in at the dropped window. Presently the bay opened its graceful arms in a welcoming gesture, as if to say "I am yours". And a heart seeking a holiday missed a beat or two. The train wriggled round a bend and its engine shrieked joyfully, as well it might. For the evening sun was kissing the grey roof tops of little Padstow which sits deep in a corner of the hills ahead, and the sight of it was very lovely.

Up West of England express near Oakley, hauled by King Arthur class 4-6-0 No. 782 Sir Brian.

'Somehow a seaside terminus always multiples one's pleasure by two. Added to which this is a very little terminus, with heaped fish boxes between the metals and a couple of trawler funnels peeping up inquisitively over the edge of the quay alongside the platform. The silence that always follows the arrival of big trains at little stations was broken sharply by throaty gutterals. I, a new arrival, was being discussed, sized up, by a long line of gulls who squatted stolidly observant on the roof of the fish market.'

And from Padstow he went on to Tintagel, Boscastle, Clovelly and other delightful places on the Atlantic coast where even the furthest tentacles of the London and South Western Railway did not extend, and the journey to them had to be completed by road. During the spring months, and until the full summer service came into operation the Atlantic Coast Express did not reach Padstow until after 5.30 pm and then of course it was only one or two through carriages. It was indeed, the furthest of all the destinations served by that remarkably comprehensive West Country train, being no less than 260 miles from Waterloo; and for those who had no particular taste for travelling by train the last two hours could be tedious. The big express that had come down from London in such dashing style was divided at Exeter, the first section going forward to Ilfracombe and Torrington, and

94

the second carrying the through portions for Plymouth, Bude, and Padstow. And on this second train a further division took place at Okehampton. I shall always remember a journey I made this way in the summer of 1936. Some West Country friends were returning from Canada. They were travelling in one of the smaller and slower Cunard liners of the 'A' class, and as they would be coming ashore at Plymouth early on a Sunday morning I went to meet them and, by way of variety, took the Southern route. It had been very stormy all the way down from London, and when we stopped at Okehampton to detach the Cornish part of the train I watched the low clouds sweeping down from the northern heights of Dartmoor. The topmost point of the Moor, High Willhays, is less than three miles from the line, and the deep ravine of the West Okement river, which comes brawling down from its source on these heights, is crossed by a spectacular lattice steel viaduct, one of the sole remaining features today of the once considerable network of the London and South Western Railway, and of course of the Southern, west of the line from Exeter to Barnstaple.

Just beyond the viaduct was Meldon Junction where the line to the Atlantic coast resorts branched off. Like the continuation to Plymouth this

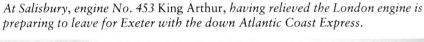

At Salisbury, engine No. 453 King Arthur, *having relieved the London engine is preparing to leave for Exeter with the down Atlantic Coast Express.*

group of branches has long been closed, and the track lifted. But the rails are still in place across Meldon Viaduct. In 1927 the Southern had a very bad accident at Sevenoaks, partly due to a poorly balanced engine and partly due to inadequate ballasting of the track. The civil engineer's department had its knuckles rapped over this in the Ministry of Transport report, with a strong recommendation for use of broken stone, instead of gravel or shingle, for ballasting on the principal main lines. There was first class granite available at the very lineside west of Okehampton, and from then the Meldon quarry was developed, and became the principal source of supply for ballast on the Southern Railway. The connecting line to the Exeter–Barnstaple route, used only by the stone trains, is the line to the Atlantic coast resorts that remains open today. I had no more than a glimpse of the great quarries as I travelled to Plymouth on that stormy day back in 1936; but today when motoring to Cornwall on the A30 the Meldon Viaduct stands out prominently against the wild moorland background.

The old London and South Western route to Plymouth reached its summit point a mile to the west of Meldon Junction, at an altitude of no less than. 950 ft above sea level; but whatever the weather it was always an enjoyable ride because of the type of locomotive used. After the fast run down from Waterloo the Plymouth section of the train used to be taken forward from Exeter by one of the veteran 'T9' class 4-4-0, designed by Dugald Drummond, and modernised to no greater extent than the fitting of superheaters. They were extraordinarily game little engines, and they climbed the stiff gradients of the Dartmoor line as readily as they swept up to 70 mph on the favourable stretches. After topping that summit point beyond Meldon Junction at just 201 miles from Waterloo, it was a steep downhill run through Lydford and Tavistock right to the banks of the Tamar. Despite the quickening speed of the train and the anticipation of journey's end, one's sightseeing is still mainly towards the heights of Dartmoor, to left of the line, and there was one delightful vista towards the west, not on any account to be missed, just after the Great Western single-tracked branch to Launceston had come alongside; this is the isolated cone of Brent Tor, just topping the thousand-foot-contour, and crowned with a tiny little church dedicated to St Micheal de la Rupe. The Ordnance Survey 1907 edition, and other cartographers, not to mention *Bradshaw*, render the name of the neighbouring village as Brentor, but an authoress whose family have lived in Devonshire for nearly two thousand years writes of it as Brent Tor; and she should know!

Before returning to Exeter to take up the working of the North Devon sections of the Atlantic Coast Express, it is interesting to reflect upon the speeds made by its various through connections once the Waterloo–Exeter speedway is left behind. During the early summer the Saturday relief train leaving Waterloo at 10.35 am covered the 171¼ miles to Exeter at an average speed of 55½ mph, with one stop, while the regular 11 am which had an additional stop at Sidmouth Junction, made 53½ mph overall. But then see what happened: the Plymouth and Cornish section left Exeter at 2.23 pm and the average speeds of the through carriages to its three western destinations were 33 mph to Plymouth, 25¾ mph to Bude, and 27 mph to Padstow. The Saturday relief service from June onwards gave rather better averages of 32 mph to Bude and 31 mph to Padstow; but Plymouth was unchanged. The overall average from Waterloo to Padstow was 39 mph normally, and 42½ mph by the early summer Saturday relief.

The Ilfracombe and Torrington sections of the Atlantic Coast Express were first away from Exeter, and after a brief call at the Great Western station made a non-stop run to Barnstaple Junction – not a rapid one for all that, because much of the route is single-tracked, and severe speed restrictions were required at each of the passing places. After grouping, most of the passenger work on this line was performed by R.E.L. Maunsell's 2-6-0 engines of South Eastern and Chatham design. Their substantial tractive power was needed, not for this first stage of the run to Ilfracombe, but for the altogether extraordinary final length. In the early 1930s Barnstaple, quite apart from its magnificent historical association, was a fascinating place from the railway point of view. The Atlantic Coast Express, which had been crossing and recrossing the River Taw for some distance draws up at the junction station, which was on the left bank of the widening estuary. A traveller would note a resplendent Great Western coach prominently roof-boarded PADDINGTON AND ILFRACOMBE. This was the through carriage off the Cornish Riviera Express, which had been slipped at Taunton, and passengers for Ilfracombe by the Atlantic Coast Express could feel distinctly superior about this because they would have left London just half an hour later than those who had come from Paddington. In the meantime the Torrington coach had been detached from the rear, and the Great Western one backed on.

The Great Western association with Barnstaple had been a hazardous business. It began in 1864 when a group of local landowners promoted a line called the Devon and Somerset, from Barnstaple to join the broad gauge Bristol and Exeter main line two miles south of Taunton. It had, of course, to be broad gauge, and it ran from a terminus in Barnstaple town, on the right bank of the River Taw. It was in the direst financial straits from its very inception, and it was not until 1873 that the 43 miles of line were finally completed. In view of the forthcoming conversion of the rail gauge by the Great Western and its associated companies the Devon and Somerset line was duly converted in 1881, and as it was then felt that the only hope of salvation was connection with the London and South Western at Barnstaple, a short line 1¾ miles was built crossing the river in 1887. This of course was standard and not broad gauge. It was nevertheless a cumbersome arrangement, because a Great Western coach, or train for Ilfracombe had to be taken into the original station, then, after reversing direction taken across the river to the L & SWR station, and then to cross back over the river to continue its journey on the right bank! In 1905 the Great Western built what was termed the 'East Loop', whereby trains from the Taunton direction could be run directly into the L & SW Barnstaple Junction, without reversal of direction. This is the way that through carriage off the Cornish Riviera Express had come.

The Torrington carriages of the Atlantic Coast Express were taken in tow by another engine for the remaining 14 miles of their journey, and run beside the widening Taw to its confluence with the equally lovely Torridge, stopping at Instow and Bideford on the way, which were change points for non-railway destinations like Appledore, Westward Ho! and Clovelly, so enticingly described and depicted by Messrs Leigh-Bennett and Richmond. I cannot remember ever having read a book that made me want to visit places more than those included in *Devon and Cornwall Days*. Of this particular 'end of the line' Leigh-Bennett writes:

'Your curiosity is awakened instantly on arrival here. Why is this one of the "ends" of the Atlantic Coast Express? Why do corridor coaches marked "Torrington" lie in the siding of what is hardly more than a village station? One or two men, obviously of the farming fraternity, lean quizzically on the low station railings expecting things off the London train; and local people, who boarded at Barnstaple, are crowding into a station 'bus somewhat in the *sauve qui peut* manner. But why have they sent me here?' And then in his own inimitable way he went on to give the answer: salmon fishing, and the utter peacefulness of village life, around the second oldest bowling green in all the world.

Meanwhile the Ilfracombe section of the Atlantic Coast Express, with that alien Great Western coach on its tail has crossed the river on a sharply curved, flimsy looking iron bridge, and stopped briefly in Barnstaple Town station. There was a time when one changed trains here for Lynton and Lynmouth. Scholarly pens have written much of the charms, the technical features, and of the sad end of the Lynton and Barnstaple Railway. Leigh-Bennett came upon it all unsuspecting, and of Barnstaple Town he wrote: 'There is a change of trains. A change of a most astonishing and amusing kind. Sitting complacently at the opposite side of your platform, looking rather self-conscious because you are staring incredulously at it, is what

At the furthest end of the line: a veteran Drummond 4-4-0, with through carriages from London is nearing Padstow.

appears to be a toy train. A tall man could lean his arms on the carriage tops. But it has a blustering little engine up in front which seems impatient to depart; and they are in fact busy round the little guard's van with your luggage. So you laugh and get into it.'

But I must press finally on to Ilfracombe, now only 14 miles away. I feel sure however there must have been many times when the management boffins in far-away Waterloo just did not want to know about that 14 miles, no matter how much holiday traffic it carried at times. It began deceptively with a level run beside the widening estuary, to a stop at Braunton; and then there was that incredible last 9 miles. The adjective 'incredible' is used rather loosely in these days, to describe things that are often no more than unusual, but the last six miles of the Ilfracombe branch really takes some believing. From Heddon Mill Crossing up to Mortehoe the gradient is continuously at 1 in 40, and the descent into Ilfracombe is at 1 in 36 – an inch in a yard, just think of it! Fortunately what was left of the Atlantic Coast Express was not very heavy by the time it left Barnstaple; but even so the train engine had to be given rear-end banking assistance from Braunton. Some of the splendid little Drummond 0-4-4 tank engines, displaced from the London commuter services by electrification, were sent to Barnstaple to help with this work, and of one of them I have a last story to tell of the route of the Atlantic Coast Express. Although the story itself belongs to a period later than that of this book generally the engine concerned was a distinguished old veteran built in 1897, and apart from the painting style completely unchanged in outward appearance.

The year was 1945 and I was collecting data for some technical articles on Mr Bulleid's latest engines. I had stayed overnight in Barnstaple, and went down to the shed early next morning intending to ride the big new 'Pacific' that would be going 'light engine' to Ilfracombe to pick up her train; but on arrival I found that one of the Drummond tanks was also going to Ilfracombe, twenty minutes earlier, and in happy anticipation I climbed aboard her. How that little engine skated along! Beside the widening estuary of the Taw, with the historic old towns of Bideford and Appledore lying across the water in the haze of a sunny autumn morning, we skimmed along at 55 mph. The track winds considerably, but that great little engine rode the curves with such ease that she seemed more to float along than to travel as one usually expected with a locomotive, especially with such an old lady as this. Naturally she had to puff a bit to get up that fearful gradient to Mortehoe. Today the rails do not go beyond Barnstaple; but I shall always remember the line to Ilfracombe with affection, if for nothing else than that ride in the cab of old No. 670, light engine, on that Sunday morning, now nearly forty years ago.

9

THE ROYAL SCOT

As a counterblast to the 'Flying Scotsman', the name 'Royal Scot' for the 10 am Anglo-Scottish express by the Royal Mail Route from Euston to Glasgow and Edinburgh was an inspiration; but by devoted partisans of the West Coast route it was received with considerably less than full-bloodied enthusiasm. In their eyes the morning departure had always played second fiddle to the prestigious 2 pm 'Corridor', even after the latter had lost some of its pre-war glamour, been decked in Midland red, and was leaving Euston at 1.30 pm. Then, with the new Royal Scot there was the thorny matter of its haulage during the first summer. The engines intended for it were not ready – nor indeed were they likely to have been, seeing the manner in which the design was initiated. This is not primarily a book about loco-motive engineering, but in the case of the Royal Scot train service its history, and the impact it made upon not only the travelling public but on all concerned with its operation, were so inextricably linked with its loco-motives that some extended reference is needed to the problems involved.

In 1926 conditions were not exactly propitious for the launching of en-terprising new train services. The coal strike, which precipitated the General Strike in May, was continued throughout the summer and autumn; and although supplies of foreign coal were imported in sufficient quantities to keep a reasonable train service going throughout the country any thoughts of major developments had naturally to be postponed. Nevertheless one major locomotive project was in hand on the LMS. In the previous year Sir Henry Fowler had succeeded George Hughes as Chief Mechanical Engineer, and locomotive headquarters was transferred from Horwich to Derby. From the moment of Grouping, in 1923, the influence of the former Midland Railway in all matters concerning train running was strong, with J.H. Follows becoming Chief General Superintendent of the enlarged system, and J.E. Anderson, Superintendent of Motive Power. Both were dyed-in-the-wool Midland men, and with Fowler's appointment the new headquarters draw-ing office was virtually the same. Fowler was a brilliant metallurgist, though

The Royal Scot in its first summer, before the new locomotives were ready: the southbound train passing Tring hauled by 4-4-0 locomotive No. 5384 S.R. Graves, and unnamed Claughton 4-6-0 No. 5958.

in no way a locomotive engine designer, and for this he relied on his drawing office. His scientific leanings attracted him to the compound system of propulsion whereby the steam is expanded in two stages. While this principle had been used to no more than a limited extent on the Midland Railway, on which he had been Chief Mechanical Engineer since 1909, he had been deeply impressed by details of test results on the latest four-cylinder compound 'Pacific' engines of the Northern Railway of France, and had received authorisation to build two similar engines for trial on the LMS.

The prospect alarmed not only the senior officers responsible for operating, who as staunch Midland men had a natural antipathy to large engines of any kind, but it brought together the previous warring factions; for those of the North Western, with lingering memories of the Webb era at Crewe, had an equally strong antipathy to compounds. The influence that Follows and Anderson wielded was indeed such that they persuaded Sir Guy Granet

OIL FIRED EXPRESS LOCOMOTIVE, GREAT EASTERN RAILWAY.

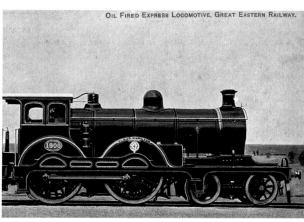

TOP (*left*): *GWR on the Broad Gauge: the up Flying Dutchman at full speed near Uffington.*
TOP (*right*): *GWR one of the broad gauge 8 ft 4-2-2 locomotives in its final form –* the Great Western.
CENTRE (*left*): *Great Eastern Railway – up Norfolk Coast Express near Brentwood, hauled by 'Claud Hamilton' class 4-4-0 locomotive.*
CENTRE (*right*): *GER: Pioneer of a very famous class:* the Claud Hamilton *engine, of 1900.*
BOTTOM (*left*): *LB & SCR: The Southern Belle leaving Victoria, hauled by superheaded 4-4-2 locomotive No. 422.*

ABOVE (left): London & North Western Railway: the southbound Corridor, (2 pm Glasgow to Euston) taking water at Tebay troughs, and hauled by 4-6-0 No. 668 Rupert Guinness of the 'Claughton' class.

ABOVE (right): The Cornish Riviera Express, leaving Parsons Tunnel, between Dawlish and Teignmouth, hauled by 'King' class 4-6-0 locomotive.

RIGHT: Southern Railway, West of England express hauled by 4-6-0 No. 739 King Leodegrance 'King Arthur' class.

BELOW: Up East Coast Anglo-Scottish express leaving Edinburgh (Waverley) hauled by two North Eastern 4-4-0s of Class 'R'.

The Golden Arrow all-Pullman boat express leaving Shakespeare's Cliff Tunnel, near Dover, hauled 4-6-0 No. 850 Lord Nelson.

ABOVE: *Route of the Aberdonian: express from Edinburgh, double-headed by North British locomotives* Aberdonian *and* Jeanie Deans *climbing to the cliffs overlooking the North Sea, by Stonehaven, about to be passed by a southbound Caledonian express.*

RIGHT: *The imposing north portal of Bramhope Tunnel, between Leeds and Harrogate, with express hauled by 'R1' class 4-4-0 No. 1238 emerging.*

BELOW: *Midland Railway, up 'Scotch' express near Hendon, hauled by 4-4-0 3-cylinder compound locomotive No. 1023.*

OPPOSITE (top): *LMS Railway: the pioneer* Royal Scot *locomotive, as running in the later 1930s with high capacity tender.*

OPPOSITE (below): *The Torbay Limited in St David's station Exeter, hauled by engine No. 6018* King Henry VI.

ABOVE: *On the Highland main line: express from Perth to Inverness climbing 'The Hill' between Struan and Dalnaspidal, hauled by the 4-6-0 locomotive* Clan Stewart, *with 4-4-0 assisting in rear.* BELOW: *First of the Gresley streamliners, the* Silver Link, *on southbound express at Grantham.*

to veto the project altogether. The motive power situation in 1927 was expected to be critical in any case. The top management was intent upon the introduction of spectacular new trains on the Anglo-Scottish service in that summer, and the projected four-cylinder compound 'Pacifics' were somewhat cynically regarded by Anderson and his running officers as likely to involve far too many teething troubles for them to be any use for the summer of 1927 – if indeed enough of them were in traffic at all by that time. In any event men brought up in Midland traditions had no objection to double heading. With work on the new compounds cancelled the drawing office at Crewe Works, in opposition to that of Derby, went ahead with the design of an enlarged boiler for the ex-London and North Western 'Claughton' class 4-6-0s; and at one time was thought that these would be the power available for the new trains of 1927.

There is no doubt that Sir Guy Granet, as thorough-going a Midland man as any prior to the amalgamation, was becoming very concerned at the continuing friction between the former North Western and Midland interests, of which the rival locomotive projects of Derby and Crewe were an example; and there is little doubt that he confided his problems to his great friend Sir Felix Pole, General Manager of the Great Western Railway. The outcome was a trial of a 'Castle' class 4-6-0 on the West Coast main line, first between Euston and Crewe, and then, with the Horwich dynamometer car, between Crewe and Carlisle. As motive power officer Anderson was satisfied that an engine of a similar capacity would meet his requirements for the summer traffic of 1927; but as the trials of the Great Western locomotive were not completed before the end of November 1926 time was running short. At that stage the traffic requirements for the new Anglo-Scottish trains had by no means been finalised, except that there was to be no acceleration of the overall times between London and Edinburgh, and London and Glasgow, in conformity with the long standing agreement with the East Coast Route.

Market research had suggested that during the peak months of tourist traffic there would be enough business to justify making the 10 am departures from Euston on the one hand, and Edinburgh and Glasgow on the other exclusive to through passengers, with no intermediate stops except for locomotive purposes. The passengers would have a completely undisturbed journey for the $8\frac{1}{4}$ hours from one terminal to the other. Forward planning took place on the basis of a nine-coach formation for Glasgow, and six-coaches for Edinburgh, both sections being self contained and having their own restaurant car facilities. Use of the new standard LMS stock, which was considerably lighter than the North Western type previously used on the West Coast main line, and including separate kitchen cars in both parts of the train, each serving first and third class open saloons, meant that the tare weight of the full 15-coach train would be about 420 tons, or perhaps a few tons less. The overall average speed required would be no more than 48½ mph, but while the 236¼ miles from Euston to Carnforth included no gradients of any great length or severity, the northern part included the mountainous climbs to Shap and Beattock summits, respectively 915, and 1015 feet above sea level. Clearly a uniform average speed throughout could not be expected.

Anderson had been so impressed with the work of the Great Western 'Castle' class engine that the latter company was actually asked to build fifty of the type, for service on the LMS. That, of course, they were not legally empowered to do, and a request for a set of drawings was refused. Help in this latter respect was however forthcoming from the Southern Railway, which had in its prototype 4-6-0 the *Lord Nelson* a locomotive of roughly similar capacity, though of a considerably different design. Instructions from the LMS top management to Sir Henry Fowler were simple enough; to get fifty new engines of capacity equal to the Great Western 'Castles' into traffic in time for the summer service of 1927. That directive was issued at the end of November 1926, and at that time the designing and manufacturing resources of the various constituent companies of the LMS had not been co-ordinated to the degree necessary to enable such an order to be executed. The job had to be put out to contract. Fortunately the immense experience and manufacturing facilities of the North British Locomotive Company, in Glasgow, could be used, though even that great firm could not possibly meet such a delivery target date as the LMS management at first stipulated. It was evident that the inauguration of the new service would have to be powered by existing locomotives.

There would have to be at least one engine change, and Carnforth, where there were adequate facilities for servicing was an appropriate place. It conveniently marked the division point between the ordinary and the mountain sections of the route. So far as the latter was concerned, although the scheduled average speed over the 130 miles between Symington, the point where the Glasgow and Edinburgh portions were combined, and Carnforth was no more than 48 mph there were then no locomotives based in Scotland that could work a load of 420 tons unassisted. Fortunately the Scottish drivers, unlike some of their North Western *confrères*, had taken to the new standard three-cylinder compounds of Midland design like 'ducks to water', and with a pair of them the working of the new Royal Scot train between Glasgow and Carnforth was a veritable holiday outing. The working of the Scottish based compounds, in pairs, was not to be confined to the Royal Scot, because in the summer service of 1927 the principal night sleeping car express between Glasgow and Euston, to be named 'The Night Scot', was to be run non-stop between Glasgow and Crewe, and also to be worked by a pair of compounds.

The Euston–Carnforth run of the Royal Scot, in the first summer of its operation, was rather a sad reflection upon the denigration of North Western motive power that had taken place under Midland influence since the formation of the LMS. In 1927 the general limit of load for the 'Claughton' class 4-6-0s was 360 tons, though a certain number of them in good condition, and designated by a letter S on their cab sides were allowed to take 380 tons. In the days of the London and North Western Railway the 'Claughton' load was 420 tons, and with such trains they worked faster schedules than were proposed for the Royal Scot between Euston and Carnforth. Furthermore in earlier days the engine crews were not averse to taking an overload. They treated such occasions as a challenge to their skills and

Early days in the North: the down Royal Scot near Burton (Lancs) hauled by two Midland compounds Nos 900 and 903.

drove and fired their engines that much harder. It had been far different on the Midland, on which the slightest excess called forth a pilot. If one should not be available I have known drivers refuse to start, or else lose a considerable amount of time deliberately. Under the reigning hierarchy on the LMS, double heading with the Royal Scot between Euston and Carnforth was mandatory, and ex-LNW 4-4-0s of the 'George the Fifth' class were used for this purpose. This also brought certain pangs to those with long memories, for in earlier days the limit of load for those engines was 400 tons, and no driver worth his salt would have hesitated to take 420 tons without assistance, if no pilot was available.

The lavish provision of engine power for the Royal Scot, while not resulting in much interest for the connoisseurs of locomotive performance, nor economy in staffing, certainly ensured very high standards of punctuality. At the northern end of the journey the train was frequently run considerably ahead of time, a situation not always to be appreciated by Edinburgh passengers. Although the load was one of only nine coaches between Symington and Glasgow both compound 4-4-0 locomotives worked throughout, leaving the six Edinburgh coaches to complete their journey behind an ex-Caledonian 4-4-0 of much earlier vintage. If as sometimes happened the main train arrived from the south at Symington anything up to ten minutes early Edinburgh passengers had the doubtful pleasure of being left, to 'cool their heels' as it were, at this wayside station until their fresh engine arrived from Carstairs, and even then to kill time to avoid too early an arrival in Edinburgh. South of Carnforth running ahead of time was not practised. The line was more densely occupied, and it was necessary for the train to adhere to its allotted timetable path. From photographs, and records of its running the Camden based 'Claughton' class used were all unnamed, but of course with the 4-4-0 pilots it was otherwise, and one of those used would have brought amusing recollections to railway enthusiasts of an earlier generation who delighted in the promiscuity of the names bestowed on London and North Western express locomotives. This was the *S.R. Graves*, which in 1927 carried the LMS number 5384.

The story takes me back to the days when that racy and often brilliant railway journalist Charles Rous-Marten was author of the monthly feature 'British Locomotive Practice and Performance' in *The Railway Magazine*. In October 1907 he wrote: 'I observe that among the "Precedents" recently scrapped is No. 1141, which bore the singularly unattractive name of *Graves* – or *S.R. Graves*, if you want it *in extenso*. Now I do not doubt for one moment that some very worthy man was worthily honoured by the placing of his name upon an engine, but I do venture to suggest that this is one of the old locomotive names which might well be dropped out of sight, regarding it merely as a name and not in connection with its human owner. I have seen passengers squirm and shudder, and heard Americans deride when they found they were to be taken in the boat train by an engine named *Graves*, which certainly has a kind of churchyardy sound. Mr Whale has been very loyal to old tradition in reproducing the names of other days, and certainly the majority of his selections have been excellent. But I do hope we shall not have a new "Precursor", or "Experiment" denominated *Graves*.' No such engine appeared in Rous-Marten's lifetime, but in March 1913, the name, which was that of a distinguished member of the Board, and a Member of Parliament for Liverpool, was revived; and the new *S.R. Graves*, No. 132 of the LNWR and later No. 5384 of the LMS, survived thus to take a part in the running of the Royal Scot, in its first summer of 1927, and was not withdrawn for scrapping until 1936.

On a fine summer evening, 14 July 1927, Sir Henry Fowler and S. J. Symes were playing golf at Long Eaton on a course beside the North Midland main line when they paused in their game to see an 'apparition' making its way slowly up the line towards Derby. It was the first of the new 4-6-0s in course of delivery from the works of the North British Locomotive Company in Glasgow. There were waves of mutual greetings from the golfers and from those on the footplate, as well there might be, for a new locomotive era was beginning on the LMS. The enthusiasts who first saw it were immediately impressed with the seemingly immense girth of the boiler, though actually it was no bigger than that of the *Lord Nelson*, the drawings of which were on hand in Glasgow when the new LMS 4-6-0 was being designed. When it was learned that its nominal tractive power was some 40 per cent greater than that of the 'Claughtons' it was not expected that there would be any difficulty in handling the 420-ton Royal Scot train single handed. What the railway world in general did *not* expect was that in the forthcoming winter service the length of non-stop run, to and from Euston, would be extended by a further 63 miles to a passenger stop at Carlisle. This run of 299·2 miles was by far the longest regularly scheduled anywhere in the world, and was indeed a most spectacular and venturesome project.

Apart from the simple mechanics of the job there were so many imponderables. The first engine of an entirely new design had only been delivered from the builders twelve weeks before the extended non-stop run was due to begin, and none of the drivers who would be involved knew the entire route. The duty was to be shared between Camden and the former London and North Western shed at Carlisle. The London men had learned the road as far as Carnforth for the summer service of 1927, but the mountain section to the north was new territory for them. The Carlisle men were still less favourably placed, because they had previously not worked further south

New power: the up Royal Scot, non-stop to Euston, leaving Carlisle, hauled by 4-6-0 No. 6139 Ajax.

than Crewe, and they had a further 158 miles of route to learn. Drivers and firemen had to master the working characteristics of an entirely new type of locomotive, while engaged on a non-stop run of 5¾ hours duration considerably longer than any of them had ever worked before, and with all the natural hindrances of wild wintry weather to be encountered on the mountain section. That the new service was inaugurated with remarkable success, was in no small measure due to the North British Locomotive Company, because the new engines proved notably free from mechanical troubles, and cases of indifferent steaming were probably due to the inexperience of some of the firemen.

As a commercial proposition the changes in working arrangements during the first five years of its operation tell their own tale. The fifteen-coach formation soon proved more than necessary, and in the very first winter the load was down to twelve, with eight for Glasgow, and four for Edinburgh. The latter included a single 12-wheeled composite dining and kitchen car of the LNWR type instead of the lavish 3-coach set originally run. The reduced

A seventeen-car train needs assistance over Shap: the train restarting from stop to attach pilot at Oxenholme, engines 4-4-0 No. 5263 Oceanic (ex-LNWR) *and 4-6-0 No. 6109* Royal Engineer.

load of the full train was 346 tons instead of the 417 tons of September 1927. Even with this reduction the train proved a difficult one to work in the depths of winter, and time-keeping overall was not too good. One of the troubles was the alarming increase in basic coal consumption of the new locomotives. They were fitted with the standard Midland type of tender carrying $5\frac{1}{2}$ tons of coal, and for the London–Carlisle non-stop run that provided for little more than 40 lb of coal per mile, not counting what was in the firebox at the start of the run. At the sheds however great care was taken to stack far more than the nominal maximum amount on to the relatively small tenders; but even so, things were running a bit fine towards the end of those long runs, with the drivers anxious that their supply of coal might not last out.

The train was made up to fifteen coaches once again for the summer service of 1928, and at times of the heaviest traffic it was sometimes sixteen, and occasionally seventeen vehicles. On such occasions a stop was made at

Oxenholme to take an assistant engine over the mountain section. But in the winter of 1928-9 the non-stop run to Carlisle was abandoned, and on the northbound journey intermediate stops were made at Rugby and Crewe. A three-coach 'tail' was added to the main train from Euston to Crewe, consisting of through carriages for Aberdeen and Dundee, and the twelve-coach train continued from Crewe to Carlisle non-stop over the 141 miles in 165 minutes. The southbound train also stopped at Crewe, but then ran the remaining 158 miles to Euston in 175 minutes, a not very exciting average speed of 54 mph, over an easily graded road. At that time however nothing more enterprising was practicable. In the design of the new engines most of the detail work had been left to the experience of the North British Locomotive Company; but certain features characteristic of standard Midland Railway practice had been insisted upon by Derby and it was one of these latter that caused the early deterioration in economic performance as represented by the increase in coal consumption. This was traced to the design of the valves controlling admission and exhaust of steam from the cylinders. Once this defect had been diagnosed, and a modified design substituted the performance of the engines was greatly improved, and anxiety as to whether the coal supply would last out vanished.

During the summer service when Anglo-Scottish traffic was at its heaviest, and the Royal Scot was carrying passengers for Glasgow and Edinburgh only, the train did not stop in Carlisle station. On the northbound run it continued for a further two miles to a stop abreast of Kingmoor engine sheds, 301·1 miles from Euston, in 347 minutes, where engines were changed. Newer and more palatial coaching stock had been introduced by 1930, and by then a fifteen car formation represented a load of 436 tons. With the improved working of the locomotives no difficulty was experienced in running the train to time. It involved passing Crewe in 175 minutes, Carnforth (236¼ miles) in 264 minutes, and climbing the 31·4 miles from there up to Shap Summit in 47 minutes. That left 36 minutes for the down-hill run to Carlisle, slowly through that station and out to Kingmoor, for the change of engines. Old North Western men would note that the Royal Scot was allowed five minutes more in which to climb from Carnforth to Shap than the old 'Corridor', and would remind us that the 'Claughton' class engines sometimes took loads of 420 tons, without assistance and without loss of time; but of course they would be running only from Crewe to Carlisle, and not from Euston.

With the improved piston valves fitted to the Royal Scot class locomotives the way was clear for acceleration of the service. In 1932 the old agreement on minimum times was ended, and from then, until the outbreak of war in 1939 there was a progressive acceleration. The introduction of the huge

'Pacific' engines in 1933, designed under the direction of Sir William Stanier, did not at first influence the working of the train to any marked degree. For a start only two were built. This was a wise step, because many features of the design were new, and untried on the LMS. Furthermore, the new engines were from the outset required to work through over the entire 401 miles between Euston and Glasgow, with a crew change at Carlisle. In the meantime the Royal Scot 4-6-0s had dealt satisfactorily with the big acceleration of 1932 by which the overall time between London and Glasgow was reduced to 7¾ hours.

The new 'Pacific' engines were named *The Princess Royal* and *Princess Elizabeth*, and the aim at first was that each of them should work daily on the Royal Scot train, one each way. But as might be expected there were many teething troubles, and there were many occasions when one or the other was not available, and until their performance had been thoroughly analysed and the faults corrected the Royal Scot 4-6-0 engines really bore the brunt of the job. But by the beginning of 1935 the troubles had been overcome, and construction of a further batch of ten 'Pacific' engines was authorised. They quickly became great favourites with their crews, and named after ladies of the British Royal Family they earned the affectionate nickname of the 'Lizzies'. With these splendid engines quickly becoming

The Stanier impact: one of the new Pacifics of 1935 No. 6204 Princess Louise *on the southbound Royal Scot at Castlethorpe troughs. Note the Caledonian style semaphore headcode (the 'bow-tie') below the chimney.*

master of any load, the summer non-stop London to Carlisle run of the Royal Scot was progressively reduced from the 345 minutes worked at the time of its inauguration to 299 minutes in the early summer of 1939, thus increasing the average speed, over the non-stop run, from 52 to 60 mph.

In that final season, southbound, the Glasgow section did not stop in Carlisle station to reman, and the 299¼ mile non-stop run to Euston was made by the Edinburgh and Aberdeen section. I shall always treasure the memory of my last journey on this latter train, before war came, and all speedy and comfortable travel became a thing of the past. I had joined the train at Stirling, and it was taken down to Carlisle by an appropriately Scottish member of the Royal Scot class of 4-6-0, the *Black Watch*. At Carlisle to haul the eleven coach train non-stop to Euston another 'Scot', *The Kings Regiment* (*Liverpool*) came on. In gloriously fine weather the mountain section was treated with complete disdain, and we passed Preston (90·1 miles) on time in 95 minutes. Then came delays, and we were 10 minutes late when passing Crewe. But some tremendous running followed, and between Stafford and Tring (102 miles) where this fast train was allowed only 94 minutes, we regained the whole of the lost time, averaging 73 mph instead of the scheduled 65 mph; and despite easy running inwards from Watford we stopped in Euston exactly on time. The maximum speed on the run was 88 mph. It was an impressive finish to pre-war memories of the Royal Scot and its locomotives.

10

THE TORBAY LIMITED

One of the new trains put on by the Great Western Railway after the opening of the new cut-off line to the West, via Castle Cary, was the 11.50 am from Paddington, non stop to Exeter in three hours, and like the Cornish Riviera Express slipping coaches for Weymouth at Westbury, and at Taunton for Ilfracombe. It was however primarily an express for the Torquay line, and in railway colloquialism became known as the 'Torquay Diner'. But its main part went through to Kingswear, and when full express speed was restored after the first world war, and its departure from Paddington was established at 12 noon, its name was officially designated as 'The Torbay Limited' and this title was displayed on the carriage roof boards. The slip coaches of pre-war days were not restored, and instead it carried a section for Penzance, which was detached at Exeter. After that the main part of the train continued non-stop to Torquay, which was reached in three hours forty minutes for the distance of 199¾ miles from Paddington. Like some other trains of that era that one can recall, it may have had the word 'limited' in its name, but it was certainly not so in weight. I have seen it leaving Paddington, when the loaded weight behind the engine's tender has varied on different occasions between 290 and 500 tons!

Although following the same route as the Cornish Riviera Express as far as Newton Abbot there was a subtle difference in attitude to the incidentals of travel on these two trains. On the 'Limited' one was bound for the far west; and while a locomotive enthusiast would log the times and speeds achieved in the most complete detail, to most passengers eager to enjoy the passing scene there was inevitably a slight impatience to get over the earlier part of the journey, and get on to the 'real stuff' west of Exeter. Even the first sight of the sea between Dawlish and Teignmouth did not do much to rouse one from a post-prandial slumber, or an excuse for a leg stretcher in the corridor. On The Torbay Limited it was far otherwise. You were nearly there! But the earlier part of the journey is full of interest. The shortened route to the West, in the 100 miles from Reading to where it rejoins the old

broad-gauge main line – the track of 'The Flying Dutchman' – at Cogload
Junction, is one of continuous and varied rural charm. One sees little of the
country towns passed on the way, Newbury, Hungerford, Westbury and
Frome, and the scene changes from the willow-flanked banks of the leisurely
Kennet to the downland of the Vale of Pewsey with its White Horses; then
after a climb over the eastern ridges of the Mendips comes a descent to the
Athelney marshes, with a distant view of Glastonbury Tor to the north.

Even though speed had to be reduced for the curves one saw little more
of Westbury and Frome than the stations, and since 1930 not even that.
Those curves meant a reduction from 70 mph or more to 30, and they not
only involved loss of time, but the slowing down and accelerating to full
speed afterwards meant an increase in coal consumption. One of the works
undertaken for the relief of unemployment in 1929 was the construction of

*The up Torbay Limited non-stop Torquay to Paddington, passing Taunton, at
75 mph hauled by engine No. 6014 King Henry VII.*

by-pass lines, avoiding both Westbury and Frome stations, and enabling the West of England expresses to continue at full speed through areas where severe reductions had been required. They saved a lot of time and a lot of coal! There was another big track improvement at Cogload Junction, where the London trains joined in the stream of traffic from the north. There was often acute congestion on the five miles of double track from there to Taunton, and things were often made worse, by restriction in the old Brunellian station at Taunton itself, through which there were only two running lines. The only way to give a fast non-stopping express preference over one that was stopping in the station was to send it round the sharply curved goods avoiding line, at very slow speed. I have more than once been taken through Taunton in this laborious way. Quadrupling the line from Cogload and the complete rebuilding of Taunton station with four running lines made a great improvement. But no track alterations could eliminate the sheer physical labour of getting heavy trains up the gradient to Whiteball tunnel, and with a maximum load on The Torbay Limited I have known the speed fall as low as 25 mph. This was just before the introduction of the full summer service, when the train had a five-coach section for Penzance behind the purely Torbay set.

Looking back to conditions as they were sixty years ago, those responsible for compiling the full summer timetables do not seem to have been gifted with much imagination, particularly when it came to weekends. Then The Torbay Limited was regularly scheduled to run in two sections, the first running non-stop to Torquay, and the second non-stop to Paignton, and conveying the normal set of coaches proceeding afterwards to Kingswear. How this second part was expected to get through Torquay while the first part was standing there discharging enormous numbers of passengers was something of a mystery. In fact, however, the nominally second part, booked to leave Paddington at 12.3 pm seems to have been sent away first, on some occasions. I was meeting my sister who was travelling by it one such day in 1925 and with the engine *Queen Matilda* and the usual eight-coach set train for Kingswear they had run well as far as Cogload, having covered the 135 miles from Paddington to passing Athelney in 137 minutes; but then they got into the Taunton 'jam', and were 18 minutes late by Exeter. Waiting for her at Paignton I was well placed to appreciate the utter confusion that reigned there, especially when the train eventually hove in sight, and was finally stopped for 25 minutes within walking distance of the station! However things were not normally as bad as that, and at mid-week the 'Torbay' was a delightful train to ride.

Having detached the Penzance section, and leaving Exeter for the west one is soon conscious of a change from the cosy pastoral country characteristic of the run down from the crest of the Blackdown Hills, pierced by the summit tunnel under White Ball Hill, to estuarine conditions and that indefinable brightening of the atmosphere, whatever the season, as one draws near to the sea. The river Exe and the canal are to the left of the line, and in an old style carriage in which one had to choose between left and right hand windows the left undoubtedly provided most of the best viewpoints on the line between Exeter and Plymouth. At first the line is straight and level and the pace is brisk. On the opposite side of the broadening estuary is the pretty little town of Topsham, and then, immediately to the left, before the line begins curving to follow the shore, is an historic site, Turf, where that magnificently original engineer, entrepreneur Isambard Brunel, built one of his picturesque pumping-engine houses for the ill-starred atmosphere system of railway propulsion. The trains were to be drawn along by suction, and air from a large pipe laid continuously between the rails was to be exhausted by a chain of pumping engines, in houses every three miles along the line. One of these was built at Turf, and to enhance rather than detract from the beauty of the countryside they were designed in the Italianate style, with the chimney disguised in the form of a campanile tower.

Just beyond Turf a quick transition to the right hand side of the train must be made for a glimpse of Powderham Castle, in its beautiful park, and then continuing on the very water's edge comes Starcross, which a writer in the *English Illustrated Magazine* of October 1891, after a ride on one of the old broad gauge engines, described as a 'nasty', risky piece of line, where it looked as if the engine would bump against the wall of the hotel, and *ricochet* on to the pier'. Another of the Brunel engine houses was just beyond the hotel, and the remains of it are still there today. Dawlish Warren comes next. When I first knew the district it used to be no more than a flat coastal wasteland looking across the water to Exmouth, but now the whole area has become a highly favoured caravan site. Many summer visitors still come by train, and the line is quadruple-tracked through the station; and then, curving to the right beside an isolated red sandstone bluff known as Langstone Cliff we come to one of the most venturesome pieces of railway engineering to be seen anywhere in Great Britain – the line by the sea. Today one should alight at Dawlish, and explore the coves and beaches between the station and the Parson Rock to appreciate just what Brunel did in 1847–8.

One might have imagined that the friable nature of those red sandstone cliffs, and their complete exposure to wild winter storms would have deterred Brunel; but as in everything else he took the likely difficulties as a challenge and built the line through and beneath those cliffs in places at

The up Torbay Limited, with many extra coaches, 14-coach load, passing Norton Fitzwarren, hauled by engine No. 6018 King Henry VI.

little more than beach level. It is impressive enough in this present age to ride in the front of a diesel rail car train, or if one is lucky enough to be so privileged, in the driver's cab of a steam or diesel locomotive; but in scrambling round the base of those cliffs and seeking out the secluded coves between the tunnels the immensity of the task essayed by Brunel will be clear enough. Between Dawlish station and the 500-yard tunnel curving through the Parson Rock there are four others varying in length from 50 up to 230 yards, and on a fast train the alternation between light and darkness is bewildering. It is not only the sea that has caused damage to this part of the line. There had been landslips, and on the open stretch between the Clerk and Parsons tunnels the line has been completely blocked, with passengers having to walk between trains parked as near as they could attain on either side of the obstruction.

Emerging from the western end of Parsons Tunnel the coastwise prospect is completely changed and extends to the rocky islets at the entrance to Tor Bay that we shall see at closer range later. The red cliffs are higher than ever here though less dramatic in their formation, but the sea wall, an invaluable protection for the railway in winter, is a favourite promenade for the holiday-makers of Teignmouth, whether they are railway enthusiasts or not. But it can be a wild stretch in the winter. I have been on the footplate of a steam locomotive when a neap tide running mountains high was crashing against the sea wall sending spray flying across the track, and those of us in the open-sided cab narrowly escaped a real ducking! The line was single-track when first built and at the Teignmouth end Brunel went through the East Cliff in a tunnel 320 yards long to reach the passenger station; but when in 1884 the line was doubled on this stretch, the tunnel was opened out and replaced by a deep cutting through the cliff. The purely coastal section between the west end of the Parsons Tunnel and Dawlish remained single track until the early years of this century.

The line runs through the back of Teignmouth town between high retaining walls, in Dartmoor granite, but quickly enough on the left hand side there come delightful glimpses across the harbour, boat yards, and the estuary of the River Teign, with the beautiful little town of Shaldon beneath the high red cliff of the Ness. The tidal part of the Teign between Teignmouth and Newton is a rare unspoilt stretch of glorious Devon countryside, with the added attraction of the broad waterway; but having changed direction considerably during the perambulation of the sandstone cliff the skyline ahead shows the unmistakable imprint of Dartmoor with the gaunt outcrops of the Hay Tor rocks showing prominently. Newton Abbot is not such an important railway centre as in the days of the Great Western Railway. Then it was the headquarters of an important Division of the Locomotive Department; there were workshops for the repair of locomotives and carriages, and the Divisional Superintendent reigned supreme over all mechanical and electrical engineering matters throughout the counties of Devon and Cornwall. Now it is no more than a traffic staging point and junction for the line to Torquay and Dartmouth.

When Brunel built the South Devon Railway, an independent company, but inevitably linked closely to the Great Western by its seven-foot rail gauge, and its through connection via Exeter and Taunton, authority to construct the branch to the Tor Bay area did not extend beyond the station for Torquay later known as Torre, up in the woods at the back of the town a mile from the seafront and the little harbour. The continuation, the Dartmouth and Torbay Railway, was a separate promotion that came later. It was always worked by the South Devon company, and eventually became part of it, and so, still later, into the Great Western. But that initial separation, which at that time did not affect the train working, and through passenger connections with the rest of the Great Western system, was prophetic of the more positive and serious separation in recent times. A great deal of the holiday business from London, South Wales, the Midlands and the North did not extend beyond Paignton, and many trains terminated there; it is this that has influenced the recent changes. Before referring to that in any detail however the outlook from the train on arrival at Torquay must be noted. When running non-stop from London in the summer months the arrival was at 3.35 pm an average speed of 55.7 mph.

The present main station, by Livermead Sands, is near enough to the beach for some enticing glimpses of the waters of Tor Bay, and as the train starts away for the south, and negotiates some sharp though short gradients the line comes right out above the beach and the full beauty of Torquay's situation and its superb and rugged coastline is displayed. At this stage in the journey the prospect is soon cut off, by the houses of Paignton. At one time the journey could be continued by 'The Torbay Limited', or a through train from Birmingham, Manchester or Leeds; but now British Railways 'operations' finish at Paignton, and to continue over one of the loveliest scenic routes anywhere in Britain, a change of trains is necessary to the steam trains of the now privately owned Dartmouth and Torbay Railway. In one respect this is a reversion to an operating practice that prevailed almost to the 1930s, because until then the large express locomotives were not permitted to run beyond Paignton. It was not so much a matter of 'permission' but of operating convenience. The line to Kingswear was

Motive power on the branch to Kingswear: a 2-6-2 tank engine climbing the bank from Paignton to Churston.

originally broad gauge, so there was plenty of side clearance in the cuttings, beneath bridges and through the one tunnel; but all engines working on the South Devon Railway, and most of them in Cornwall too were of the tank type which could be run just as conveniently chimney or bunker first. So there was no need for a turntable at the end of the Kingswear branch, and it was not until some years after I first knew the line that one was installed. Any express engine that went down to Kingswear would have had to return tender first, and to avoid that inconvenience engines were changed at Paignton, even on The Torbay Limited. The '45XX' class 2-6-2 tank engines were used for all trains on the branch. The subsequent installation of a large turntable at Kingswear enabled the 'King' class engines to be used, and so avoid the inconvenience of changing engines at Paignton.

On leaving Paignton, and climbing on to the cliff edge beyond Goodrington Sands the wide panorama over the entire sweep of Tor Bay reveals some of its interesting and complex geological features. The red sandstone cliffs of Dawlish and Teignmouth recur at Paignton, in an even deeper shade of red, but at each end of the bay, on the north side extending outwards from Torquay to Hope's Nose, and at the south beyond Brixham to Berry Head, the tattered and splintered rock formations from 'London Bridge' to the outlying Thatcher and Oar Stones, and Berry Head itself are examples of carboniferous limestone, and provide such striking and spectacular cliff structure as to cause at least one eminent geographer to compare it with those of Mediterranean Riviera resorts. The prospect, as the train climbs the gradient, extends much farther east than Tor Bay. One cannot see Teignmouth and Dawlish from the train, but eastward from the Exe the red cliffs are prominent around Sidmouth and bring to mind the amusing couplet by the Rev. Richard Barham, author of the *Ingoldsby Legends*:

> 'It is certainly odd that this part of the coast
> While neighbouring Dorset gleams white as a ghost,
> Should look like anchovy sauce, spread upon toast.'

In clear weather the view certainly extends to the white cliffs between Seaton and Lyme Regis.

In the meantime the railway is climbing to breast the ridge between Tor Bay and the deep valley of the Dart. Churston station, on the crest of the ridge used to be the junction for the short branch line running down to Brixham; but this little section, only 2 miles long, was closed before the preservationists took over the main part of the Dartmouth and Torbay Railway. It always seemed strange however that the Brixham line was constructed to make a 'trailing' connection at Churston; for while the passenger service was never more than a shuttle up and down the 2 miles of

The Brixham connection: branch train with antiquated rolling stock arriving at Churston.

the branch, and involving passengers going farther in a change at the junction, goods trains, including considerable fish traffic in the appropriate season, always had to change direction at Churston before continuing to Paignton, Newton Abbot, or farther afield. When I first knew it the branch passenger train would have provided a good study in railway archaeology, for it consisted of some of the smallest and most antiquated coaches the Great Western possessed, even though they were always kept beautifully clean.

On leaving Churston the sightseer should be sure to cross from the left hand to the right hand side of the carriage, because in less than a mile, coming on to a high embankment there is a first glimpse of the River Dart; and when this is briefly cut off by the passage through Greenway Tunnel it is only a prelude to the train's emerging upon one of the most beautiful of all railway based prospects. I always think that the estuary of the River Dart, with the twin castles of Dartmouth and Kingswear facing each other across the waterway, and the majestic grouping of the hills and the tree-clad shores on either side, is one of the loveliest places in all England. For me, too, the names have a greatly enhanced significance, perhaps, than for those who gaze enchanted upon a scene more like that of a fairy tale than of reality. When, in 1923, the Great Western Railway introduced their ever-famous 'Castle' class of 4-6-0 express passenger locomotives, although the first batch was named mostly after Welsh strongholds it was not long before one of them, No. 4088 was named *Dartmouth Castle*, and in 1932 there followed No. 5015 *Kingswear Castle*. It so happens that I have special memories of those two engines. I was a passenger on the 6.10 pm from Paddington to Wolverhampton on the Friday before Whitsun 1930, when owing to holiday traffic we had a load much heavier than normal; and with *Dartmouth Castle* the driver made a tremendous run, the best I ever had on that route. Then in 1934 I had been at Swindon with a party of young engineers, and to take us back to London on the 'Cheltenham Flyer' we had *Kingswear Castle*. She ran the 77¼ miles in a little under 63 minutes, with a top speed of 85 mph. Railway operations down at Kingswear, or indeed on any part of the branch line from Newton Abbot, are nevertheless far removed from the haste involved in working trains like the Cheltenham Flyer; and I like to recall two occasions when I travelled away from King-swear on The Torbay Limited. The first was between the two world wars, after the big turntable had been installed, and 'King' class locomotives stationed at Newton Abbot worked the train through to Paddington. The fact that it was the end of a holiday made me look with an even greater appreciation upon the beauties of the scene. It was a lovely morning, with just a few fleecy clouds sailing overhead; sunshine dancing on the water, and the cottage gardens gay with flowers. Across the waterway ferries were coming and going, for Dartmouth has a station of its own, at which one can book tickets to any part of the British railway network. From the Dartmouth water front we could see on the farther shore a long line of the familiar chocolate and cream Great Western coaches being propelled into Kingswear station – The Torbay Limited, due to leave at 11.25 am and over there with the flowing tide lapping to within a few feet of the permanent way, the scene became more aminated as departure time drew near.

Passengers were coming over from Dartmouth by the ferries, while more were coming from trim little houses on the Kingswear shore. In the sartorial conventions of the day those who were indeed homeward bound looked a little self-conscious in their town clothes among the gay dresses, white flannels and gaudy blazers of those gathering to wave them off. The res-taurant car conductor was on the platform taking orders for lunch, and at the head of the train, with the morning sun flashing on its polished brass and copper work, was the engine, the *King Henry VI*. Instinctively one took a last look round this beloved corner of England. Ships were lying up the river. The square tower of St Saviour's rising above the roof tops of Dart-mouth brought memories of the decorative work put so lovingly into the Devon churches, but then as passengers sank with resignment behind their magazines and newspapers the signals were pulled off, and the fireman was looking back from the engine cab. The guard with a Devon rose in his buttonhole, was chatting to the stationmaster, but in a moment the forward inspector's whistle was blowing. The green flag was waved, and The Torbay Limited was on its way.

One of the pleasures of travelling by a highly scenic route like that of the Dartmouth and Torbay Railway is that the return journey so frequently reveals new delights. It is certainly so when starting away from the water side terminus in Kingswear, and heading up beside the Dart estuary. On a route like this when the constantly unfolding beauty of the landscape rivets the spectator inevitably to what is happening forward, the rearward-looking scene escapes unnoticed. It is here, when returning from Kingswear, that the ride is full of pleasures anew, as the single tracked railway climbs higher above the tide water of the Dart estuary, and affords glimpses up stream of the higher hills lying to the north. Then comes the crossing of Greenway viaduct, a brief sight of the curves of the river at Dittisham ferry, and then into Greenway Tunnel. So, to the crest of the ridge and a quick change from left to right hand side of the carriage; round the curve past the one-time junction with the Brixham line at Churston and downhill, to enjoy once again the broad prospect over Tor Bay.

It was nearly twenty years later when I made another memorable journey on this splendid train, which although decked in British Railway colours was still leaving Kingswear at the same time and still worked by a Great Western locomotive. I had an engine pass, and began the journey at Newton Abbot. The engine itself, a 'Castle' class 4-6-0 No. 5059 *Earl St Aldwyn*, was working down to Kingswear on a local train to pick up the 'Torbay'. In its revival, after being suspended during World War II, there was a slight change in the name, with the rather incongruous word 'Limited' dropped in favour of 'express'; and indeed on this very occasion, such were the numbers of passengers travelling that arrangements were made to attach an extra coach at Exeter. From Kingswear we had the then standard ten-coach set, amounting to within a ton of the maximum load of 350 tons that a 'Castle' class locomotive was expected to take on this fast train. But to me the main interest of the journey was to observe how this high speed express engine would tackle the very severe gradients of the Torbay and Dartmouth branch line. It was no light task to lift a heavy train of more than 350 tons up those steep inclines at the very start of a long run. Undue pounding, and the fierce draught created could easily disturb the most carefully prepared firebed, and lead to poor steaming later in the run.

From the waterside the gradient is 1 in 66 up through Greenway Tunnel, and here to the accompaniment of a sharp exhaust beat we climbed steadily at 21 to 23 mph. The valves were set to cut off steam in the cylinders at 40 per cent of the piston stroke, and the steaming remained quite steady. I was riding in the left hand corner of the cab, and was well placed to appreciate the beauty of the river scenery as we mounted high on the wooded slopes. It took us just ten minutes to climb the 3¾ miles to Churston, where we stopped briefly to pick up some passengers from Brixham. Then we ran very cautiously down the steep gradients towards Paignton, where the curves are so severe that we barely exceeded 30 mph. We continued similarly over the sharp gradients on the cliff edge to Torquay, and so far there had not been much like an express in the manner of our running. We were still only 9 miles on our way to London, and inclusive of the two stops we had taken 29 minutes to cover those miles. Moreover, the restart from Torquay is even worse than that out of Kingswear graded at 1 in 55 at first; and when we reached the summit point, above Torre station the speed had not increased beyond 19 mph. But once we were through Newton Abbot, and still more so after we left Exeter we began to run to some purpose, as indeed we needed to with only 175 minutes in which to cover the 173½ miles from Exeter to Paddington. There was that extra coach too, and such crowds of passengers that the gross load behind the tender was at least 420 tons. On a busy Friday afternoon there were traffic delays; but this fine engine ran magnificently and made up no less than 8 minutes of lost time. In contrast to that laborious start from Kingswear our maximum speed east of Exeter was 86 mph.

11

THE THAMES-FORTH EXPRESS

This train, so attractively named in 1927, was one of the last relics of that burgeoning era when the Midland Railway was waging fierce competition for the Anglo-Scottish traffic, not only from London, but also from the West of England, to Glasgow, Edinburgh and Aberdeen, and for a time to the Highland line. It is not always realised that the Midland Railway was the largest single contributor to the capital needed to build the Forth Bridge. At the time of which I am now writing however I would imagine that very few passengers made the complete journey from St Pancras to Edinburgh Waverley. I used it for business visits to Chesterfield and Sheffield, and occasionally when I had to go to West Cumberland, when The Royal Scot was running non-stop to its summer engine-change at Kingmoor. But for anyone bound for Edinburgh who was prepared to leave London an hour before the Royal Scot or the Flying Scotsman, and to enjoy the journey it could be a most enthralling ride.

For one thing, it would hardly have been possible to pack a greater variety of scene into a single day's journey in Great Britain. Over the Chilterns, on, at high speed through the green shires, the hunting shires of Leicester and Rutland, having turned off the principal main line to the north just after Kettering. This direct line to Nottingham, now closed, was an important relief route for the almost continuous procession of coal trains from the north-midland pits to London, when coal traffic was the very life-blood of the Midland Railway; but passing trains apart this line was a veritable epitome of rural English country, with its rich farmlands, broad vistas – especially when crossing the Welland valley on the 82–arch Harringworth viaduct. Passing Oakham in the inter-war years one would never have thought that a time would come when not only the railway but the county itself, proud Rutland, would be no more. Beyond Melton Mowbray the line is still in existence, but as no more than a single track, and at one time used for experimental running with the prototype Advanced Passenger Train. The first stop was Nottingham, reached at an average speed of 60 mph from St Pancras.

Leaving Nottingham the Thames-Forth Express took a sinuous route at first, at appropriately slow speed, until re-joining the principal main line to the north at Trowell, in the Erewash Valley; and there everything used to be subjugated to coal. Even this important trunk route was punctuated by frequent areas of severely restricted speed, where the ground had subsided because of mining activities far underground; and on the adjoining relief lines the south bound coal trains would sometimes be queued up buffer to buffer waiting for a clear line to proceed. Compared to the booked average speed of 60 mph to Nottingham, no more than 42½ mph was scheduled for the next 28¼ miles to Chesterfield. On one journey when I was a passenger, what with the three regular slowings for the junctions at Radford, Trowell, and Clay Cross, and three sections of dead slow running where there had been mining subsidences we could not even keep this slow timing. But while one looked out upon a landscape scarred with the signs of industrialism one could equally reflect that it was here that the Midland Railway collected the traffic that enabled such handsome dividends to be paid to its share-holders, rather than in the running of lightly loaded, if spectacular express passenger trains.

Even in this outwardly gloomy environment however there is one 'sight in a thousand' for the traveller, the parish church of Chesterfield, dedicated to St Mary and All Saints. Standing prominently on a hill to the west of the line it is the 228 ft high spire that rivets the attention, because it is most grotesquely twisted. It is believed that the deformation was caused by the use of unseasoned timber, though local legend ascribes it to the work of the devil! But in any event no attempt has ever been made to repair or rebuild it. Rather, it has always been regarded as a heritage of the town, to be cherished and maintained in its traditionally warped condition. Shortly after leaving Chesterfield, on the opposite side of the line is Tapton House, where George Stephenson lived in his retirement, and died in 1848. At this point The Thames-Forth Express is briefly travelling on the line of the one-time North Midland Railway which ran from Derby to Leeds and is generally considered to be one of the greatest of George Stephenson's works. We joined its route at Clay Cross Junction, to leave it again at Tapton Junction only a mile north of Chesterfield. When the North Midland Railway was projected in 1837, steel was a material of the future; the great city of Sheffield scarcely existed, and the pioneer line was taken, at river-level grades down the valley of the Rother, linking up all the collieries, to its confluence with the Don at Rotherham.

An independent company, the Sheffield and Rotherham, was actually completed and in operation before the North Midland was finished, not without a great deal of local opposition however, because the denizens of

On the Settle and Carlisle line in Midland days: express from Glasgow and Edinburgh approaching Armathwaite, hauled by two 6 ft 6 in 4-4-0 locomotives, Nos 444 and 450.

the quiet little town of Rotherham, to quote a contemporary report, 'dreaded an incursion of the idle, drunken, and dissolute portion of the Sheffield people as a consequence of increasing the facilities of transit'. But this short line, only 5½ miles long, was the only connection Sheffield had with the Midland Railway main line until nearly thirty years later, when the hotly contested direct line from Chesterfield was built, costing the Company half a million pounds for its 11½ miles from Tapton Junction. And travelling by the Thames-Forth Express the discerning passenger could well appreciate why it was so expensive, and why George Stephenson did not take the North Midland Railway through Sheffield. From river-level grades the railway climbs into rough upland country, the eastern boundaries of the Peak District, with the engine pounding uphill at little more than 30 mph, and after passing Dronfield entering the long Bradway tunnel. The outlet is at a dramatic railway location, the triangle junction amid the deep cuttings by Dore and Totley station. Here the line makes connection with a one-time competitive, and now the only trans-Pennine route westwards from Sheffield, the highly scenic 'Dore and Chinley' line. It began with the longest-but-one of all British railway tunnels, Totley, 3½ miles of it, under the 1300 ft moorland ridge separating Dore from the delightful river scenery of the Derbyshire Derwent.

From the Thames-Forth Express there is no more than a glimpse of the beginning of that line as the speed rises to 60 mph probably for the first time since leaving Nottingham, on the descent of the Abbey Dale towards Sheffield. On resuming the journey north, passing the dramatically impressive industrialism of Brightside, and rejoining the North Midland line at Rotherham the train continues to make no speed records, being allowed 48 minutes for the 39½ miles from Sheffield to Leeds. The necessarily slow progress over this part of the line affords an opportunity to say something of the locomotives, both pre- and post-grouping; because there was a continuity here that was rare on railways north of the Thames in this era. For

Familiar power on the Settle and Carlisle line: Midland Railway 4-4-0 No. 480, rebuilt from an earlier smaller boilered design.

one thing, the old Midland colour for engines and carriages, Derby 'red', had been retained by the LMS, not, it is true, so lavishly applied to the carriages, and restricted to only the principal express passenger locomotives; but the long-lived three-cylinder Deeley compounds, and their LMS successors were still much in evidence, and the No. 2 class 4-4-0s frequently turned out to pilot them in any case of overload. On the Midland the old traditions died hard, and even with the powerful modern 4-6-0 locomotives introduced from 1932 onwards the slightest excess over the stipulated maximum load called forth a pilot engine.

The first of the larger engines were the 'Baby Scots', Derby's riposte to Crewe's successful rebuilding of the ex-LNWR 'Claughton' class 4-6-0s with larger boilers. Derby took the enlarged 'Claughton' boiler and put it on to the 'Royal Scot' chassis. It made a handsome and efficient express passenger unit mid-way in power between the No. 5 class, and the 'Royal Scots', and many of them were put to work on the Midland line. But after Sir William Stanier, from the Great Western Railway, had been appointed Chief Mechanical Engineer they were largely superseded by his new Jubilee class, of the same nominal tractive power, but having in the Swindon type of taper boiler, features that eventually resulted in lower maintenance costs. Several of the 'Jubilee' class have been preserved in full working order, and in particular the *Leander* frequently works special trains on the Midland line north of Leeds. The celebrated 'Black Five' 4-6-0s although designated 'mixed traffic' units, were regularly used on express passenger trains in the steam era.

Arrival in Leeds marked an important stage in the Anglo-Scottish run by the Midland route. Not only was one nearly half way from London to Edinburgh or Glasgow, but on leaving the relatively slow running of the heavily industrialised part of the journey was quickly cast aside and the going was noticeably brisker from the outset. Another evidence of change was the change of direction. The former Midland station in Leeds, the 'Wellington', was a terminus and the engine to take the train forward to Carlisle coupled on to what, up to now, had been the rear of the train. Until May 1932 the train included a through carriage from St Pancras to Aberdeen, but so few passengers used it that it was then withdrawn, and after that the only continuing justification for the original Midland investment in the Forth Bridge was one night through carriage service. The Thames-Forth Express also had a through carriage from Nottingham to Glasgow. As from May 1932 this carriage was detached from the Edinburgh train at Leeds to await the arrival of the morning Glasgow express from St Pancras. There was good reason for lightening the load of the Thames-Forth Express north of Leeds, because it had a pretty sharp timing over the mountain section, with only 94 minutes to cover the 86¾ miles from Skipton to Carlisle and the 1151 ft altitude of Aisgill Summit to be mounted on the way. At its lightest the train consisted of no more than five carriages, and the three cylinder compound 4-4-0s could handle this fast train quite competently.

While the locomotive enthusiast would delight in logging the details of the run, how speed was maintained up what railwaymen called the 'Long Drag', the 14 miles of almost continuous ascent from Settle Junction to Blea Moor, and of the exciting speeds sometimes attained on the long descent from Aisgill summit to Carlisle, those less technically minded could sit back and enjoy the swiftly changing pageant of mountain grandeur that began to unfold when the train was about a quarter of an hour on its way from Skipton. I have said 'sit back'; but actually this is one of the few scenic routes in Great Britain on which there is as much to see on one side of the line as on the other. To avoid dashes from a window corner on one side of the train to the corridor on the other one really needed to make several journeys to absorb it all. At the time of which I am now writing the open saloon type of carriages were confined to the dining cars. This was certainly a route where the stop-watcher had an advantage over the general sightseer, because the mileposts, at least, were all on one side, the right-hand going north. But before plunging into the mountain country proper there is one sight that no traveller should miss. Far on the left, as the Thames-Forth Express was racing down from Hellifield to its point of parting from the line to Carnforth and the Lake District, could be seen the great 1800 ft whaleback profile of Pendle Hill. There, on the summit, at the Malkin Tower, the 'Lancashire Witches' are said to have held their grand council – one of them in particular being regarded as a local agent of the devil! Satan apart, however, the LMS named one of the 'Royal Scot' class locomotives after her – No. 6125 *Lancashire Witch*.

Then, just as the train is entering upon the Long Drag, several miles ahead there is a glimpse of a landmark of a very different kind, all the more striking for standing out so vividly against the range of limestone scars behind. It is a most brilliant green dome, looking for all the world like the cupola of some oriental mosque. Actually it is the school chapel of Giggleswick, the munificent gift of a multi-millionaire governor of the school to celebrate the Diamond Jubilee of Queen Victoria's reign. As an 'old boy' of Giggleswick School I must be forgiven for drawing special attention to a place where I worshipped during five formative years of my life. So past Settle, and into the highest and wildest parts of Ribblesdale. A topographical writer of my boyhood, Arthur H. Norway, wrote that in her river scenery the great county of Yorkshire was peerless. No doubt he was thinking of the dale country through which rivers run south and east from the Pennines. North Ribblesdale is not among these, though the Settle and Carlisle line runs beside one brief, but exquisite stretch in the Stainforth gorge just before the railway comes out upon the open moor at Helwith Bridge in full view of the fine peak Pen-y-Ghent. Thenceforward, as the train pounds uphill, the dale is bleak in the extreme, till reaching the boggy wastes of Ribble-head, set in an amphitheatre of great hills, from which there is no outlet to the north save through a long, dank tunnel beneath the flanks of Whernside. Blea Moor: the very name seems to epitomise the eerie solitude of the place.

Nearby, of course, is the great 110-year-old Ribblehead viaduct the condition of which threatens the very life of the line itself. In such a remote and exposed location maintenance of a huge masonry structure is all-important, and the cost over the years of this, and the smaller but equally spectacular viaducts farther north has been out of proportion to the volume of traffic conveyed. There have never been nose-to-tail processions of freight trains up here to roll in the money, and at last the crunch has come. No such inhibitions beset the line in the 1930s however, and I recall clocking the Thames-Forth Express, double-handed it is true, to climb the Long Drag at a steady 45 to 46 mph and then to go careering downhill in such style as to pass Appleby five minutes early, in 59 minutes for the 56 miles from Skipton. In relating this experience I have nevertheless skated over the most fascinating part of the whole line, the high tableland section between the northern end of Blea Moor Tunnel and the summit point at Aisgill Moor. It is a stretch where perhaps the most outstanding engineering characteristic of this great line is becoming increasingly apparent; and it was made even more apparent to me on the occasions when I was privileged to ride on the footplate of locomotives – there were no speed restrictions! The Midland Railway was bent upon running on equality of times to Scotland with the established East Coast and West Coast routes. Whatever the terrain was like between Skipton and Carlisle which the line must go through, it had to be straight enough to permit of the highest speeds the locomotives could make. If there was a deep valley ahead there could be no detour; a high viaduct must take the line straight across. If there was any obstruction, be it a rocky out-jutting bluff, or a mountain, there was no way other than to tunnel clean through it! And along this high level stretch, across high viaducts and through long tunnels, all at an altitude of more than 1100 ft above sea level the Thames-Forth Express raced at between 62 and 70 mph.

From the left hand carriage window the scenery at times is breathtaking. At Dent station, where one looks westwards down the valley of the Dee, four miles to the village itself, the railway is 400 ft sheer above the valley floor, and after storming through Rise Hill Tunnel the line emerges high above another westward valley Garsdale, scarcely less dramatic in its setting. The railway itself is dead level hereabouts, so much so for a set of water troughs to be laid in. They give a welcome fillip to the crews of locomotives that had been steamed hard up the Long Drag, and still more so after the lengthy upward ascent southbound from Carlisle. Just beyond the water troughs at Garsdale Head, was the station that used to be known as Hawes Junction. From it a branch went eastwards down Wensleydale for six miles to Hawes itself, where it made an end-on junction with the North Eastern Railway branch that had climbed up the dale from Northallerton. Hawes Junction was an extraordinary place. There have been certain remote locations on the British railway system described as 'railway colonies', but at Hawes Junction there was at one time hardly a house in sight. Yet apart from providing connection to the few trains on the branch it had quite a vital part to play in Midland Railway operating, that once led to a tragedy.

Company policy was to run the passenger train service, of light trains, with locomotives of no more than medium power. The loading limits were strict, and for any excess a second engine was to be provided. On the mountain section these pilots were needed only in the uphill direction, and to save engine mileages a stop was made at Aisgill summit to detach them, so that they could return light to their home station as soon as possible. But before they could do this they had to be turned, and because there was no turntable at Aisgill they had to run the three miles to Hawes Junction, where there was one on the northbound side of the line. It was an awkward arrangement in any case and at times of heavy seasonal traffic, when many trains were conveying more than their normal loads, there was sometimes a positive glut of engines at this remote outpost, amid the high fells. It was certainly so in the early hours of Christmas Eve 1910, when from just before 5 am there were no fewer than *nine* at this tiny station. Amid all the pressure of work dealing with them, in addition to the regular traffic, two of them were moved out on to the down main line, ready to return to Carlisle, and then, alas, forgotten. They moved away in response to a signal that was not intended for them, but for the midnight express from St Pancras; and it was not until the latter came on at full speed, caught them up and crashed into them that the unfortunate signalman at Hawes Junction realised his mistake.

From Aisgill, starting beneath the crags of Wild Boar Fell, the descent to Carlisle provides 46 miles of unrestricted racing ground. At its fastest the Thames-Forth Express was scheduled to take 47 minutes over the 48¼ miles from the summit into the Citadel station; but this provided, indirectly, a considerable margin for recovery. Until 1963 the record, so far as I can trace, dates back to a run in 1902, when one of the big non-compound 4-4-0s sometimes referred to as the 'Belpaires', from the design of their fire-boxes, covered the 40·9 miles from Mallerstang signal box to Cumwhinton at an average speed of 76·3 mph with a maximum of 90 mph; but in 1963 I personally saw this record beaten by a clear minute, on a special train hauled by a visiting LNER streamlined 'Pacific' of the 'A4' class, the *Golden Eagle*, when the average was stepped up to 78·4 mph. Had we begun the descent as vigorously as on one of my fastest trips on the Thames-Forth Express this fine average would have been increased still further to just over 80 mph. The last stages of that fast descent provide some of the most beautiful scenery of all on the journey of the Thames-Forth Express, because after Lazonby the line runs high above the lower reaches of the Eden Valley, and the sightseer might wish that the train would travel a little slower, that the succession of delightful vistas might be more thoroughly enjoyed. So into Carlisle, at 3.14 pm 323¼ miles from St Pancras at an overall average of 52½ mph, despite the enforcedly slow running between Nottingham and

The Thames-Forth Express, southbound, leaving Nottingham, hauled by standard 3-cylinder compound 4-4-0 No. 1093, with a tremendous stack of coal on the tender.

Leeds, and the 17 minutes standing at the five intermediate stops. The running average speed was 54¼ mph.

At Carlisle haulage of the train passed into the hands of the London and North Eastern Railway, and a complete change in the character of the running was soon to be noted. This was not due to any variation in competence or lack of engine power – rather the reverse – but because of the fundamental nature of the road itself. Whereas the Midland line between Settle and Carlisle was from its very inception planned as a fast express route, through extremely difficult country, the continuation to Edinburgh over what was part of the former North British Railway was quite the opposite. It was the linking up of 'bits and pieces' that began in 1831, and took the line as far as Hawick in 1849. There it terminated for ten years, and was duly described in official North British Railway documents and plans as the 'Hawick Branch'. But the Company had, in Richard Hodgson, a Chairman of boundless energy and enterprise, and he was determined to carry the line southward to tap some of the increasing traffic from the south that was even then beginning to come into Carlisle. Other interests sought to block his way. The Caledonian Railway had a scheme to build a line northwards through Langholm, and by Ewes Water and Teviothead into Teviotdale, the route of the present 'A7' highway. But Hodgson had a beter idea. If the line from Carlisle was taken up Liddesdale, instead of via Langholm, a junction could be made, high in the Cheviot Hills, with another of his protégés, the Border Counties Railway, which made a precarious and impecunious way up the North Tyne Valley from Hexham. Despite support from the Duke of Buccleuch the Caledonian scheme was rejected, and Hodgson got his Border Union Railway. It was opened for traffic of a sort in 1862; but it was not until 14 years later, when the Settle and Carlisle line was completed, that the North British teamed up with the Midland to run a through service from St Pancras to Edinburgh.

The way the line had originally been built up proved an almost crippling hindrance to fast running. The gradients were severe in any case, toiling up the side of Liddesdale to the Whitrope summit in the Cheviots, and then on an equally steep and winding descent into Hawick. Then from Galashiels there was hard climbing to Falahill, a summit point in the Lammermuir Hills before the final precipitous run down into Edinburgh. But while the gradients were bad enough it was the incessant and severe curvature that precluded any fast running. One could not run at more than about 60 mph anywhere, so that it is not surprising that the Thames-Forth Express took 2½ hours to do the 98 miles from Carlisle to Edinburgh, an average speed of only 39 mph. But romantic associations amply made up for any lack of thrills in running speeds. In the nineteenth century Sir Walter Scott wove an aura of romance into the literature of the day and the North British Railway carrying its Carlisle–Edinburgh line within sight of Abbotsford, his beautiful home on Tweedside, capitalised on this close association with he who was often called, 'The Author of Waverley'. Their principal station in Edinburgh was named Waverley; the line to Carlisle was the Waverley Route, and the largest engines working the Anglo-Scottish trains over it had appropriately fine names: *Holyrood*, *Abbotsford*, *Tweeddale*, *Hazeldene*, *Teribus*, *Liddesdale*, and even the nobleman who backed their opponents in trying to block construction of the Border Union Railway, *Buccleuch*. Needless to add, there was also one of them named *Waverley*.

These magnificent 'Atlantic' engines, dating from 1906 were still on the job when I first travelled in Scotland over the route of the Thames-Forth Express and their work was spectacular, not in the speeds they made but in the precision of the point-to-point timekeeping. In September 1928 I travelled by the southbound train behind the engine *Holyrood*, and at twelve intermediate points at which working times were laid down we were nowhere more than 45 seconds out, ultimately clocking into Carlisle 35 seconds ahead of time. At first the old North British system of engine headboards was carried on into London and North Eastern days, whereby the destination board was for operating convenience rather than for passengers, and indicated where the particular engine was going. Thus, on this journey of mine with the southbound Thames-Forth Express the engine *Holyrood* carried a headboard labelled CARLISLE. In writing of the origins of the Waverley Route, now alas no more, I have inadvertently been concerned with its northern end, rather than in logical continuation of the journey northwards from London to Edinburgh; so I must return to the Citadel station in Carlisle where the Midland engines have just coupled off, and the apple-green LNER successor is backing on.

Although the North British 'Atlantics' were the most powerful of their type ever to run in Great Britain, because of the length and severity of the gradient the maximum load they were permitted to take without assistance over the Waverley Route was 290 tons – ten of the standard Midland type coaches; and in climbing the often storm-swept flanks of Liddesdale, where the gradient was 1 in 75 without a break for $9\frac{1}{4}$ miles, the train was allowed 22 minutes to climb the $10\frac{1}{4}$ miles from Newcastleton to the Whitrope summit. Sustained speed on the bank was rarely much more than 25 mph and then one had to run cautiously round the many curves on the equally steep descent to Hawick, only briefly topping 60 mph. By then we were in the very heart of the Scott country, stopping briefly at St Boswell's and Melrose before coming to Galashiels, the last stop before Edinburgh. This was a stretch where one needed eyes for the sights on both sides of the line.

From St Boswells one made a leftward turn through a full right-angle round the base of the triple-crowned Eildon Hills; then on the right came Melrose Abbey, and, two miles beyond, the final crossing of the River Tweed and a sight leftwards up the dale to the woodlands planted by Sir Walter Scott around Abbotsford.

Restarting from Galashiels, and climbing up the glen of Gala Water, the merest glance at even a moderate scale map is enough to show why no sustained fast running can be made while coming down from Falahill on the southbound run, because its course by Bowland, Stow, and Fountainhall is like that of a wriggling eel! There were times, indeed, when the *uphill* speeds seemed a trifle hot for some of those curves, especially after some of the Gresley 'A3' class 'Pacifics' had been put to work on the Waverley Route. They, of course, could take a considerably heavier load than the 'Atlantics', though in lighter working conditions one could sometimes see some quite spectacular regaining of lost time. I was on the footplate of one of these engines one afternoon when we were leaving Galashiels some minutes behind time, with a load of no more than 275 tons, and we cut 5½ minutes off the timing of 26 minutes for the 15½ miles up to Falahill. For much of the way we were sweeping round those curves at 54 mph, yet when it came to the steep final descent towards Edinburgh the engine was so severely held in that we did not exceed 56 mph. After the majestic scenery of the last four hours journey's end comes as much of an anti-climax, and in days before the 'clean-air' regulations 'Auld Reekie' often lived up to its nickname lying under a pall of smoke, when it was not obscured by a sea-fog of the kind known locally as 'haar'.

There was in any case not much to see from the carriage window in those last miles. There was no risk of a repetition of that hair-raising negotiation of the notorious S-curve at Portobello, where the night 'sleeper' from Kings Cross threw the passengers out of their beds by going round it at 80 mph during the 'racing' days of 1895, because the Waverley Route comes down from Niddrie South Junction to join the East Main line in a 'dog's hind leg' of a junction, and the speed is appropriately slow. After that there is a glimpse over the roof-tops of the Palace of Holyrood House, and a dive through the final tunnel to arrive in Waverley station, beside The Mound, crowned by buildings once apostrophised by a Cockney tourist as 'the fimous Castle of Edinburgh', but which was actually the Calton Gaol! Such was the run of the Thames-Forth Express. In the days of the nationalised British Railways it was renamed 'The Waverley' and as such it ran until the line from Carlisle was closed in 1969.

Brief Encounter – The Queen of Scots

For most of its run from Kings Cross to Edinburgh this handsome 'Pullman' train followed the route of the Flying Scotsman. Only between Doncaster and Northallerton, no more than $62\frac{1}{4}$ out of the inter-capital mileage of $392\frac{3}{4}$ did it make a diversion to the west, to serve Leeds and Harrogate. The first stage, the concluding stage of the fast non-stop run from London, is best forgotten scenically, because it runs past a seemingly continuous succession of coal tips; but the next 18 miles, northwards from Leeds to Harrogate, are exceptionally interesting, both scenically and engineering-wise. It would have been worth while joining the Queen of Scots for this brief journey to enjoy the passing scene to the full from the big Pullman windows. And if time pressed, after a stop-over time of no more than nineteen minutes in Harrogate one could have returned to Leeds by the southbound Queen of Scots, gazing upon the beauty of Wharfedale in reverse. The origin of this route between Leeds and Harrogate was twofold, both parts dating back to the wild days of the Railway Mania, in the 1840s.

The businessmen of Leeds were suspicious of the entrepreneurial activities of the former linen draper of York, the chimerical George Hudson, and they determined to have a line of their own to the north. They projected, and eventually obtained an act authorising construction of what was first called the Leeds and Thirsk Railway. It was an expensive line through very hilly country, and in the relatively short distance between Leeds and Harrogate there were some impressive works. Thomas Grainger, of Edinburgh, was the engineer, and he made a splendid job of it. Climbing steeply out of Leeds, towards the high ridge between the Aire and Wharfe valleys, when little more than a mile on our way is a fine viaduct of twenty-three arches; but the ridge itself is pierced by the tremendous Bramhope Tunnel, just over two miles long, and marked at its northern end by one of the finest tunnel facades anywhere in Great Britain. Castellated, in weathered stone, it looks most impressive against the background of wooded hills. From the Pullman windows one naturally gained a better idea of it when travelling south; but

The Harrogate Pullman train, in 1926, passing the Kings Cross goods station yards, hauled by ex-Great Central 4-6-0 No. 6169 Lord Faringdon.

The Edinburgh Pullman – non-stop to Harrogate – climbing the Holloway bank, hauled by ex-Great Central 4-4-0 No. 5507 Gerard Powys Dewhurst.

The Queen of Scots Pullman, passing Croft Spa (County Durham) hauled by Class 'A1' Gresley 4-6-2 No. 2582 Sir Hugo.

The Queen of Scots Pullman, leaving Edinburgh Waverley, hauled by Class 'A2' Raven 4-6-2 No. 2401 City of Kingston-upon-Hull. Note the tender, coaled up for the run through to Leeds.

of course the best view of all is from the front seat of a modern diesel railcar. This part of the line is still open.

After leaving Bramhope Tunnel the Queen of Scots Pullman crossed the valley of the Wharfe on another splendid viaduct of twenty-one arches, but like the earlier one crossed, near Leeds, the passengers would have little or no chance to see or appreciate its fine architecture, because it is on no more than a slight curve. But as the train sped northward, passing the village station of Pannal, those passengers on the left hand side, looking ahead, would soon see stretching across the valley, completely athwart the present direction of travel, a tremendous viaduct of thirty-one arches, that carried another railway 100 ft above the level of the valley. This was actually part of the first line to reach Harrogate, and was a branch of George Hudson's own York and North Midland Railway, that came up through Tadcaster and Wetherby, and emerged at high level from a tunnel called the Prospect, to cross the valley on the Crimple viaduct. When it was first built the Leeds and Thirsk line passed underneath at right angles, and continued to circumvent the hill on which Harrogate is perched, and to serve the town by a

The Queen of Scots Pullman, down grade at high speed towards Grantham, hauled by GNR Atlantic No. 4433.

low level station to the east, named Starbeck.

When the Leeds and Thirsk had extended to Tees-side, and had become the Leeds Northern, (after a disgraced Hudson had quit the scene, and his York and North Midland, and other enterprises had been amalgamated to form the North Eastern) a connecting line was put in. This was on a very sharp curve and a steep gradient to enable trains from the Leeds and Thirsk line to head round on to the great Crimple Viaduct and the high level station in the most fashionable part of Harrogate. For those who enjoy the scenic aspects of railway travel this was a most spectacular ride, if not a very rapid one. In view of the many beautiful photographs that were taken of the Queen of Scots Pullman train it is a pity that none of the expert photographers visited the picturesque section between Harrogate and the north end of Bramhope Tunnel. The train continued over the one-time Leeds Northern line, through Ripon, with a glimpse of yet another famous English cathedral, to its intersection with the East Coast main line at Nor-thallerton, and so back again on to the route of the Flying Scotsman. But the line north of Harrogate is now closed, and the track removed.

The Queen of Scots north of Newcastle, hauled by ex-North Eastern 3-cylinder Atlantic No. 2211, accelerating after slowing round Morpeth curve.

BOAT TRAINS:

THE GOLDEN ARROW - THE NIGHT FERRY

From the very inception of railways in Kent the boat trains running in connection with the cross-Channel packets, and carrying the Continental and Imperial Indian mails on the first stages of their journey overland to Brindisi, had been some of the most prestigious trains in the South of England. By 1910, when patronage, both in numbers and affluence, demanded a degree of additional luxury in travel the South Eastern and Chatham Railway began running Pullman cars on the boat trains, though in contrast to the similar cars running on the Southern Belle and other seaside services of the neighbouring Brighton Railway the boat train cars were painted in a maroon livery to match the colour of the ordinary SE & CR coaching stock. These facilities were withdrawn during the first world war, but in 1921 when some fine new coaches for ordinary boat train passengers were put on, the 11 am from Victoria to Dover always included at least three of the maroon Pullman cars. As conditions gradually returned to normal on the Continent boat train traffic increased by leaps and bounds, and the more popular services were regularly run in duplicate; and the first break-away from older traditions came in 1925 when a set of seven new Pullmans, allocated to the 10.50 am relief to the old-established 11 am service from Victoria were finished in the chocolate and cream livery instead of the hitherto standard SE & CR maroon.

In pre-war years the principal boat train services had been operated from Charing Cross, with some running into and out of Cannon Street, to collect mail vans; but for future development the former Chatham lines in the London area with their various alternative routes, plus the system of interconnecting junctions between the Chatham and South Eastern lines at Chislehurst provided so many advantages in working relief, and delayed inward services through the increasingly crowded London suburban area, that in post-war years all Continental traffic was concentrated at Victoria. This brought a temporary handicap in that the largest and most powerful locomotives of the South Eastern and Chatham Railway could not be used, because of axle-loading restrictions; but R. E. L. Maunsell's rebuilding of the 'E' class 4-4-0s with superheaters in 1919 produced an excellent engine, and this type was used on the boat trains until the summer of 1925. It was then that the celebrated 'King Arthur' class 4-6-0s were introduced, and the first of those built in Glasgow, by the North British Locomotive Company, and always known on the Southern as the 'Scotchmen', were sent new to Stewarts Lane shed, Battersea, to work the Continental boat expresses. The first four were *Sir Bors de Ganis*, *Sir Gawain*, *Sir Gareth* and *Sir Geraint*, and one could imagine the more erudite of the locomotive enthusiasts turning to Malory to find out just who these chaps were! Rumour had it that the fifth of the batch, by some howling bloomer, was originally to be named after the traitor *Sir Mordred*, but that the *faux pas* was discovered in time, and it went in to traffic as *Sir Valence*.

With locomotives of such enhanced power available the traffic department was not long in piling on extra coaches, and the all-Pullman 'relief' to the 11 am boat train, with further chocolate and cream cars added to the original seven became nicknamed among Southern railwaymen as 'The White Elephant', wholly on account of its weight, and not, I hasten to add, from any resemblance to the doubtful attributes of that metaphorical monster! In keeping with traditional Pullman practice these beautiful new cars were all named, the seven of 1925 being *Aurelia*, *Marjorie*, *Medusa*, *Pauline*, *Sappho*, *Viking* and *Montana*. The last mentioned was a brake and luggage van finished externally to match the passenger cars and so avoid the incongruous appearance of an ordinary van at one end of a rake of Pullmans, as happened on the post-war 'Southern Belle'. As patronage of this very popular train rapidly increased, it became necessary to add other vehicles before additional Pullmans were available, and also the open trucks for conveying the containers of registered through luggage, to be lifted direct on to the ship at Dover. To avoid 'spoiling the look' of the train from the front these miscellaneous vehicles were marshalled discreetly at the rear end. 'The White Elephant' was no record breaker for speed; it was allowed 98 minutes to cover the 78¼ miles from Victoria to Dover Marine, and to allow ample time for transfer of its affluent patrons from train to boat before the regular 11 am arrived the departure from London was made 10.45 am.

The new Pullmans were beautiful cars, and differed in many respects from those previously in use on both the Brighton and the SE & C railways. Although carried on four-wheeled bogies they were considerably heavier than the maroon cars, turning the scale at 40 tons tare, against 34 tons. Each had seating for 22 passengers in high backed individual armchairs, and each had its own kitchen and pantry. As with the cars of the Southern Belle (see Chapter 3) each of the new cars had its own distinctive style of interior decoration. That applied to the car *Pauline* will give an indication of the tasteful artistry invoked in all of them. In this car the panelling was in mahogany with black band and light line border to panels which had floral and ribbon marquetry with oval inlaid medallions bearing a classic figure. The pilasters were inlaid with light lines, and the moulded cornice cross-banded with light and dark lines. The pleasing effect was completed with a green trellis carpet, and a light ground floral pattern moquette on the chairs. All the fittings were in gilt. In all the cars the armchairs were movable, and could be disposed, from information given by passengers at the time of reservation to suit parties travelling together or in ones or twos.

In the following year contracts for no fewer than 150 Pullman cars for service on the continent of Europe were secured by British firms, and one set of the new cars was put into service on the Calais–Paris *rapide* connecting with the 10.45 Pullman train from Victoria to Dover. The French all-Pullman service was inaugurated in September 1926 and was from the outset named *La Flèche d'Or* – The Golden Arrow; but it was not until May 1929 that the really striking developments took place on the English side. By then the demand for luxurious first class travel between London and Paris had increased to such an extent that the 10.45 am departure from Victoria was loading daily to ten Pullmans, all first class, and in sharing the steamer accommodation with the passengers off the 11 am train conditions were often becoming uncomfortably crowded. So the decision was taken to give the Pullman passengers a ship of their own, with appropriately lavish furnishings, and a number of de-luxe private cabins. This was the beautiful new turbine steamer *Canterbury* built by Denny, of Dumbarton, specially and exclusively for this service. In keeping with the name given to the connecting French train, in 1926, the English all-Pullman boat train, retimed to leave Victoria at 11 am was named 'The Golden Arrow'.

This beautiful train, more so perhaps than any other of those featured in this book, was representative of what is now a by-gone age in first class travel. Commercial air services were in their infancy. Trains and ships were the main means of getting about, and the speed of transit, with an arrival at the Gare du Nord in Paris at 5.35 pm was considered a remarkable achievement. The acceleration of service was achieved not by faster running of the trains but by the reduced time in transferring between train and boat: 17 minutes at Dover and 15 minutes at Calais. On the English side the boat train had seats for 220 passengers, and the *Canterbury* was designed to accommodate about 250, thus allowing for a few 'extras' who might arrive at Dover in chauffeur-driven cars. In addition to the ten Pullman cars the Golden Arrow included a four-wheeled luggage van, and a six-wheeled truck for the containers carrying through registered luggage. These vehicles were marshalled at the rear of the train on the outward journey, conveniently placed on arrival at Dover for quick detachment and shunting to the tracks alongside the steamer berth.

The official maximum tonnage for any of the Continental boat trains run from Victoria was 425 tons tare. This would cover the ten 40-ton Pullmans of the Golden Arrow plus the smaller vehicles. By the time the new service was introduced further engines of the 'Lord Nelson' class were in traffic, eventually totalling sixteen by the end of 1929. But these powerful machines had to be shared between Stewarts Lane shed, for the boat trains, and Nine Elms, for the Bournemouth and West of England trains, and the boat train loading was fixed so that the duties could be satisfactorily worked by 'King Arthur' class 4-6-0s if a 'Nelson' was not available. The first eight of the new engines, Nos 851 to 858 were put on to the boat train workings, and of the first of them there is a good story to be told. In England locomotive enginemen, and those responsible for regulating the working, up to the lower ranks of the running departments, never seem to have paid much attention to the names bestowed upon their locomotives. On the Southern, with the fearful and wonderful collection of names given to the 'King Arthur' class this was more than easily understandable, while it is doubtful if the names of the famous 'sea dogs' of English maritime history bestowed upon the 'Lord Nelsons' meant very much more. But on one occasion, so

The outward bound Golden Arrow, hauled by King Arthur class 4-6-0 locomotive No. 769 Sir Balan.

I have it on very good authority, that ignorance, or rather indifference to it led to a very amusing, though slightly embarrassing situation.

The Spanish ambassador was travelling to London on official business, and it was intimated in advance that he would be on the inward bound Golden Arrow on a certain day. From other sources it was known that he was something of a locomotive enthusiast, and High Authority requested that everything should be done to give him a good run. It was even hinted that as he would probably take a look at the locomotive on arrival at Victoria, it would be a good thing to have the engine nicely 'spruced up'. Well the day came, the ambassador duly landed at Dover and was conveyed in good style up to London; and as was expected, before leaving Victoria he asked to see the engine. And it was named, believe it or not, *Sir Francis Drake*! Until that moment no one on the Southern seems to have realised the colossal 'brick' that had been dropped. Knowing something of the inner workings of the locomotive department I can quite imagine someone at Stewards Lane saying: '851's our best engine; see she's put on to that Spanish ambassador job', without any thought as to the unfortunate engine's name.

I do not suppose many of the affluent patrons of the Golden Arrow spared much of a glance for the passing scene on the way down to Dover until the train was drawing near to journey's end. Then there could well be many an anxious glance seaward. There were no such things as stabilisers on the Channel packets of those days, and even on so luxurious a ship as the *Canterbury* the 75-minute crossing from Dover to Calais could have a devastating effect upon weak stomachs! Fortunately I have always been a good sailor, and the first sight of the sea, just after the train passed through Folkestone Central station, was exhilarating. The line was then running at high level, and it crossed the deep valley of the river Foord on a splendid nineteen arch viaduct, having a maximum height of 100 feet above the valley below. From this altitude one looks down to the oldest and most congested part of Folkestone, clustered behind a largely man-made harbour. As a supplementary facility to Dover, Folkestone has always played an important part, though the railway approach to the harbour pier could scarcely be more inconvenient, with reversal of direction for the boat trains at Folkestone Junction, and then a precipitous descent from the high ground to harbour level.

It is after passing Folkestone Junction however that trains bound for Dover enter upon a section resulting from one of the most venturesome examples of railway engineering construction to be found anywhere in Great Britain. Sir William Cubitt was the engineer and like other railways that he built the South Eastern was laid out for high speed. There was no circumventing of physical obstructions; if there was anything in the path of the

The Golden Arrow emerging from the highly distinctive Shakespeare's Cliff Tunnel at Dover, hauled by Lord Nelson class 4-6-0 locomotive No. 859 Lord Hood.

Engine No. 856 Lord St Vincent on the turntable at Folkestone Junction, preparatory to working an inward bound boat train.

The inward bound Golden Arrow, with container trucks next to the locomotive, near Dunton Green, hauled by engine No. 856 Lord St Vincent.

direct line he wanted it must be tunnelled through, or swept aside. And in the six miles between Folkestone Junction and the original town station at Dover he did both things, most spectacularly. Down the years poets have waxed lyrical about the 'White Cliffs of Dover' but Cubitt set himself the task of carrying a first class main line railway amid their tumbled array; and while careful preliminary surveys showed that the chalk was sound enough in the great headlands of Abbots Cliff, and Shakespeare's Cliff there were other stretches where it seemed unstable, notably in the Folkestone Warren, and at a lesser headland known as the Round Down Cliff, between the Abbots and the Shakespeare cliffs. Nevertheless, in the Warren the range of high cliffs lay well back from the proposed line of the railway, and by grading the cutting slopes appropriately an excellent alignment was obtained; and though there have been blockages due to landslips, in the 140 years since it was first opened for traffic on the whole it has functioned well, and is now electrified.

The passengers saw little of this majestic scenery from the curtained windows of the Golden Arrow Pullmans with the imminence of journey's end, and apprehension as to the possible effects of the sea crossing more likely to be uppermost in mind. One needed to travel on the footplate of the locomotive, as I have many times been privileged to do, to appreciate the grandeur of the cliffs as the train approaches the Abbotscliff Tunnel, and even more so when it emerges on to a high ledge just above the sea, and to recall it was here that Cubitt blasted the unstable Round Down Cliff out of the way, in one gigantic explosive operation. This seemingly hazardous part of the line has given no trouble from the day it was built; and while reflecting upon this the twin bores of Shakespeare's Cliff Tunnel are looming ahead. Beneath this great headland immortalised for all time in the matchless blank-verse of the Bard himself, Cubitt adopted a tall Gothic-pointed arch formation for each of the single-line bores, that themselves made the outward appearance of the tunnel unique. Unlike some distinctive and ornamental facades elsewhere however the shape was continued unchanged from end to end, probably as a precaution as to any disturbance in the chalk. Actually, like Abbotscliff, the tunnel has stood four-square ever since its construction.

So, the Golden Arrow comes gently down into Dover passing on the left the famous Lord Warden Hotel, as much a symbol of an English homecoming as the White Cliffs themselves, and into the fine Marine station. What stories could be told by earlier travellers, before the South Eastern and Chatham Railway built that station when the transfer between train and boat was made on the open Admiralty Pier! In times of storm waves would crash clean over the high parapet wall and descend in a cascade upon trains and passengers; in extreme weather coaches have been overturned. But the Marine Station was once described by a widely travelled *littèrateur* as 'a haven of tranquillity'; and so it would certainly be for most passengers travelling by the Golden Arrow in its earlier days. But life had not moved far into the nineteen thirties before the world-wide recession began to cast a blight upon luxury travel. Fewer and fewer passengers were travelling, and eventually the number of Pullman cars had to be drastically reduced and the train re-combined with the ordinary mid-morning service to Paris, from which the all-Pullman section had originally been an offshoot. I have seen the train with no more than three Pullman cars and five ordinary coaches together with the usual van and luggage truck at the rear end. It was a sign more perhaps of the changing trends of cross-Channel travel than of the lingering effects of the depression.

Business travellers, begrudging the working hours wasted in lengthy day-time journeys between London and Paris, and between London and Brussels

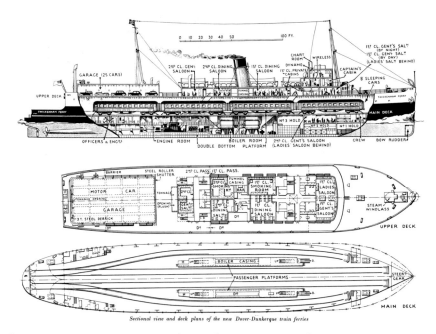

Sectional view and deck plans of the new Dover-Dunkerque train ferries

had given some patronage to the night routes, Newhaven to Dieppe, and Southampton to Le Havre, even though these involved longer sea passages, and in the former case particularly changes from train to boat at highly uncongenial hours. Consequently the introduction in October 1936 of a through express train service between London and Paris, conveying first and second class sleeping cars, across the Channel by train ferry and involving no change en route was widely welcomed. The ferry berths were constructed at Dover and Dunkirk, although this involved a considerably longer sea passage than to Calais. I have used the term 'ferry berth', and this was how it was referred in the public timetables of the Southern Railway; but actually it gives no real idea of the work that was involved at Dover. While across the Channel, at Dunkirk, the ferry berth was located inside the dock area, and was thus unaffected by the tides, at Dover there is no less than 25 ft difference between high and low tides, and to have used a sloping bridge to connect the ferry boat with the shore would have involved a quite impracticable length of bridge. So it was decided to build a totally enclosed dock, adjacent to the Marine Station, in which the water level could be raised or lowered at will, and the ferry deck brought level with the tracks on the quayside at any state of the tide.

Although it might be imagined that the building of such a dock in the innermost part of Dover Harbour, itself seemingly sheltered from the worst of the Channel storms by the long arm of the Admiralty pier on the western side, and the breakwaters shielding all but the relatively narrow entrances

150

on the seaward side, the constructional work on the new dock was seriously affected; and in the very first winter all the first stages were washed completely away. But I must not dwell upon the engineering problems, which began in 1932, and which continued for more than three years. The work went on, day and night below water, until the beginning of 1936, and apparently with little or no progress. Then at last the vital underwater work was completed; the superstructure on the dockside was rapidly built, and in October of that year the new service was inaugurated. At that time the through sleeping cars were run only between London and Paris; but when the service was re-introduced after the second world war additional cars were run between London and Brussels.

The service had not long been in operation when I made my first journey, on a winter's night when there was ample opportunity to appreciate the comforts of all the accommodation provided. Although the through first and second class sleeping cars formed the main feature of the new service the boat trains on both sides of the Channel included ordinary accommodation for those who did not wish to go to the expense of a sleeping berth, and to take what rest they could in the very pleasant lounges of the ferry boat. On the English side, for the benefit of passengers used to Continental rather than British hours of dining a restaurant car serving an attractive variety of menus was attached to the train between Victoria and Dover. Furthermore, the new service had not been long in operation before a Pullman car was added, for those who desired a little extra luxury on the run down from Victoria to Dover. The sleeping cars were of the traditional French *Wagon-Lit* design, though modified in overall dimensions to conform to the more restricted loading gauge of the British railways. They were nevertheless massive things of all-steel construction, and whereas the usual form of first class sleeping car run on the night trains in Great Britain weighed no more than 42 or 43 tons tare these *Wagon-Lits* turned the scale at no less than 55 tons.

Normally there were four sleeping cars working through from London to Paris, but sometimes there were five, and occasionally six. This, with the various through luggage vans, and the English restaurant car, Pullman, and ordinary coaches made up some exceedingly heavy trains, well beyond the unaided capacity of the Southern Railway 4-6-0s. As with the daytime boat trains the maximum tare load for an unassisted engine was 425 tons. When double-headed two 4-4-0s were used, variously of the 'L', 'L1', 'E1' or 'D1' classes. A number of these were stationed at Dover at the time, and a pair of them was the most frequently seen combination on the inward bound train, which left Dover Marine station at 7.20 am. For convenience in marshalling at Dover the through luggage vans were always at the rear end of

*The inward-bound Night Ferry train, double-headed with ex-Southern Railway
4-4-0s Nos 1758 (Class L1) and 1757.*

the outward bound train, and the sleeping cars immediately ahead of them.
From that position they could be quickly detached on arrival in Dover
Marine, and shunted round to the train ferry dock.

Early in 1937 I went through to Paris by the new service, and I shall not
forget the sight that greeted me when I went on the Continental platform
of Victoria station late one evening in March. There the Paris express was
drawn up, four huge cars in the Royal blue livery of the International
Sleeping Car Company. Blinds drawn aside revealed the brilliant saxe-blue
of the berth interiors, and the chocolate-uniformed attendants, receiving
patrons, gesticulating, and bringing a vivid foreign atmosphere to this otherwise very English railway station. Ten pm as we knew it then, now 22 00
hours, brought farewells in many languages. Along the corridor of the
sleeper I was in were a German businessman waving to some British associ-
ates, an English playwright being seen off by his actress wife, and another,
whose speech was strange to me. In the meantime the dynamic little French
steward, who spoke many languages fluently, was here, there and every-
where, settling all questions, going from berth to berth making sure every-
one was comfortable. I went to the restaurant car for a late drink. This was
indeed a train for men of affairs. Scraps of conversation that one overheard
brought mining in France, sport in Hungary, and the commerce of the Baltic
within the confines of a single railway carriage. Before we started I had

The inward-bound Night Ferry train, near Bromley, hauled by Lord Nelson class 4-6-0 No. 858 Lord Duncan.

gone up to the front end and seen that our engine was the *Howard of Effingham*, a very satisfying English contribution to the general cosmopolitanism of this great train.

We were sweeping down the gradient towards Folkestone at 77 mph when a fellow traveller announced he was going to bed. I went back to my berth and switched off the lights so as to get a better view of the Channel as we crossed the great Foord Viaduct, and entered the Folkestone Warren. There, over the sea, the French lighthouses were making brilliant play. Threading our way through the long tunnels, Abbotscliff, Shakespeare's Cliff, with that ledge, just above the sea where Sir William Cubitt blasted the Round Down Cliff out of the way, in between, and so finally round the curve into Dover Marine station. But we had scarcely stopped when a local tank engine was attached in rear, and soon the through luggage trucks and the sleeping cars were being drawn out round the eastern spar of the triangle, in front of the Lord Warden Hotel, to Hawkesbury Street Junction. In the dock, amid a blaze of quayside lights, lay the *Twickenham Ferry*. Behind her the lights of Dover twinkled up the steep hillside to the Castle, and farther away the South Foreland lighthouse was sweeping the sky with a huge fan-shaped beam of light. The little engine backed us towards the ship; green lights shone ahead, and then the heavy sleeping cars passed smoothly and quietly over the connecting bridge on to the vessel.

Although the train deck of the ship was approximately level with the quayside during loading operations there was bound to be a certain amount of tilting, both sideways and longitudinally, as the train was pushed on board. The connecting bridge, which was 70 ft long, was articulated so as to accommodate this movement; but no little skill and good judgement was needed on the part of the officer in charge in order to carry out that manœuvre with the very minimum of tilting. As we came on to the bridge I waited keenly to see how much tilting could be felt as the coaches passed on board. After all, the time was approaching midnight, and one could appreciate that by then many of the sleeping car passengers would already be in bed. I personally, was standing in the corridor watching the whole operation, and was, perhaps, not in the best position to sense any unwelcome movement; but certainly I felt not the slightest tilting action. Once on to the ship I got out of the sleeping car to watch the rest of the proceedings. During the voyage the cars were secured to the deck of the ferry. Powerful jacks were used to take all the weight off the springs, and chains attached to the main frames of the coaches anchored them to the deck. Every care was taken to ensure that passengers' rest was not disturbed; the men securing the chains moved about almost noiselessly, and the chains themselves were bound with rope to deaden the noise, should one of them have been accidently dropped.

With the loading of the sleeping cars the novel part of the railway journey on the English side was completed. But the *Twickenham Ferry* was conveying much more than passengers that night. The accompanying cross-sectional plan drawings of the ship show that there were four railway tracks on the main deck, with the two central ones reserved for the sleeping cars, and having access via the platforms and staircases to the dining saloons, and lounges on the upper deck. Outwards of these tracks, on both sides of the ship, and outward of the twin funnel casings, were two more tracks, occupied on this particular night with many covered vans containing through goods traffic to the Continent. I stayed on deck for a little time after we sailed to enjoy the ever-fascinating spectacle of Dover Harbour and it was about 1 am before I decided to turn in. I went down to bed – in the train. The feeling was a little queer at first; one could just feel the movement of the waves, but all the usual noises of a ship were entirely absent. I was soon fast asleep. I had intended to rouse fully again at Dunkirk and watch the loading operation in reverse; but I very nearly slept through it. I was awakened by some slight noise and then realised it was complete and the French train was starting away for Paris. I turned over and went to sleep again, and it was not until we were nearing Arras that I wakened in earnest. It was an impressive trip.

13

THE ABERDONIAN

This resounding name has been variously applied over the years to both locomotives and trains working over the most northerly part of the East Coast main line. At present it belongs to the diesel-powered high speed train leaving King's Cross at 10.00 hours, and covering the 523 miles to Aberdeen in 419 minutes; but in the period with which this book is principally connected 'The Aberdonian' was the very heavy sleeping car express leaving Kings Cross at 7.30 pm and, its counterpart leaving Aberdeen at 7.35 pm. Apart from the through accommodation both these trains were rendered still heavier on the earlier stages of their journey by conveying dining cars, from Kings Cross to York going north, and from Aberdeen to Edinburgh. In the railway world however the name 'Aberdonian' goes back to 1906. In that year competition between the Caledonian and North British Railways for traffic between Edinburgh and Glasgow, on the one hand, and Aberdeen reached a new intensity with the North British putting on new 'block' trains to make the 130½ mile journey between Edinburgh and Aberdeen in the level three hours. Authorisation was given for the purchase, from the North British Locomotive Company of fourteen new locomotives of a greatly enlarged design, 'Atlantic' type, to maintain the accelerated schedules.

In this latter investment there was a good deal more in it than the competitive Aberdeen service. The North British were anxious to improve their Anglo-Scottish service in partnership with the Midland Railway, and this involved hard working over the heavily graded Waverley Route to Carlisle, referred to at some length in the earlier chapter of this book, dealing with the Thames-Forth Express. But apart from their technical features, some of which were not to the liking of the North British Railway's civil engineer of that period, they broke new ground in being named in an attractive and imaginative way. In the nineteenth century, when the great Dugald Drummond was Locomotive Superintendent, he had introduced the practice of his former chief, William Stroudley of the London Brighton and South Coast Railway, of naming all the passenger locomotives, express passenger and local tanks alike, after stations on the line; and in so prominent a manner that the public were sometimes confused into imagining that the name of the engine signified the destination of the train, and got taken to somewhere they did not want to go. Drummond's successor, Matthew Holmes, abolished the names; but when the new 'Atlantics' were introduced in 1906, naming was resumed, and in a much happier way.

The first six of them were allocated to Ferryhill shed, Aberdeen, for the accelerated trains to Edinburgh and Glasgow, and they were named appropriately *Aberdonian, Dundonian, Bon Accord, Thane of Fife, Auld Reekie* and *Saint Mungo*, thus covering the three cities at the extremities, and the route traversed. The remaining eight, covering the balancing turns from Edinburgh, and the Midland expresses over the Waverley route to Carlisle were *Dunedin, Midlothian, Waverley, Liddesdale, Hazeldean, Abbotsford, Tweeddale* and *Borderer*. This class of locomotive was perhaps exceptional on the railways of Great Britain for the way in which their workings were kept in accordance with their fine names. When I first went to Aberdeen, in

The Night Scotsman during its early morning call at Stonehaven, hauled by the Atlantic engine Auld Reekie *and a 4-4-0 the* Jeanie Deans.

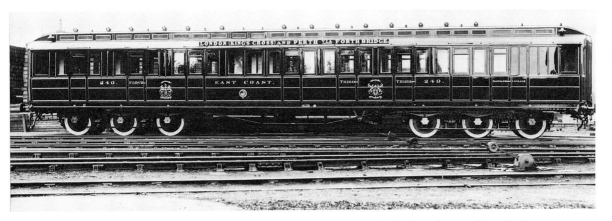

An example of the beautiful clerestory-roofed 12-wheeled coaches used on the East Coast expresses to Highland stations.

1928, five of the original six were still regularly working over that route, more than twenty years after their first introduction. By that time, however, there had been a change in the diagrams. Following the introduction of the eight-hour day for locomotive enginemen it was found convenient for all through expresses to change engines at Dundee, rather than work through between Edinburgh and Aberdeen; and the 'Atlantics' thence forward stationed at Dundee Tay Bridge shed, each worked two return trips to Aberdeen, with different crews on each trip. Similarly, the Edinburgh engines worked to Dundee and back.

When the new 'block' trains were first introduced, in 1906, the Glasgow section consisted of no more than three coaches; but in those highly competitive days, purely for prestige purposes those light loads had to be hauled by 'Atlantics', and it was doubtless for this reason that one of the class originally allocated to Aberdeen shed was named *Saint Mungo*. But the original through engine workings were not revived after the first world war. The Glasgow and Edinburgh portions of the day Aberdeen trains were combined at Kirkcaldy, and the engine *Saint Mungo* was transferred to Haymarket shed, Edinburgh. I travelled behind it on the midday London express down to Carlisle in 1927. But in this chapter I am concerned with the Aberdonian train itself, the Kings Cross 'sleeper', which was officially named in 1927, and thenceforth carried its title on the carriage roof boards. I have some stirring memories of this train. Although making no speed records its great weight made this one of the most severe locomotive duties in Scotland, because of the awkward physical characteristics of the route.

None of the gradients encountered in the 130 miles between Edinburgh and Aberdeen are very long in themselves, but the route includes many sharp curves and awkward junctions where speed had to be drastically reduced, and it so happened that some of the worst gradients came immediately after sections of severely restricted speed. Few, if any of these inclines are what the Americans call 'momentum grades' – that is, one could use the impetus of express speed to help in climbing them. North of Dundee in particular where station stops were made at Arbroath, Montrose and Stonehaven, the restart from rest had to be made against a severe gradient. Even so, the 'Atlantic' engines were required to haul remarkably big loads before an assistant engine could be claimed. The prevailing situation became still more onerous in the winter of 1928 when sleeping cars for third class passengers were introduced on to the 'Aberdonian' and several other important Anglo-Scottish night trains. In consideration of the physical difficulties of the route the loading limits for the 'Atlantic' engines were high, being no less than 380 tons going north, though 340 tons on the southbound run, which was the more difficult of the two.

Great store was always set upon accurate timekeeping, and for any excess over the stipulated maximum loads an assistant engine was provided. On other lines where double heading was frequent it was usual for the assistant engine to be coupled ahead of the regular one, and on railways like the Midland and the London and North Western it was usual to see small vintage engines leading larger and relatively modern ones; but on the North British, on double-headed trains the regularly allocated 'train engine', and on it, of course, the senior driver, was always in the lead. After the grouping of 1923, and the building of successive batches of the new 'Pacifics' of Gresley design a few of these engines were made available for the Aberdeen route, with the civil engineering proviso that they must not on any account be double-headed. When their load limits were laid down as 480 tons northbound, and 420 tons southbound one might have imagined that such a contingency was hardly likely to arise; but I have later to tell of an amusing contretemps that I witnessed in the early hours of an August morning in Edinburgh Waverley station.

It was always in a spirit of expectancy that one boarded the Aberdonian in Kings Cross station. Having been greeted by the friendly sleeping car attendant, and stowed the luggage the next thing was dinner, served as soon as the train left London. I travelled by the Aberdonian at various seasons, but a trip I shall always vividly remember was one on a bitterly cold February night in 1935. In connection with some technical writing on which I was then engaged the Locomotive Running Superintendent of the Scottish Area of the London and North Eastern Railway had given me an 'open' footplate pass to ride as often as I liked between Edinburgh and Aberdeen. Fifty years ago, being a good deal more energetic than my old bones now permit, and determined to make the most of my opportunity I surprised the sleeping car steward by asking him to call me half an hour before we reached Edinburgh, so that I should be dressed and ready to ride the engine that was taking us forward to Dundee. He brought tea and biscuits as we were passing Dunbar, and the cheerful news that it was snowing! Wind howled in the ventilators; snow and sleet spluttered against the window panes, but I shrugged my shoulders and wrapped up well, beneath my overalls ready for a cold ride.

During the winter months the Aberdonian used to bring a very heavy load down from London. In addition to the main part of the train, and a section that went forward from Aberdeen to Lossiemouth there were through carriages and sleeping cars for Inverness and Fort William, and these were detached in Edinburgh. Although there was an eerie solitude about most of that great station at four in the morning all was animation at the front end, where three fresh engines were waiting. Even after the portions to be taken forward by these latter had been detached the main train still topped the 400-ton mark, because several heavily-freighted parcel vans were being attached in rear. The load would have been too heavy for an 'Atlantic' to take forward unassisted but Waverley had one of the latest 'Super-Pacifics' for us, an engine almost as well known to the 'train spotters' of Kings Cross as in Scotland – *Call Boy*. During the summer months, when the Flying Scotsman was running non-stop between London and Edinburgh, it was a favourite engine on the job, and later that same year it was coming to Kings Cross regularly, three times a week.

It was still stormy and bitterly cold when I climbed aboard, and as we rode out into the open country still very dark. Few would be stirring at that hour. There was no airport at Turnhouse then, but as we passed its site there were signs of a break in the weather, and just ahead of us was the Forth Bridge. The passage that morning was an unforgettable experience. Through rifts in the stormy sky the moon shone out and revealed great banks of snow-laden clouds over the sea. The mighty girders were silhouetted weirdly against the night sky, and as we passed beneath each cross-member was lit up by the glare from the open firedoor. Down the steep descent from the bridge speed rose quickly to nearly 60 mph but then the brakes were put hard on, to reduce to 25 mph through the junctions at Inverkeithing, a characteristic prelude, on this route, to the next stiff ascent, to Dalgetty, where the most we could do was 27 mph. Then down through Aberdour to the shores of the Firth of Forth, immediately abreast of Edinburgh, with the port of Leith ablaze with lights, even at this hour. So, northwards through Fife, running hard where we could, slowing for more curves and junctions: 25 mph at Burntisland, 25 through Kinghorn Tunnel,

15 over Thornton Junction, 35 at Ladybank. This was never meant to be a main line, just a lot of bits and pieces joined up, and the engineering was not very expert in places, especially in the boring of Kinghorn Tunnel. It is not very long, but like some of the great Alpine constructions it was bored from each end; but the surveys were not accurate, and instead of meeting neatly in the middle the two bores missed by almost the complete width of the tunnel! To join up they had to put an S-curve in the middle with a 25 mph speed restriction for all time!

One can get going in more express train style after Ladybank; but after St Fort we came to the wide estuary of the Firth of Tay, and as we swung leftwards over Tay Bridge South Junction, there, two miles across the water was Dundee. It was then just after half past five, and while the waterfront was a far-stretching chain of twinkling lights, across the sea there was a faint gleam of dawn. Any northbound crossing of the Tay Bridge can arouse a variety of emotions, especially on a run like this, on which the driver, faithfully observing all the speed restrictions, is pounding the engine hard intermediately, as indeed he had to, for an average speed of 44 mph from Edinburgh to Dundee. And he had a final thrill for me, even as we entered upon the Tay Bridge. The regulator was opened again, wide, and across those dark heaving waters speed rose rapidly. The great bridge is straight

Southbound express from Aberdeen entering upon the Forth Bridge, with the Atlantic engine Dunedin *leading an old unnamed 4-4-0 on a heavy train.*

for most of its length, but at its northern end it curves round sharply to the right, through the one-time Esplanade station, and past the engine sheds. From my stance on the right hand side of the cab I looked ahead, peering through the darkness for a sight of that curve, which we were now approaching at nearly 60 mph. The very name 'Tay Bridge' has an ominous sound, and in my inexperience of the route I just wondered if we might be going too fast, jump the rails at the curve and head over the side! But our fine engine took the curve without a tremor, and brought us smoothly into Dundee, after a notable run.

In August of that same year I was travelling north again to ride on the first two of Sir Nigel Gresley's giant 'Mikado' type engines, designed specially for the difficult conditions of the Aberdeen route. Traffic conditions were very heavy and the Aberdonian was running in two portions throughout; and I was told beforehand that the second of the new engines, the *Earl Marischal*, would be working the first portion of the train northwards from Dundee. As previously my authority to ride on the footplate began at Edinburgh, and when we arrived I was ready, in overalls, and went up to the front end. We had a load of 483 tons, and a North British 'Atlantic' and a 'Scott' class 4-4-0 were waiting to take us to Dundee. Waverley had a 'Pacific' waiting on the far side of the station to take the second portion

The giant Gresley 2-8-2 engine, the Earl Marischal *at Aberdeen, having hauled The Aberdonian express from Dundee.*

of the train. Then it was discovered that this second portion had collected so many 'extras' on its run north that it was considerably heavier than our train, and thus greater than the 'Pacific' limit of load, 480 tons. Ours was just fractionally greater, but of no consequence in such pressure of traffic, so 'control' acting with the utmost promptitude, switched the two sets of engines over. The 'Pacific' was brought from the south side of the station, and coupled on to the first portion, while the 'Atlantic' and its assistant were crossed over to wait for the second portion. Incidentally the 'Pacific' we had that morning had one of those names that always seemed to me rather puerile – *Salmon Trout!*

It is on the track of the Aberdonian, north of Dundee, that I have my happiest memories: photographing at the lineside, stop-watching in the trains or from the engines, or just enjoying the passing scene. For it is indeed one of the most interesting and appealing of British coastal routes, no matter what the season, or what the time of day. I shall always remember that February occasion when the approach to Dundee from the Tay Bridge had been so dramatic for me. At that time there were no 'Pacific' engines stationed at Dundee, and with such a load as we had brought north we should have to be double-headed on the final stage of the journey to Aberdeen; and there, on the track next to the west wall of the station, were waiting an 'Atlantic', the *Duke of Rothesay*, and a 'Scott' class 4-4-0 the *Lady of Avenel*. I climbed aboard the former, and I still say now, after fifty years of such experiences, that I have never been made more welcome on the footplate. John Ogilvie was then the senior driver at Dundee, and he and his fireman, John Macdonald, had a quiet, but nevertheless infectious pride in their engine, their job, and their evident pleasure in having a visitor. Of course their task that morning was lessened by their having an assistant engine behind. Only one coach less in the train and they would have been on their own, but in the gradually strengthening light of a cold winter's dawn it was a fascinating ride up the coast.

First of all beside the broadening Firth of Tay it was level pegging at a steady 60 mph past Monifieth and the cherished golf links of Carnoustie; but then, after leaving Arbroath we were faced with the gradients as severe as those south of Dundee. We pounded up to Letham Grange at 30 mph, dashed downhill at nearly 70 mph to cross the Water of Inverkeilor, and then up on to the cliffs overlooking the sands of Lunan Bay. Forlorn though that seashore looked at that hour in the morning, with the waves crashing in, it had nevertheless the appeal of all remote, lonely places, while the steep gradient, for all our two engines, brought the speed down to less than 40 mph before we had topped the bank. Then steeply down into the beautiful coastal town of Montrose. The wide view to the west, across the

Montrose Basin, that opens out as the Aberdonian makes its cautious way down the gradient was at one time a viewpoint of deep significance for North British enginemen, and for that I must take the story briefly back to the exciting summer of 1895, when the rival night expresses from London that left Euston and Kings Cross at 8 pm were racing for Aberdeen; and at a point 2½ miles north of Montrose, the vital Kinnaber Junction, their routes converged. It was across the Montrose Basin that North British men might get their first sight of their rival, coming from Perth and Forfar.

There is irony in those old memories today. In the Beeching rationalisation schemes of the 1960s it was considered un-economic to have two routes to Aberdeen parallelling each other so closely; and as the former Caledonian Railway had a good line from Perth to Dundee it was decided to close the former direct line through Strathmore, by Coupar Angus, Glamis and Forfar, and put all traffic for Aberdeen from Perth, Stirling, Glasgow and the West Coast through Dundee, and thence up the North British line. It added less than three miles to the total distance from Perth and places south, but unfortunately it left the country towns of Strathmore, which had been on the Euston to Aberdeen main line without any railway communication. And the point of convergence on the hill above Montrose was no longer a junction. After the great Railway Race of 1895, a celebrated railway *littérateur* of the day, the Rev. W. J. Scott, wrote a forty-six-page pamphlet entitled *Kinnaber*, which he prefaced with a parody on the well-known Highland lament *Lochaber No More*. He called it *Kinnaber No More*, and it was indeed a lament for the end of the racing between the Euston and Kings Cross routes to Aberdeen. But could he have foreseen a time when Kinnaber would no longer be a junction at all!

When I made my first footplate journeys to Aberdeen one could still travel there from Euston in the comfort of a sleeping car. The Royal Highlander, which then left London at the same time as did the Aberdonian was primarily a train for Inverness, as the next chapter of this book will describe in detail; but it had a section for Aberdeen. There was no racing in the 1930s, and the train conveying the through sleeping cars from Euston was booked to pass Kinnaber ten minutes after the Aberdonian. The junction layout was then very awkward for the train from Kings Cross, and required a speed reduction to no more than 15 mph; but after that we were soon going ahead in fine style. The gradient is slightly favourable for a time, and the speed rose towards 60 mph, and as we neared the viaduct over the North Esk John Ogilvie beckoned to me to come over to the left hand side of the cab, and he pointed to the line of the Grampian Mountains away to the west. After a night of snow they hung wraith-like across the sky, ethereal almost, in the half-light before full day. He pointed to Lochnagar, the highest at present to be seen, and spoke of the Royal deer forests there-abouts. Then, with mingled modesty and pride in the highest achievement of his calling, he added: 'I've driven the King seven times'.

We were now in the Mearns country, passing Laurencekirk, and in fine upland farmland, doing 65 mph; but we had to climb again to reach the watershed before the wild glen of the Carron Water, and descend steeply towards the coast again at Stonehaven. Half way down this incline there was a signal box named Dunnottar. It took its name from a castle once described as 'romantically invincible over the sea along that redoubtable coast line, but not too ruined to be pleasing'. The signal box was some three miles away from the castle, but I recall there was a hamlet of the same name rather nearer at hand. The speed usually rises to nearly 70 mph coming down the bank, and the Aberdonian stops at Stonehaven only by request, to set down passengers from Newcastle, or stations still further south. We went through at full speed on this particular morning, and were soon climbing again to the cliffs, where the railway completely divides the Stone-haven golf course. I have spent many happy hours photographing trains in this pleasant locality, though my presence on the line was once misconstrued by a young lady golfer who drove 'out of bounds'. When I retrieved her ball for her, it having landed right in the 'four-foot', I was embarrassed when she offered me a not inconsiderable tip!

The last miles to Aberdeen are delightful. The line is hardly ever out of sight of the sea, and on this February morning the skies were clearing to show patches of brilliant colour. When we came to the final descent, past Cove Bay, the great lighthouse of Girdleness was gleaming white in the first near-horizontal rays of the sun, and we swung through a full right-angle to come alongside the estuary of the Dee, and to enjoy the prospect of the City of Aberdeen, silver grey on the further bank. We coasted in to arrive three minutes early, just that much short of the level twelve hours from Kings Cross, and an overall average speed of 43½ mph over the 523 miles. Writing of the Aberdonian of those years it may indeed seem slow today. The fastest ever by the East Coast train in the Race of 1895 was 520 minutes, whereas the fastest sleeping car service of today, by the 2200 hours southbound from Aberdeen, takes 573 minutes, an average of 54·8 mph. This, of course, is substantially beaten by the daytime HSTs, the quickest of which takes no more than a minute under seven hours, 419 minutes, and a very spectacular average speed of 74·8 mph. For my own part however, much as I applaud the technology built into the modern trains, I like to recall the days when those tough old North British 'Atlantics' took over the haulage of the train in Edinburgh and one could listen to the fierce tattoo of their exhaust beats pounding up the steep inclines.

Of the southbound train I have two particularly lasting memories. The first was just after Easter in 1934 when, with returning holidaymakers, an enormous train was necessary. The passenger portion of the HSTs of today weigh no more than 270 tons, and on that night in April 1934 the Aberdonian totalled up to 523 tons, not counting the crowds of passengers and their luggage. As usual we had an 'Atlantic' leading – the one originally named *Dundonian* but later changed to *Bonnie Dundee*. The second engine was a 'Scott', the *Caleb Balderstone*. That enormous train was not far short of the maximum tonnage for two such engines. I was not on the footplate that night, but from one of the leading coaches the combined roar of their exhausts when climbing the gradients was terrific. Just over a year later I rode the second of Sir Nigel Gresley's great 'Mikado' 2-8-2 engines, the *Earl Marischal*, with a load nearly as great. It was for these trains that the engines were specifically designed, and when I came to compare the notes of the two runs I was astonished to see how closely they corresponded in timing. At most of the passing stations the differences did not amount to more than a few seconds, and they exemplified the precision in running that was a characteristic feature of the North British section of the LNER. The gross trailing loads hauled were 565 tons by *Bonnie Dundee* and *Caleb Balderstone*, and 530 tons by the *Earl Marischal*.

When travelling by the southbound Aberdonian the changing of engines at Dundee always brought new heights of expectation; it would then be nearly half past nine, and glinting in the platform lights, out beyond the covered-in part of the station, the fresh engines would be waiting. On that Easter journey of 1934 we had a similar pair to those that had brought us down from Aberdeen: an 'Atlantic' *The Lord Provost*, leading, and a 'Scott', the *Lord Glenvarloch* next to the train. On the second journey, the first and most highly publicised of the new 'Mikados', the *Cock o' the North*, was waiting; and briefly, before the *Earl Marischal* coupled off and drew ahead we had the impressive spectacle, in the station lights, of these two huge engines alongside. It is worth recalling that the tractive power of each of them was slightly greater than that of a North British 'Atlantic' and a 'Scott' combined. Furthermore, the improved technology built into them enabled them to do the job on little more coal than the two older engines would have used between them.

Yet for all my professional lifetime's involvement in engineering, and the design and production of machinery to have greater efficiency, when it comes down to memories of the Aberdonian and its locomotives I become a sentimentalist again, and it is the older engines and of the 'all-out' manner in which they were driven that I like best to recall. At Dundee, from the very moment the guard of the Aberdonian gave the 'right away', one was treated to an evocation of steam power enough to stir the blood of even the most prosaic of travellers. Tay Bridge station, the principal one in Dundee, is at very low level, so much beneath the Esplanade indeed as to make it seem below river level, a situation accentuated by passengers having to descend to its platforms by staircases. From that low level heavy trains have to be lifted, immediately on starting, to cross the Esplanade and enter upon the Tay Bridge, climbing steeply all the way until reaching the high girders in mid-firth, where the head-room beneath has to be great enough to allow shipping to pass under. So, to the thunderous music of two roaring exhaust beats the enginemen of *The Lord Provost* and of the *Lord Glenvarloch* lifted that huge load up on to the Tay Bridge; and the speed had reached 30 mph even before the level gradient at the southern end of the bridge had been attained.

The 'Scott' class engines have rather smaller driving wheels than the 'Atlantics', so the exhausts do not regularly synchronise. At one time they are exactly in unison; then they step out into syncopation before pulling back again. The noise is thrilling, but it is reserved for passengers in the leading coaches, or for watchers at the lineside. On the footplate at such times the racket is such that one cannot hear the noise of the second engine, even though it is just behind. Once the gradient is climbed those reverberating exhausts quieten into almost complete silence as speed mounts towards 60 mph; but their fierce tattoo is only to be renewed again from Ladybank Junction up to Lochmuir, from Burntisland up to Dalgetty, and most of all on the terrific pull from Inverkeithing up on to the Forth Bridge. Even these two stalwart locomotives could not manage more than 23 mph on that last incline. But it was enough. At Dalmeny junction just south of the bridge they were nearly two minutes early, before a brisk spin at 64 to 65 mph over the nearly level last miles brought us into Edinburgh. I was not travelling further south that night, and at Waverley station I went forward to watch *The Lord Provost* and *Lord Glenvarloch* coupled off, and take with them the carriages put on for local people, and the dining cars. From the darkness outside the station a 'Pacific' came backing silently down, and I knew that on easier gradients and not too exacting a schedule the sleeping passengers on the 'Aberdonian' would have a placid and quiet run to the south.

14

THE ROYAL HIGHLANDER

In 1927 when the LMS named some of its principal express passenger trains it was only natural that recognition was taken of the historic position of the West Coast main line as the Royal Mail route to Scotland to use the prefix 'royal' in some of the new titles. In the case of the Highland express leaving Euston each evening at 7.30 pm it was particularly appropriate, because its Aberdeen section followed the route taken by the Royal Train each summer when King George V paid his annual visit to Balmoral. So the 7.30 pm from Euston became 'The Royal Highlander'. For nine months in the year however for stations on the Highland line itself, with which this chapter is particularly concerned, it was not a very fast train, and the 'Direct Line' section from Aviemore did not reach Inverness until 9.50 am – 14 hours and 20 minutes for a journey of 568 miles, an average of only 39·6 mph. During the three months of the summer service it was about an hour faster, yet still averaging no more than 42 mph. It was then the only through express from London to Inverness. It was nevertheless a fascinating train, as lineal descendant of one of the rival trains that made such history in the exciting summer of 1895. When I was travelling, in the early 1930s, there was however not much likeness so far as weight was concerned; for against the three-coach 70-ton racer of August 1895 we pulled out of Crewe for the north with a train of 475 tons.

My authority to ride on the footplate on that journey did not begin until we left Perth, at 6.25 am; but although I was cosily ensconced in a 'sleeper' until then, with the enthusiasm of youth I sat up for most of the night logging the speeds. With a 'Royal Scot' class engine, the *Lancashire Fusilier*, we were double-headed over Shap, but with a slight reduction in the load we went on unassisted from Carlisle. At 4.40 am at Stirling we detached the through portion from Euston for Oban, and then went on to make a fast finish into Perth, with a top speed of 84 mph down the bank from Gleneagles. It was then, though fully in accord with the timetable, that the time began to slip by. Considerable remarshalling of the train began in these chill early hours. The Aberdeen portion, with a fresh engine attached, was

A glimpse of a past age at Inverness: one of Alexander Allan's 2-2-2s No. 32 Cluny, *built 1863, finally withdrawn from service in 1898.*

soon away, and in the meantime the North British train from Edinburgh had arrived bringing the sleeping cars that had come north from Kings Cross on the Aberdonian; but all our connections had not yet arrived, and at 6.02 am the famous West Coast Postal Special drew in. Leaving Euston at 8.30 pm it was exclusive to postal business as far north as Stirling; but by that time having shed portions for Edinburgh and Glasgow no more than three vans remained for Aberdeen, and at Stirling it attached a short passenger section from Glasgow. The postal part of the train had brought a big tally of mails for the Highlands, and transfer of these now began to the travelling post office van of the Inverness train.

By the time the remarshalling was complete, and the train was made up with its sleeping car portions from both Kings Cross and Euston, a breakfast car, carriages for local passengers and the post office vans we had an enormous train, weighing nearly 500 tons and necessarily, two engines. The train engine, with the regular driver and fireman, was a new LMS 'Black Five' 4-6-0, and the assistant, one of the Lancashire and Yorkshire type 2-6-0s, nicknamed the 'Crabs' from the ungainly appearance of their valve gear when in action. We left on time at 6.25 am, so that passengers from the south had a full hour in and around Perth station during the remarshalling and waiting time. It was still quite dark when we left, and would remain so for nearly an hour on this January morning; and since some of the most beautiful scenery on the Highland line is passed in that first hour I am switching the story to a journey I enjoyed on the same train in August 1932, when I was a passenger, and noting points from the breakfast car. In the height of the tourist season the sleeping car sections from London were heavy enough to make a train of their own, and they were taken on ahead, without waiting for coupling up to the mail portion. On that earlier occasion the dining car in which I had breakfast was the very last vehicle in the train. I do not think it had been coupled very tightly to the rest of the stock, and on the faster stretches and round the many curves we had a very rough ride! Enough of that however, for it was a glorious morning, and the scenery entrancing.

The Highland line proper begins at Stanley Junction, 7¼ miles north of Perth, and its first 8½ miles began independently as a curious little offshoot of the then-Scottish Central Railway, which later became part of the Caledonian. But the Perth and Dunkeld Railway, as it was known, did not take the seemingly obvious, if more circuitous route to Dunkeld, following river level grades beside the Tay, but took a hilly course involving some steep gradients, direct across country from Stanley. This was the more odd because it had to depend upon the Scottish Central for its motive power, and the latter company was not exactly blessed with any powerful locomotives. It is after passing the first station, Murthly, that the line climbs high in the pine forests to left of the river, and at Kingswood Crossing loop single-line tablets were exchanged for the second time in the run. The fluctuations in speed were always very rapid here in steam days. One went through the loop at Murthly at nearly 60 mph, the speed fell to little more than 30 by Kingswood, and in less than three minutes were dashing downhill – 'dashing' that is for the old Highland line – at a full sixty before taking the Dunkeld loop at full speed. The trees are so dense on this ragged hillside, and curves so continuous that it is rather like weaving one's way into an unknown country, and there are moments when it is impossible from the carriage windows to guess how the railway is going to find its way through the heights crowding into the picture ahead.

In the great project launched in 1861 to build the Inverness and Perth Junction Railway, as it was at first known, there were only two tunnels in the entire 104 miles, linking the existing line in the north at Forres, with the little Perth and Dunkeld Railway. Joseph Mitchell, the Engineer, was a native of Inverness. He was an expert geologist, as well as being an outstanding civil engineer. In designing bridges to suit the many different conditions experienced on the route he felt it was necessary to build massively, seeing that the whole line was exposed to every vicissitude of climate and flood. He did indeed; and from the time it was opened for traffic in 1863 it has stood four-square ever since, carrying vastly heavier locomotives and trains, and now, with the introduction of the diesel HSTs to Inverness in 1984, speeds of up to 90 mph on certain sections of the route.

There is a dramatic scene in the very first mile of Mitchell's road northward from Dunkeld the full impact of which was not brought home until a good thirty years after my first journeys into the Highlands, and then only when I rode north on this same early morning train, but in the driver's cab of one of the new diesels. The extent to which one could run 'in blinkers' as it were, on large modern steam locomotives was amazing, especially those with high, vertical sided Belpaire fireboxes. All the essentials for train running could be clearly seen, but the outlook was otherwise most restricted. From the cab of a diesel however one sees it all, and here, running at about 60 mph the great crags jutting out from the range of hills on the right bank of the Tay can be seen in all their majesty. One can also see the single-line railway heading for a tunnel-mouth flat on a vertical rock face, without anything of a preliminary cutting which is the usual prelude to entering a tunnel. The men who drove and fired the tough little 'F' class 4-4-0s of a hundred years ago would have seen that spectacular tunnel entrance clearly enough through the large round spectacle glasses above the small boilers of their engines; but on Christopher Cumming's 'Clan' class 4-6-0s, and the LMS 'Black Fives' that I rode, one saw less than half the full picture.

The tunnel is a short one, only 350 yards long, but with mention of the 'Clan' class locomotives, the last of the true Highland dynasty, some reference to its history and the beautiful engine names is appropriate while the train is speeding at 55 to 60 mph up the broad inner reaches of Strathtay. I first saw Highland engines in 1923. The grouping had taken effect in the previous January; but on the LMS in Scotland so far as engine colours were concerned it might never have occurred. The Caledonians were all still in their beautiful blue, and although I did not get very far north of Glasgow in that year I had a treat one afternoon when I was out on the line photographing near Glenboig. After grouping it was arranged that instead of changing from Highland to Caledonian engines at Perth one Highland engine on the morning express from Inverness should work right through to Glasgow. Its crew should lodge, and then take the morning train back next day, with a second Highland engine taking up the working on alternate days. The two most senior drivers at Inverness had the job to themselves for the whole of the summer of 1923: Bob Ross and 'Tam' Gordon, and their engines were the *Clan Chattan* and the *Clan Mackinnon*, so magnificently turned out that one might have imagined they were going to work a Royal Train. It was of no consequence that the Highland livery was then plain green, without any lining. The last four 'Clans' were in a lighter shade, a beautiful moss green, and when I saw the *Mackinnon*, in 1923, it was a positive apparition.

I went to Inverness first in 1927, when most of the Highland passenger engines had been repainted in Midland red. They were looking quite smart though one detected a certain falling off of that pride in the job that had once so deeply permeated all the goings and comings of Highland locomotives. I was too late to see any of the celebrated Class 'F' 4-4-0s at work. When they were first introduced by David Jones in 1874 they were the most powerful passenger engines in Great Britain, and at that time they might have been known as the 'County' class. Seven out of the first ten were named after the shires through which the line ran, the exceptions being *Bruce*, *The Duke* and *The Lord Provost*. I should add that the first of these three was not in honour of the great national hero of medieval times, but the Hon. C.T. Bruce, the Chairman of the Company, while *The Duke* was the Duke of Sutherland. All these engines, personalities as well as 'counties', changed their names several times, indeed *Perthshire* became successively *Stemster*, then *Huntingtower* and finally *Ault Wharrie*. Six more of this class of locomotive were built later, and some of these also had names that might baffle a visitor from south of the Border.

The most picturesque of these was *Clachnacuddin*. While an interested visitor might well ponder as to who, where, or what was the bearer of this resounding name no native of Inverness would have been in any doubt. As displayed on the locomotive it was a slightly anglicised version of the Gaelic *clach-na-cudainn*, of which a literal translation is, 'the stone of the tubs'. By tradition, long before the days of organised urban water supplies, it was the stone where the citizens carrying water up from the river for their domestic needs rested their water tubs. Another version, equally old, attributes the name to the resting place of the wash-tubs of the womenfolk returning from the river bank after carrying out the weekly wash in traditional Highland fashion, pummelling the clothes in the clear running water with their bare feet. Karl Baedeker, in one of his classic Guide Books for Travellers, not only lists the Clach-na-cudden (yet another spelling!) as a feature of interest for tourists, but adds that it is 'regarded as the palladium of Inverness'. The first edition of his guide book is dated 1887, only three years after the engine was built. This engine put in more than forty years of hard work before it was withdrawn in 1915.

The 'F' class 4-4-0 locomotive named Clachnacuddin.

The Royal Highlander in 1927, going hard above Daviot, and hauled by Loch Ruthven *(pilot to Slochd Summit only) and* Gordon Castle.

A span of forty-five momentous years separates the years of introduction of 'F' class, and the 'Clans', and when I first travelled to Inverness, many years before I had any footplate passes, the load was heavy enough for us to have two 'Clans' from the very start, *Munro* and *Mackinnon* in partnership for a 420-ton train. But while I have been gossipping about engine names 'The Royal Highlander' of my footplating days had speeded over the level miles of Strathtay, made a brief stop at Pitlochry, and its two engines were pounding up into the Pass of Killiecrankie. It was then nearly 7.30 am and daylight was just breaking – a magical cloudless dawn, amid the delicate leafless tracery of the wooded mountain slopes of the pass. Mitchell, an artist as well as an engineer and a geologist, was very sensitive to the environment; and here he was able to carry the single line unobtrusively through the trees until it came to the head of the pass, where it had to curve sharply round to the left, crossing the Allt Girnaigburn and diving through a short tunnel into the more open landscape of Strathgarry. To cross that burn Mitchell built a beautiful ten-arch viaduct. When the line was opened in 1863 it was considered that the viaduct was so graceful as to enhance the beauty of the scene; but in the intervening years the trees on the river banks below have grown to such an extent that the viaduct can scarcely be seen, except from the engine of an approaching train. So we came to Blair Atholl, in steam days one of the most important intermediate stations on the Highland line.

As a tourist centre Blair Atholl is in no way comparable to Pitlochry, but it owed its status to railway geography, lying at the foot of the longest and most severe incline on British main line railways. 'The Hill', as it was modestly known among the Highland railwaymen, begins just a mile beyond Blair Atholl, abreast of the ducal policies of Blair Castle, so happily described by the attractive train hostesses travelling on the present 'Highland Chieftain' high-speed diesel express from Kings Cross. But with a solid fourteen miles of ascent, on gradients varying between 1 in 70 and 1 in 85, leading eventually to the highest railway summit in Great Britain there is little time for even sidelong glances at the passing scene from the engines of trains like the Royal Highlander. Blair Atholl in steam days was essentially a bank engine station. Engines were based there with the sole function of assisting trains up 'The Hill'. Some of the slightly larger successors of the old 'F' class 4-4-0s, known as the 'Clyde Bogies' finished their working days at Blair, because the 4-6-0 engines of the 'Clan' and 'Black Five' types were expected to bring quite heavy loads thus far from Perth, without assistance. The 'Clyde Bogies', and the later 4-4-0s banked them in rear up to Dalnaspidal. The biggest loads I have seen taken unassisted from Perth were 345 tons by a 'Clan' and 415 tons by a 'Black Five'.

On my January trip with the Royal Highlander we got away from Blair Atholl in good style, and on a brief easing of the gradient before Struan station the speed rose to as much as 40 mph. There is an interesting engineering feature here that I had been to see in a short holiday in the neighbourhood. To get a good gradient on the steepening ascent of Glen Garry Mitchell had to cross the river somewhere near the clachan of Calvine; but as the land here was within the demesne of the Duke of Atholl any structure had to meet with his approval. At Calvine there was a road junction, where the one running up Glen Errochty and over the mountains to Kinloch Rannoch branched from the main highway to Inverness. It crossed the Garry on a handsome stone arched bridge, and Mitchell secured the approval of the Duke by designing a three-arch bridge to carry the railway striding diagonally across the road bridge at a higher level. The railway bridge was built in matching stone, and its unusual siting, straddling the existing bridge made it an object of considerable local interest. In 1898 work began on doubling the line between Blair Atholl and Dalwhinnie, and the widening of the bridge at Calvine, near to Struan station, was effected by an entirely separate single-span Warren girder bridge alongside.

Beyond the woods of Struan, now on a continuous ascent of 1 in 70, the speed settled down to a steady 27 mph and the snow clad mountains made a constantly changing picture of great beauty. Across the Braes of Atholl, where bracken glowed warm russet in the strengthening light, the hill-tops with a light covering of snow looked like so many phantom peaks. Then we turned into the narrowest and wildest part of Glen Garry, with deeper snow drifts, and the turbulent river sparkling under a clear lemon-coloured sky. By the time we neared Dalnaspidal, and the hill-range to the left of the line opened out to reveal a partly frozen Loch Garry with the heights of Badenoch towering above it we were ushered into a world of gleaming white. On trains that were assisted in rear from Blair Atholl the 'pusher' engine dropped behind at Dalnaspidal, leaving the train engine to mount the last two miles up to Drumochter summit unaided. Our two engines had accelerated to 41 mph past Dalnaspidal, and topped the summit, at 1484 ft above sea level, at 39 mph.

Once over the watershed, also the Perth–Inverness County March, speed quickly rose to nearly 70 mph, but the weather, as well as the speed, changed very rapidly. The sky darkened, and descending into Strath Spey we were soon running into the teeth of a blizzard. Ice packed up against the cab glasses, the mountains were hidden in a flying welter of sleet and snow, and with the visibility reduced practically to nil we had to ease up considerably. But these Highland enginemen were born and bred in such conditions and I shall always recall another driver once introduced to me as being able to find his way to Inverness blindfold! We ran out of the storm soon after leaving Kingussie, 36 miles from Blair Atholl in $57\frac{1}{2}$ minutes – nicely inside schedule time despite 'The Hill' and the storm; and by the time we were completing the next short run, to Aviemore, the skies had cleared somewhat and eastwards we could see the great Cairngorm range gleaming white. Aviemore, now an increasingly popular tourist centre, and a base for the winter sports activities, used to be a major junction in the Highland railway network; but it is no longer so, because the original line that Mitchell built in 1863, down Strath Spey at first, then through Grantown, over Dava Moor and down to Forres, is now closed. Only the first short section to Boat of Garten which is privately owned is now operating.

In former days, with the big trains from the south, there was always some remarshalling at Aviemore. The Royal Highlander carried through carriages and sleeping cars for the stations on the old line, Grantown-on-Spey, Forres and Nairn; and the train engine from Perth coupled off, and took the Forres line section of the train. It was a much longer way round, and with many intermediate stops, and the engine did not arrive in Inverness, via the coast route, until nearly two hours after the 'direct' portion, with the mails. It was the same when the old Highland engines were still on the job, and on my first journey in 1927, when I was travelling to Nairn the *Clan Mackinnon* continued as our engine from Aviemore. But on that snowy January morning when I was on the footplate we had two fresh engines from Aviemore, for a reduced load of 430 tons. Another 'Black Five' was the train engine, going through to Inverness, and to assist in the heavy pulling up to Slochd Crossing, including one stretch as steep as 1 in 60, we had a rare old veteran in one of Peter Drummond's 'Castle' class 4-6-0s the *Beaufort Castle*, built as long ago as 1902, and still then of unchanged design. I could not resist climbing on to her footplate for the climb up to Slochd, though in such weather the ride was likely to be distinctly air-conditioned!

The 'Castles' were always great favourites with the Highland enginemen, and although this one was then a veteran with thirty-four years of hard service behind her, she was still in excellent condition. I was very pleased to get a ride on this engine, because about twenty-five years earlier, when she was in her prime, she was a star performer on the Aviemore–Inverness direct line, and held what was thought to be the record for a non-stop run, in $48\frac{3}{4}$ minutes, though with a train of no more than 175 tons. That however, was just about her share of the 430 tons we took up to Slochd on my run. We looked out through large round windows over the boiler, though there were times when there was precious little to see ahead – or behind for that matter. Like most Highland engines engaged on piloting work *Beaufort Castle* did a considerable mileage tender first, returning 'light engine' to

The great viaduct across Strathnairn, just south of Culloden Moor.

Aviemore either from Slochd or Dalnaspidal; and to give some protection to the crew in the small cab a tarpaulin was stretched from the cab roof to the tender front. We had a brief stop to put down some sleeping car passengers at Carrbridge, and then we tore into it on the worst gradient of the whole northbound journey to Inverness. The wind caught us viciously, and snow was driving horizontally, clean through the cab, but a steady 30 mph was maintained up the 1 in 60 gradient, with both engines going very nearly all out.

So we reached the summit, a wilderness of rocks 1315 ft above sea level, and there the *Beaufort Castle* coupled off, to return tender first to Aviemore. The snow was driving well nigh level and I was glad to climb up into the shelter of the big engine's cab, for the remaining twenty-two downhill miles to Inverness. The gradient is 1 in 60 downhill at first, and we soon got into speed. Ahead of us was the Findhorn valley, with its tall curving viaduct silhouetted against the snow like some delicate trestle. Over it, at 63 mph, and then on, in driving sleet to Culloden Moor, doing a steady but carefully restrained 60 mph down the steep gradients. The wind was furious on these exposed heights, and where on a clear day one could see and recognise

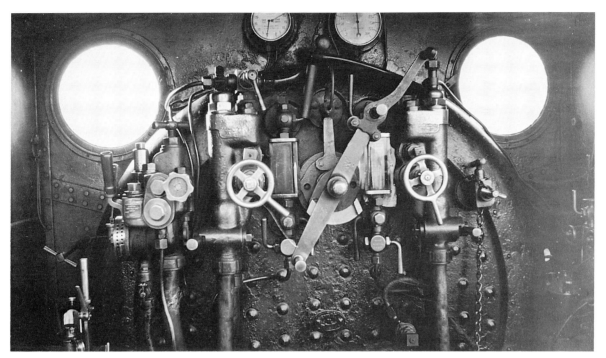

In the cab of the Beaufort Castle *on which the author rode from Aviemore to Slochd on a snowy January morning.*

mountains fifty miles away to the west there was now only a whirling curtain of white, through which, below on our right the Moray Firth could be no more than vaguely seen. We ran cautiously down the last miles into Inverness and arrived practically on time. But one had only to look at our engine to see something of the weather we had been through, even on the relatively short run from Aviemore, just over an hour's travelling. The snow plough on our engine, the buffer beam, and the cab front were thickly coated with ice. In view of the weather reports Inverness was preparing to send out the big patrol snow ploughs, to run constantly over the line, and prevent snow drifts accumulating.

As well as these vivid winter memories of the Royal Highlander I recall many more benign occasions, on summer holiday visits to the Highlands, when I enjoyed photography 'out the line' as the local phrase goes. The southbound Royal Highlander left Inverness at 4.15 pm as the centre-piece of a procession of expresses to the south, and in early September they all carried very heavy loads. First, leaving at 3.20 pm came a relief train, run only when required, and made up to the maximum load that could be taken by one engine. On days like that there was not 'even half an engine to spare', to quote the famous poster of the second world war. The three 'heavy weights' of those late summer afternoons were the 3.45 pm Mail, the Royal Highlander itself, and the 4.35 pm which was a combined train with a lavish amount of sleeping accommodation for both Kings Cross and Euston. The train engines in the late 1920s were usually 'Clans' working through to Perth. Inverness had to provide assistance only up to the Slochd, and they had a very neat way of doing it. Within the hour before the departure of the mail three connecting trains arrived, one from the Kyle of Lochalsh, one from Elgin, Keith and Aberdeen, and the north mail from Wick. Inverness remanned the three engines concerned, topped up their tender tanks, and sent them out again as pilots for the three heavy south-bound expresses.

The Royal Highlander got the engine from Keith, always a 4-4-0 at that time, either one of the outside cylindered 'Loch' class, a vintage design of 1896, or one of Peter Drummond's small 'Bens', that looked so like his elder brother's famous 'T9' 4-4-0s on the London and South Western Railway. The train itself was non-stop from Inverness to Aviemore, leaving the succeeding 4.35 pm to pick up all the sleeping car passengers from the intermediate stations. It brings waves of nostalgia to me to recall those serene afternoons of long ago, when I relaxed in the heather by the lineside, with camera set up ready. It was a good place for the rather primitive apparatus I was then using, because the speed on the 1 in 60 between Culloden Moor and Daviot was rarely much more than 20 mph. On one occasion the Royal

4-6-0 express locomotive Clan Cameron, *the final Highland passenger engine design.*

Highlander engines were *Ben Loyal* and *Clan Stewart*; on another the *Loch Ruthven* and *Gordon Castle*. But there was one more spectacle that was worth waiting to see. After arrival up at the Slochd, and coupling off their respective trains, the three pilots joined up, and returned to Inverness. It was quite a sight to see the three engines, all running tender first, and drifting lazily downhill, with the 4-4-0 that had assisted the 'Royal Highlander' sandwiched between a mixed traffic 4-6-0 that had earlier come up from the Kyle of Lochalsh, and the 'Castle' that had come down from Wick.

Although I was too late to see the beautiful and historic 'F' class 4-4-0s in action there were still a few of their smaller wheeled, and unnamed contemporaries at work in 1927. Through their regular use on the mountainous route from Dingwall to the Kyle of Lochalsh they were always known as the 'Skye Bogies'. In later years, when steam locomotives were nearing the end of their useful life little trouble was taken to keep them reasonably clean; but it was not so with the 'Skye Bogies'. In 1927 there were six out of the original nine still in active service, and in 'Midland red' they were all kept looking very smart. I photographed one of them out on the high moors above Loch Luichart bringing up the mails from the Kyle, and I wondered if she had gone through to Inverness, and as was usual on that duty double-headed the 3.45 pm south mail up to Slochd. She would have made a brave sight pounding up the 1 in 60 past Daviot, leading a 'Castle' or a 'Clan'. For the record, that 'Skye Bogie', No. 14284 of the LMS, was the former Highland No. 7, built in 1898, and was the last one of the class to survive, not being withdrawn until April 1930.

In referring to some of the problems involved in getting the southbound trains away from Inverness I have not yet mentioned one interesting sequel to the arrival of the down train during the winter months, when it had waited at Perth and been incorporated in the 6.25 am mail train. The travelling post office, and its attendant stowage van was the only part of the train that continued to the far north, even so not to the very ultimate end of the line. Two connecting trains left Inverness, after 10 am. That for the Kyle of Lochalsh went first, and it actually took the TPO van as far as Dingwall. In the height of the tourist season there would be a heavy mail for the popular fishing and shooting resorts towards the western end of the Kyle line, not to mention for Skye itself and the Outer Isles, and the half-hour run between Inverness and Dingwall gave the opportunity to get this separated from that destined for the north main line. The TPO was transferred to the following Wick train at Dingwall, though it did not proceed farther north than Helmsdale. But it is on the threshold of this lone, fascinating area of the northern Highlands that the Royal Highlander decamps its passengers, and it is at Inverness that this chapter must end.

15

THE SILVER JUBILEE

When Sir Nigel Gresley was knighted in 1936 *The Times* succinctly described him as 'Engineer and Speeder-up to the LNER'. For some years prior to that he had been the principal inspiration behind certain runs, with both 'Atlantic' and 'Pacific' engines at considerably higher speeds than required by the current timetables; but the catalyst towards one of the greatest passenger train developments seen on the British railways this century came in May 1933 with the inauguration of the high-speed diesel railcar train the *Flying Hamburger*, between Berlin and Hamburg, at an average speed of 77·4 mph. Gresley was impressed by the way this train, and the newly introduced fast services in France and the USA, had not only done much to re-establish railways in public estimation, but had recovered a considerable number of passengers from alternative forms of transport. In the late summer of 1934 he visited Germany and travelled on the *Flying Hamburger* and he was so impressed with the smooth running of the train at 100 mph that he felt it was advisable to explore the possibilities of extra high speed on the LNER, by having such a train for trial.

He therefore approached the makers of the German train, and invited their proposals for a similar high speed train for running between Kings Cross and Newcastle. Furnished with full details of the gradient, curves and speed restrictions of the route they submitted a design of a three-coach articulated train that would convey 140 passengers. After a very thorough examination of all the physical conditions they estimated that the 268·3 miles could be covered in 234 minutes, but recommended that a 10 per cent recovery margin should be added, to quote Gresley's own report 'to meet varying weather conditions and to have sufficient time in reserve to make up for such decelerations or delays as might normally be expected'. The extra 24 minutes added in their schedule was much the same as the basic 4 minutes recovery time for each 50 miles recommended in the scientific train timing procedure adopted in British Railway's days, where accelerations of steam worked services were being planned in the 1950s. The outcome of this investigation was that the Germans could not promise anything better than a non-stop time of 257 minutes. The difference between this average of only 62·7 mph and the 77·4 mph of the *Flying Hamburger* was not only a result of the limitation, then, on the LNER to a maximum speed of 90 mph inclusive, as compared to 100, but also of the numerous intermediate speed restrictions, quite apart from the major ones at Peterborough, Selby, York and Durham.

More than any question of high overall speed, however, there was the nature of the passenger accommodation provided in the proposed three-car articulated train. It was far more cramped than that provided for ordinary third-class passengers on main line trains in Great Britain, let alone on a service on which there would probably be a supplementary charge for the higher speed. On this one's thoughts stray briefly to today's French *Trains à Grande Vitesse*, on which the accommodation is like that of the tourist class on an airliner, only worse, in that half the passengers are sitting back to the direction of travel in the same conditions. With Gresley faced with such a situation Sir Ralph Wedgwood, Chief General Manager of the LNER then took a hand, and suggested that with an ordinary steam Pacific engine faster overall speeds could be maintained with a train of much greater weight, capacity and comfort. Thus followed the ever-memorable trial runs of 5 March 1935, with the 'Super Pacific' engine *Papyrus*, when with a train of five ordinary coaches and the dynamometer car, 217 tons, and nearly double the weight of the proposed German diesel train, the journey from

Inspiration for the Silver Jubilee streamlining: Bugatti high speed railcar on the State Railways of France.

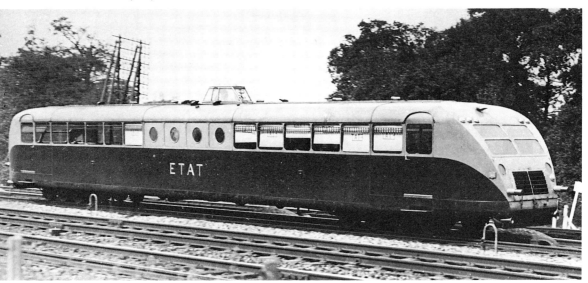

Kings Cross to Newcastle was made in 237 minutes, despite seven minutes delay en route, and the return in 231¾ minutes. By a special dispensation a higher speed was permitted on the famous racing stretch down from Stoke Tunnel to Peterborough, and there a world-record maximum speed of 108 mph was attained.

The suggestion that existing LNER steam power could provide the haulage capacity for a four-hour London-Newcastle service was amply demonstrated by these runs. Furthermore, within the weight actually conveyed there would be accommodation for no fewer than 204 first class passengers, in the comfort to which they had been accustomed on the Kings Cross route to the north for so many years. At the same time the conditions on that March day in 1935 had been very favourable, with good weather, and a picked engine in perfect condition. Moreover examination of the data recorded in the dynamometer car showed that the engine had been worked relatively hard, and that for regular working a greater margin of power would be desirable. In addition, the coaching stock was of the standard LNER teak-bodied type, with ribbed and panelled sides. They were very attractive to look at, but at very high speed would probably offer something in the way of what is often termed skin-friction. Now Gresley was nothing if not a publicist, and on receiving authority to construct a new train for the proposed London–Newcastle high speed service he decided to streamline both engine and train, as effectively as practicable.

The timing of this innovation was important. It was the year of King George V's Silver Jubilee and it was also the centenary of the Great Western Railway, and one could be fairly sure that this latter event would be marked by the publicity and pageantry characteristic of that great company. The new LNER train was essentially to be a service for the business clientele rather than tourist, or summer seasonal traffic, and so to have its full impact, and to counter any similar innovations from Paddington, in their centenary year, it must be ready for introduction in the winter timetables. There was not much time: only five months for the design and building of an entirely new train. Modifications to the locomotive were not confined merely to the addition of streamlining. It was felt that the thermodynamic performance could be improved by use of a higher boiler pressure, and smaller cylinders, while the freedom of running at high speed could be increased by larger piston valves to facilitate the free flow of the steam at entry to, and exhaust from the cylinders.

The actual form of the external streamlining of the locomotive led to criticism from certain engineers in the aerodynamic field, who argued that the shape was not true streamlining in that it did not follow a perfect aerofoil contour in all directions. In that respect it certainly was very much

Inaugural public run of the Silver Jubilee: 10 am Newcastle to Kings Cross, on 30 September 1935, with the engine Silver Link.

of a compromise, albeit an ingenious and highly effective one. As the boilers of steam locomotives grew progressively larger, and the chimney dwarfed in consequence, so that it projected no more than an inch or two above the line of the barrel, trouble had been experienced, particularly when the engine was being lightly steamed, of the exhaust clinging to the outside of the barrel, and drifting downwards to obscure the driver's look-out from the cab. Gresley's own staff had considerable difficulty with the second of the large 2-8-2 engines, the *Earl Marischal*. On the new 'Pacific' engines for the high-speed Newcastle train the aerodynamic form of the streamlining was that used on the Bugatti high-speed railcars running on the Western Railway of France, and included as its principal feature a sloping front that was flat in transverse cross-section.

When the new train did take the road in September 1935, and was named 'The Silver Jubilee', it created an absolute sensation. Breaking clean away from East Coast traditions, engine and train alike were finished throughout in silver-grey, and the air-smoothing of the coaches was complete from end to end of the seven-car formation. The principle of coach articulation had been successfully used on the LNER in the three-car dining sets used on the Flying Scotsman and the afternoon Anglo-Scottish express, and the Silver

Jubilee had a two-car articulated set on either side of the central three-car restaurant unit. There were thus only ten bogies to carry the seven cars, making possible a considerable reduction in total weight, which amounted to 220 tons tare. Including the accommodation in the restaurant cars there were seats for 78 first, and 120 third class passengers, in probably the most spacious and comfortable stock yet provided in this country for non-Pullman patrons. While the exterior, in the all-pervading silver-grey, without any lining or external decoration was one of austerity, the coach interiors were delightful, with a soft-blue colour scheme in the first class, and pale green in the thirds.

Externally the very look of the train was such as to generate an impression of breathless haste, though actually, before it had turned a wheel in express speed running there had to be some fairly deep heart-searching over the matter of its brake power. For sometime previously no braking other than on the driving wheels had been applied on the large express locomotives of the LNER. The complication of flexible connections to the bogie wheels were not considered worth the trouble they involved. So, on the Gresley 'Pacific' engines only about two-thirds of the total engine weight was braked. With the ordinary Anglo-Scottish expresses, with 500 tons of train and a 150-ton engine, the proportion of unbraked weight was relatively small; but it was a very different matter with the Silver Jubilee with the new engines weighing 165 tons, and the train only 220 tons. Furthermore, the cruising speed of the train would be 85 to 90 mph instead of 55 to 70 mph. Accordingly, for most of the distance between Kings Cross and Newcastle the Operating Department determined that instead of one section, from one signal box to the next ahead being clear before the train could be signalled through, there must be two sections clear – a space interval of about four miles, instead of two. But while this method of working, termed 'double-blocking', could be applied over the bulk of the route, where the signalling consisted of manually operated semaphores, it was not possible between York and Northallerton, where most of the signals were automatic. Consequently, over what would otherwise have been one of the fastest stretches of the whole journey a speed limit of 70 mph was imposed so as not to exceed the safe limits of braking distance. This would add about 6 minutes on to the total journey time.

Although the overall schedule that was planned was carefully adjusted to provide for faster running south of York, to compensate for this restriction, without requiring any excess above the generally accepted maximum line speed of 90 mph, when the time came for a demonstration run for the guests of the LNER and for the national press authority was given for a faster run than would normally be required to see how much time was in hand. A remarkable degree of confidence in the new power was shown from the outset, because at the time the new public service was programmed to begin only one of the new streamlined locomotives was ready. This was the *Silver Link*, so named as representing the new high-speed link between London and Tyneside. At this distance in time a story may be told about the naming of this engine. Gresley's younger daughter, Mrs Violet Godfrey, had always been a keen follower of her father's locomotive work, and on completion of the *Silver Link* she accompanied him to Doncaster Works to see the new engine. The name was rendered in a cast plate, chromium plated, in the same style as that used on the large 2-8-2 engines used north of Edinburgh

The two 10 am departures from Newcastle, crossing the King Edward Bridge: on left, the Silver Jubilee, on right express for Liverpool via Sunderland.

on the Aberdonian. Mrs Godfrey felt that this large cast plate, standing somewhat proud of the streamlined flanks of the locomotive rather destroyed the effect; and at her prompting the plates were taken off and the name painted on the boiler side, above the middle pair of driving wheels.

It is fairly safe to suggest that very few of the LNER officers and their guests, probably not even Gresley himself, anticipated what would happen with the driver having been given instructions to go a bit harder, to see how much there was in hand on the new schedule. This allowed just half an hour for the $41\frac{1}{4}$ miles from Hatfield to Huntingdon, requiring an average speed of $82\frac{1}{2}$ mph; believe it or not, the actual time was a few seconds over $24\frac{1}{2}$ minutes, a then sensational average of $100\frac{1}{4}$ mph and Peterborough was passed $9\frac{1}{2}$ minutes ahead of the planned schedule. But if the senior railway officers on board were impressed, in a variety of ways, by the astonishing speed developed by the new locomotives they were concerned, not to say

The down Silver Jubilee near Hadley Wood, hauled by Class 'A4' 4-6-2 No. 2510 Quicksilver.

outrightly *scared*, by the tempestuous riding of the coaches. One by one they made their way to the front of the train to find Gresley ensconced behind an enormous stop-watch clocking off the mileposts and enjoying every minute of it. And when the hapless Civil Engineer looked into the compartment, just as there was a particularly bad lurch, Gresley cheerily chaffed him about the poor state of his track! After passing St Neots however, doing 110 mph and approaching the S-curve on the banks of the River Ouse, at Offord, even Gresley was moved to go through the corridor tender and tell the driver to ease up a little.

The wild riding of the coaches was far more the fault of the method of suspension than of the track, though at that time the method of laying in the transitions between straight track and curves had not been perfected. The trial run of the new train took place on the Friday before the regular service was to begin, on the very next Monday; and in that brief intervening weekend some considerable adjustments were made to the coach suspension. In any case the service train was not required to run at anything approaching the terrific speeds attained on that exciting Friday. The irony of it all was that throughout that breathtaking spell, with maximum speeds up to 112½ mph, the *Silver Link* was riding perfectly, and the driver and fireman and the senior locomotive superintendent who was riding on the footplate with them had not the slightest conception of the way the coaches were tossing about. From the very inception of the Silver Jubilee project insistence had been placed on the strict observance of all the speed restrictions, which of course included the line maximum of 90 mph south of York, and 70 mph between there and Darlington. The locomotives were fitted with recording speedometers on which a 'trace' of the actual speed throughout every run was made. At journey's end a running inspector removed the chart, which was then sent to locomotive running headquarters for scrutiny, and woe betide any driver who had stepped outside the rules.

Actually that scrutiny soon became a mere formality. For very many months after the train was first put on it was worked by a special link of only four crews, all based at Kings Cross. The drivers were all senior men of the highest reputation; and although the Silver Jubilee was only one of their regular assignments, in view of the marvellous record of punctual running that they established during that first winter their names should certainly go on record: H. Gutteridge, G.H. Haygreen, W. Payne, and A.J. Taylor. It was the last mentioned who made the record running on the demonstration trip. When the new train went into regular service *Silver Link* was the only streamlined engine that was ready for high-speed running, and for the first fortnight she worked the train in both directions, 536½ miles daily, without the slightest trouble. The three subsequent engines were

187

Quicksilver, Silver King and *Silver Fox*. The first and third of this trio were stationed at Kings Cross and took turns regularly on the Jubilee, while *Silver King* was stationed at Gateshead, and stood pilot for the southbound Jubilee, which left for London at 10 am. Such was the reliability of the regulars however that *Silver King* was hardly ever seen at Kings Cross. After the up Jubilee had left Newcastle it had a 408-mile stint of its own to run daily: Newcastle to Edinburgh: Edinburgh to York: and then York back to Newcastle.

After that tremendously exciting demonstration run, details of which were 'splashed', even in those journals most famed for sobriety of utterance, it would have been difficult to write of the Silver Jubilee without some reference to the thrills of high speed, and although I had no occasion to travel on it until some months later, I shall always remember the excitement with which a Hartlepool friend regaled us after a trip. 'It was absolutely marvellous' he said. 'Even the engine driver is streamlined, wearing a black beret, instead of a cap, and they let you go into the guard's van to watch the speedometer. We did 97!' Incidentally, the black beret was not worn by the driver but by George Haygreen's regular fireman. It was his usual headgear on any train. There was certainly a welter of thrill-mongering about The Silver Jubilee when it was first put on, so much so that its real purpose became somewhat obscured, except to its regular patrons. The ordinary LNER expresses were second to none for smooth riding, and even though the new streamliner took him home in $1\frac{1}{2}$ hours less time than the old 5.30 pm a Newcastle business man would hardly appreciate a burst of speed at 90 to 95 mph if the train rolled and lurched, the coach bogies jangled and 'hunted' and all the ingredients of a 'thrill' were present.

Nevertheless as a popular spectacle the train achieved something of a pre-eminence, not confined to railway enthusiasts, or thrill-merchants. *The Railway Gazette*, that pillar of senior management and engineering sentiment, aptly expressed the feelings of the day in an editorial note published a few weeks after the train had commenced to run: under the heading 'A London Spectacle' it stated: 'The departures of the Silver Jubilee from Kings Cross qualify to rank with the established sights of the capital, for the crowds that congregate on No. 6 platform as much as half an hour before 5.30 pm represent that range of ages, types and interest that characterise spectators of the older London institutions. All the ingredients of spectacle are there, from the military smartness of the train attendants to the growing tension as half past five approaches. Nature has added to the pleasure of the beholders by providing a twilight which emphasises the glow of the fire in the engine cab, and a darkening sky against which the tall and spreading column of *Silver Link*'s exhaust stands out with startling whiteness and solidity. Like most London crowds, this one makes no great display of its feelings, contenting itself with a little desultory hand-waving and a communal sigh of satisfaction as the last coach vanishes into the tunnel. But the symbolism of speed and distance epitomised in this little nightly pageant, staged at the moment when its spectators have just earned a few hours' freedom from the circumscribed atmosphere of office or factory, must surely react to the benefit of the railways as a whole by awakening a wider consciousness of how travel can relieve the uniformity of life.'

No mention of a black beret however! But the atmosphere of spectacle did not seem to cloy with the passing of time. I travelled to Darlington by the train in the late summer of 1936, nearly a year after its first introduction, and I was interested to see little groups of sightseers had gathered at points all down the line to watch the 'flyer' pass. Not only around the bigger towns, but even in the depths of the country we were greeted by many a waving handkerchief. She seemed to cast her spell over young and old alike, so that even a cold, matter of fact engineer, whom I never suspected of having the slightest interest in railways other than his immediate preoccupation as a signal contractors' man, came back from the north and described to me in glowing terms the spectacle of the Jubilee picking up water at the Wiske Moor troughs, just north of Northallerton. The odd thing was that the train would often be travelling slower than many ordinary trains at this particular place. With the normal cruising speed at 85 to 90 mph a vast amount of water would be flung about and wasted if the scoop was lowered at such a speed, and with the Jubilee it was customary to ease up to 70 mph or even less when picking up water. On that day it was the train, more than anything else, that impressed my colleague; the Flying Scotsman or the Queen of Scots Pullman might have given him a still more spectacular water-splash!

On that journey of mine in September 1936 we kept very closely to booked time until after Peterborough, though at no time exceeding 92 mph, and while keeping to the same careful parameter we drew slightly ahead, passing Retford $4\frac{1}{4}$ minutes early, in $111\frac{3}{4}$ minutes for the 138·6 miles from Kings Cross. But we were delayed by signal through Doncaster, and lost about 5 minutes in running, and it was while the engine was being opened out a little to recover the lost time that I found the actual travelling so very impressive. Passing through York at the usual 15 mph under the fascinated gaze of a hundred or more sightseers, we then accelerated rapidly to a very thrilling finish. But as always on this train the thrills were apparent only to a man with a stop watch. It was dark by that time and inside a cosy compartment we seemed cut off completely from the outside world. Noise of travelling was very effectively deadened by double-glazing, the space

A green class 'A3' super-Pacific deputising for a streamliner on the up Silver Jubilee in September 1937. Engine No. 2501 Colombo *passing Peterborough, on time.*

between the two panes acting as a sound insulator, and the beat of the wheels came in a distant pleasing rhythm. Those were the days before rails were welded together in long lengths, and the gentle tattoo was that apostrophised by the child of immortal memory as the *'diddly-da's'*.

Vertical strip lights in the four corners of the compartment and the blue walls combined to produce a soft restful light; loose cushions on the seats, a thick Wilton carpet, and curtained windows gave one the impression of a quiet corner in a private house rather a railway train. It seemed incredible that we were speeding through the dark, late evening countryside at nearly 90 mph. One of my fellow travellers was deep in a book; another was hard at work surrounded by a mass of documents and calculations. And so we sped on. By Thirsk the slight arrears of time occasioned by the delay at Doncaster had been more than recovered, and the engine was being eased slightly. With clear signals all the way we swept across the Tees viaduct at Croft Spa, entered County Durham, and in 195¼ minutes from Kings Cross, nearly three minutes early, stopped at Darlington. Our actual average speed for the 232¼ miles was 71·5 mph – an excellent run, but no more than typical of a nightly performance on the Silver Jubilee.

A week or so before this journey of mine two test runs were made on which the dynamometer car was added to the train, and a continuous record taken of the actual horsepower needed to run the train. On the very straight and favourably graded length between Stoke Tunnel and Peterborough an attempt was made to secure a maximum speed record, in fully observed test conditions; and with the train riding with perfect smoothness and the many passengers on board quite unaware of what was being attempted a maximum speed of 113 mph was attained. This was the British record for a train carrying ordinary fare paying passengers, and it remained the record until the advent of the diesel-powered High Speed Trains with which the speed limit on certain routes was increased to 125 mph.

16

RIVALS IN CORONATION YEAR

The success of the Silver Jubilee was absolute. In the technical performance of its locomotives and rolling stock it was an engineering triumph for Sir Nigel Gresley and his staff; it was a marvellous advertisement for the LNER, and by loading to capacity, or nearly so every day, month in month out, it was a money spinner. It was not surprising that the management began to look for other fields in which to introduce similar streamlined high speed trains. The early autumn of 1936 was full of rumours. While the dynamometer car test runs on the Silver Jubilee itself on 27 August created much technical interest, quite apart from the maximum speed of 113 mph, the carrying out of a second trial between Newcastle and Edinburgh on 26 September gave the first indication that thoughts of extending the streamline service into Scotland were already in the air. At that time only the one streamlined train existed in public service from Monday to Friday. The Edinburgh run had therefore to be made on a Saturday, when the train would in any case be at Newcastle. No passengers were carried. On the return journey, without unduly hard running the 124 miles from Edinburgh to Newcastle were covered in 114 minutes, and keen observers were already pointing out that with the already established standards of locomotive performance a six-hour service between Kings Cross and Edinburgh was practicable.

Until then the LNER had the field to themselves. The London–Darlington–Newcastle run posed no rivalry to any existing LMS services, and from informal conversations with various LMS officers during the summer of 1936 one gained the impression that the top management then had no intention of introducing high-speed streamlined services on such lucrative business routes as Euston–Liverpool, or Euston–Manchester. Rather, there was a policy of more gradual acceleration of all services, to a uniformly high standard. At the beginning of October however it was announced that one of the new batch of 'Pacific' engines to be built at Crewe in the following year was to be named *Coronation*, in honour of the forthcoming Royal occasion of 1937, thus following the precedent set by the London and North

Western Railway in 1911, in so naming one of the latest 4-4-0 express locomotives of the 'George the Fifth' class. At that time in 1936 it was thought that the coronation would be that of King Edward VIII, and there was no indication that any new, or accelerated train services would be made in celebration of the event. But then, at the beginning of November the LNER announced that in the following year new high-speed streamlined services would be introduced between Kings Cross and Leeds, and Kings Cross and Edinburgh, at Silver Jubilee standards of speed. The last mentioned was to involve an overall time of six hours, and clearly constituted a threat to the Anglo-Scottish business of the LMS.

Whether the LMS had any advance intelligence of these important new proposals I cannot say; but so far as the timing was concerned their riposte was as immediate as it was brilliantly successful. For within a fortnight of the LNER announcement a special train had been run non-stop over the longer distance of 401 miles from Euston to Glasgow, northbound in 5 hr 53 min and returning next day in 5 hr 44 min. As in the case of the preliminary LNER run of March 1935, these record-breaking LMS performances were made with a standard 'Pacific' engine and ordinary coaches. The only additions to the locomotive equipment were the fittings normally necessary for connecting to the recording instruments in the dynamometer car. From this test it was confidently expected that the LMS would match the already announced six-hour Kings Cross–Edinburgh service with one of six hours from Euston to Glasgow. The LMS locomotive concerned was the *Princess Elizabeth*, now happily preserved in working order, and used from time to time on special trains – though not at the speed she was run in November 1936! It was some months after those brilliant performances however before the LMS announced their intentions of a faster Anglo-Scottish service for Coronation Year.

In the meantime there had been considerable discussion in the correspondence columns of the railway press as to the probable running times of the new LNER streamliners. The Leeds train was generally expected to follow the pattern of the Silver Jubilee, leaving about mid-morning, giving a full afternoon for business in London, and then returning in the early evening; but the Scottish service was a more difficult matter. Edinburgh already had three popular and heavily loaded services from Kings Cross, in the Flying Scotsman, and its summer appendage at 10.05 am, the Queen of Scots Pullman, also serving Leeds, and the 1.20 pm. A new streamlined train at Silver Jubilee speed would be difficult to slot in, without disturbing trains at well-established and commercially viable times. Suggestions for a later afternoon departure, to provide an arrival in Edinburgh around 10 pm or 10.30 met with objections from certain correspondents who felt that

Edinburgh should not be treated on a business basis but rather on a tourist one. It was of course clear that in any case the new facility could not be provided by a single train-set, as in the case of Newcastle and Leeds. There would have to be two trains, making roughly simultaneous departures from Kings Cross and Edinburgh.

Developing the tourist possibilities certain erudite correspondents suggested that a noon departure from London would enable a greatly improved service to be given north of Edinburgh, and would make unnecessary the running of the Queen of Scots Pullman north of Harrogate. The patronage of the latter beautiful train had always been relatively sparse north of Leeds. On the other hand, with a 4 pm departure from London evening connections could be made from Hull and the cities of the West Riding to give a greatly accelerated service to Scotland at that time. Authorisation had been given for construction of seventeen more streamlined 'Pacific' engines, and at New Year the names of the first five were announced – all being the fleetest 'birds of the air' – *Golden Eagle*, *Falcon*, *Merlin*, *Kingfisher* and *Kestrel*. The names were chosen by Mrs Violet Godfrey, the younger daughter of Sir Nigel Gresley, and when the first of them came to Kings Cross on 6 January, to take the 1.20 pm Scotsman to Newcastle, the spectators were interested to see it was painted in the standard apple-green livery, and not the special silver-grey finish of the Silver Jubilee engines. This suggested that the coaches of the Leeds and Edinburgh streamlined trains then under construction would be in the standard LNER coach livery, and not grey.

The interest and anticipation also spread to the West Coast route, on which it was confidently expected that a six-hour service between Euston and Glasgow would be inaugurated in the forthcoming summer season. Again the speculation centred upon the likely running times, while the margin of time in hand demonstrated on the trial runs in the previous November suggested that one, or perhaps even two stops could be included within the six-hour schedule. In the well-informed correspondence flowing at the time Preston was generally favoured for one stop, because of the convenience it gave for connections to and from the Lancashire towns. Although by then it had become a regular practice for one 'Pacific' engine to work through from Euston to Glasgow, being remanned either at Crewe or Carlisle, in view of the arduous nature of the expected six-hour schedule, and the need for strict punctuality at all times, it was also suggested that changing engines at Preston might be desirable. The LNER was charging a small high-speed supplement over the ordinary fares for travelling on the Silver Jubilee and anticipating that the same would be done on the expected Glasgow 'flyer' one correspondent made the pertinent suggestion that in the event of late running the supplement should be refunded!

So, during the early months of 1937 hopes and expectations remained in a state of suspended animation until March, when the LMS announced that the new service between Euston and Glasgow would have an overall time of 6¼, and not the expected 6 hours, with one intermediate stop, at Carlisle. There was also considerable surprise in that the departure time, from each terminus, would be at 1.30 pm, thus realising no more than a quickening of the long-established service provided by the old North Western 'Corridor', referred to in Chapter 4, and its LMS successor, the Midday Scot. The new Coronation Scot was a permanent separation – Mondays to Fridays – of the Glasgow section of the Midday Scot, from the sections for Edinburgh and Aberdeen. In the previous summer the train had been accelerated to a 7¼ hour run from Euston to Glasgow, but it carried such an enormous load, not to mention the addition of a through portion from Plymouth at Crewe that considerable difficulty was experienced in keeping time. On the other hand with the 9-coach load proposed for the Coronation Scot, the 6¼ hour run with only one stop promised to be fairly easy. Much was made of the proposed non-stop run between Euston and Carlisle, to be made in 283 minutes for the distance of 299 miles, in both directions. The average speed of 63·4 mph made them the longest non-stop runs anywhere in the world at an average of more than 60 mph. While the non-stop run to Carlisle ensured the setting up of this record, one could not help feeling that a stop at Preston would have been more advantageous from the business point of view.

While the Coronation Scot, with its departures at 1.30 pm provided an improved service for a long-established clientele, the decision of the LNER upon a late afternoon departure for the rival Coronation express, at 4 pm from Kings Cross and 4.30 pm from Edinburgh Waverley bid fair to build up an entirely new market. The down train would call only at York, making good forward connections from Leeds, Hull, Sheffield, and so on, to Edinburgh, while the up train would call only at Newcastle. The locomotives, like those of the Silver Jubilee were to be fitted with corridor tenders, but although working throughout between London and Edinburgh re-manning was to take place at the station stops. The regular working of the Silver Jubilee and the trial runs made between Newcastle and Edinburgh in September 1936 had given the impression that no difficulty would be experienced in observing the six-hour schedule; but as matters eventuated it became one of the most arduous assignments ever presented to British steam locomotives.

In what could be termed the 'run-up' to the introduction of the new Anglo-Scottish train services on both routes on 5 July 1937, interest moved to the new streamlined locomotives of the LMS. The appearance of the

LNER *Golden Eagle* in January had shown that nothing new was to be expected from Doncaster, and with the British speed record standing at 113 mph there was some hope in the rival camp that an attempt might at some time be made to surpass it. So far as the design of the new engines was concerned the interesting thing is that Stanier himself was in India, as a member of a Government inquiry, for nearly all the time the work was in progress. But he was not primarily an innovative engine designer. In addition to being an outstanding workshop man he was a born leader of men who had unerring skill in getting the right men on to the job, and this was exemplified in the way two of his leading assistants, in his absence, settled the design of the streamlined 'Pacifics' for the Coronation Scot. These two were R.A. Riddles, Principal Assistant to the Chief Mechanical Engineer, and T.F. Coleman, Chief Locomotive Draughtsman.

The first of the new engines, the streamlined *Coronation* was outshopped at Crewe Works in May 1937, and by a superb feat of journalistic enterprise readers of *The Railway Gazette* were presented with a fully comprehensive, and lavishly illustrated description of the locomotive and the new train no later than that journal's regular issue of May 28. Intense interest was im-

The Coronation Scot passing Crewe hauled by blue streamlined Pacific engine No. 6222 Queen Mary.

mediately created by the form of the streamlining of the locomotive which was so different in appearance from that of Gresley's *Silver Link*, and its successors. Controversy quickly arose as to which was the better. Partisanship, right down to junior school level, was joined with the utmost vehemence, regardless of anything that might be contained inside those streamlined casings, and when the LNER announced that five new engines specially allocated to the Coronation train were to be painted, not in silver or in green, but in 'Garter Blue', and named after the five largest overseas territories of the British Empire the heat was on in earnest. These five locomotives were to be: *Dominion of Canada, Commonwealth of Australia, Dominion of New Zealand, Empire of India, Union of South Africa.*

In opposition, from the West Coast route, the remaining four of the new streamlined 'Pacifics' followed the tradition set with the earlier Stanier 'Pacifics' of the 'Princess Royal' class, and were named after 'Royal' ladies : *Queen Elizabeth, Queen Mary, Princess Alice* and *Princess Alexandra.*

The style of painting of the new engines was most cleverly devised, to be as different and distinctive from that of their East Coast rivals, and yet give a vivid impression of speed worthiness. The streamlining was of true aero-

The Coronation Scot passing Rugby, in September 1937, hauled by engine No. 6221 Queen Elizabeth.

The southbound Coronation Scot taking water at Tebay troughs: engine No. 6224 Princess Alexandra.

dynamic form, beautifully shaped and rounded, and accentuated by silver stripes springing from a point immediately above the coupling on what would be the buffer beam of a non-streamlined engine. A group of two broad and two narrow stripes swept to each side of the engine from this originating point, and were continued from end to end of the train. The blue and silver colour-scheme was finely captured in a painting by M. Secretan, published at the time. It was then said that an attempt had been made to recreate the original dark blue livery of the Caledonian Railway, in·view of the northern destination of the train, and the need to have something different from the 'Garter Blue' of the LNER. But no other adornments of the old Caledonian livery were incorporated, such as the purple-lake underframes and red backgrounds to the number plates. The 'Coronation' engines of the LMS were finished entirely in the blue and silver style, with the wheel rims as well as the motion parts polished bright – at any rate when they were new. The five new engines were known officially as the 'Princess-Coronation' class.

In early June 1937 news filtered through of many dashing feats of speed by the new engines, and then I was invited to accompany a demonstration run from Euston to Crewe and back on 19 June, only a few days before the

The Coronation of the LNER near Hadley Wood hauled by Class 'A4' Pacific
Dominion of Canada *before addition of the presentation Canadian bell.*

public service with the Coronation Scot was due to begin. When it became known that the LNER were arranging a similar run from Kings Cross to Grantham and back with the Coronation train on the very next day the excitement rose almost to fever pitch. By that time the more discerning of outside observers had come to appreciate that the working of the Coronation train was to be very much more strenuous than that of the Silver Jubilee. Not only was there one extra passenger coach, but at the rear end was the spectacular, beautifully styled beaver-tail observation car, making up a tare load of 312 tons, as compared to the 220 tons of the Silver Jubilee. Furthermore the one engine was going to work through between London and Edinburgh. In that last week however there is no doubt that most of the interest and the anticipation rested upon the LMS. I was in the confidence of some of their senior officers, and although no previous announcement was made to their distinguished visitors, or to the press, on the demonstration run it was hoped to surpass the existing British speed record of 113 mph at that time held by the LNER.

With the same Crewe driver who had made the record London–Glasgow non-stop runs in the previous November, a senior locomotive inspector, and Riddles himself on the footplate the northbound run was fast, if not

A fine rearward shot of the Coronation about to enter Potters Bar Tunnel.

exceptionally so as far as Stafford, which station, 133·6 miles from Euston, was passed in 109¾ minutes. Up to that point careful attention had been paid to all the existing speed restrictions and the maximum at any point had not exceeded 89 mph. North of Stafford also there was then a speed restriction to 60 mph over the junction at Norton Bridge; but once clear of that point a special dispensation had been given by the Chief Civil Engineer for them to 'have a go'. The line rises gradually, though on easy gradients, to a summit near Whitmore, after which there is 10½ miles of straight, falling gradient to the outskirts of Crewe. I knew the locomotive inspector who was concerned, and some months afterwards he confided to me that they had been instructed to try and reach a maximum of about 120 mph.

The attempt was however somewhat mismanaged. After passing Norton Bridge at exactly the prescribed 60 mph the acceleration up the gradual rise to Whitmore was unexpectedly slow. The official line maximum was 90 mph, but no one would have minded if the speed had been pushed a little above that figure, possibly even up to 95, which would have been easily possible with that locomotive, and a load of only eight coaches. Instead, the speed crept up until we were doing no more than 85 mph at the summit; and that deficiency was fatal to the attainment of the record maximum speed desired. What happened in the 7 minutes 6 seconds that remained before we were safely at rest in Crewe station was exciting enough, but not *quite* in accordance with the 'book'! There were four of us in the first two compartments of the leading coach taking detailed records of the speed, including the late Cecil J. Allen, then the doyen of stop-watchers, and we agreed, to the second, on the minutiae of the running. For some reason, instead of being pressed a little the engine was allowed to make its own pace on the very favourable, and splendidly straight track north of Whitmore. At Madeley, 2½ miles beyond the summit the speed was 97 mph; the 3¼ miles of the bank itself, the steepest part of the line anywhere between Euston and Crewe, brought it up to no more than 107, and we were then less than five miles from Crewe station. Then, perilously near to our stopping point and a long way from the desired maximum the engine was opened out!

Studied today, in cold print, the facts of that last 4¾ miles take some believing. On the footplate Riddles allowed acceleration to continue until we were two miles from Crewe, by which time all four of us agreed that the speed was 112½ mph. Two successive half miles were covered in exactly 16 seconds, showing that the speed was then being sustained at that figure. We were then however near to outright disaster, because to fit in with other train movements we were signalled into No. 3 platform, which from the down main line involved the negotiation of three crossover roads in succession. The brakes were fully applied just two miles from the centre of the station, and we did in fact make a smooth stop exactly at the correct place; but the run through those crossovers was hair raising! We were still doing 57 mph, when we struck the first one, and although the engine itself rode steadily through the coaches were tossed about in a frightening manner, the effect getting worse towards the rear of the train. Many years later when I was in a diesel-hauled train that did the same, but at still higher speed, the last three coaches were derailed, lost their bogies, and were dragged on their sides for some distance, though again the locomotive and the leading coaches kept to the rails. At Crewe in 1937, while some of the guests preparing to alight were flung against each other, and the floor of the dining car was strewn with a mosaic of broken crockery there were no casualties. Some of the press men came surging up to the engine to know if a record had been broken, and the LMS spokesman on the spot had to tell them 'no'.

Then we all went over to the Crewe Arms Hotel for a lunch presided over by E.J.H. Lemon the Vice-President of the Company responsible for engineering and operation. At the top table was a galaxy of senior officers, some of whom were still clearly discomfited from the precipitate nature of our arrival in Crewe. But after lunch Lemon, welcoming the guests in a spirit of the most disarming *bonhomie*, made light of the incident, until he was handed a slip of paper. As he read it a broad smile spread over his face, and he interrupted the flow of that post-luncheon speech to say that the speed recorder chart from the locomotive had now been examined, and the maximum speed was 114 mph. I shall never forget the look that Cecil J. Allen gave me, and the other two recorders, because quite frankly none of us believed it! There was, of course, no gainsaying it. The claim had come from Riddles himself, who had stayed with the locomotive during the lunch break. But of course its significance lay in its surpassing the existing LNER record by one mile per hour. The day was completed by a very fast and smoothly accomplished trip back to Euston, with most of the guests happy in the belief that a new British record speed in railway travel had been made that day. But like some other famous occasions it had, in more ways than one been 'a close-run thing'!

That it left uneasy feelings in the minds of some of the guests was shown by an incident the next day, and told me by one of my closest friends on the LNER at Kings Cross. He was rung up by the 'Special Correspondent' of *The Times*, who on the previous day had an honoured place at the top table, next to W.A. Stanier. On the following morning he asked my friend: 'Are you doing any speeding today, because if so I'm not coming; and my newspaper will be told why!' Actually there was a general desire at Kings Cross to surpass the day-old LMS claim of 114 mph; but with the heavy load of the Coronation train, and the need to work up speed after a lengthy stop at Barkston, 4½ miles north of Grantham, waiting for a lengthy stretch of clear road, the circumstances were not favourable, though in a very different way from those facing their rivals on the previous day. They managed to attain 109 mph but although there were still about ten miles of straight clear road ahead the engine was beginning to run short of steam, and they had to ease up.

When it came to regular service running with the rival Anglo-Scottish streamlined trains, the power potential was in inverse ratio to the traffic demands. The Coronation Scot, hauled by locomotives having a nominal tractive power some 15 per cent greater than that of the Gresley stream-liners, could be run to time without the speed greatly exceeding 80 mph anywhere, so relatively generous were the booked running times, whereas with the sharply timed Coronation there seemed very little time to spare even in calm summer weather. Quite apart from the greater tractive power the LMS locomotives had two advantages over their rivals: their tenders carried 10 tons of coal, instead of 9, and they had the boon of a steam operated coal pusher. Only those with footplate experience of long-mileage runs will appreciate the misery, for a hard-worked fireman, of having to get dwindling supplies of coal forward from the back of the tender, and Stanier's coal pushers were indeed the answer to a fireman's prayer! Furthermore these LMS engines, although having a huge firegrate area of 50 square feet were among the easiest to fire, the coal tending to spread itself uniformly over the entire grate. The LNER engines needed a specially acquired knack to keep the vital back corners of the firebox adequately fed.

Footplate craft apart, the Coronation was a lovely train to ride. Externally the two-tone colour scheme was a delight, with Cambridge blue upper panels, and the bodies in Garter blue to match the locomotives. The beaver-tail observation car might have been thought a gimmick, albeit a very attractive one, because the seating in it was not additional to the revenue earning capacity of the train, except that a small fee was charged for a brief sojourn in the car. Such a spell was very interesting in showing how that streamlined tail smoothed out the eddies and swirls in the air currents immediately in the wake of a very fast train. Because the train ran in the late evening however the observation cars were not run during the winter months, and this made a welcome reduction in the load to be hauled during the days when adverse weather conditions could considerably increase the haulage effort required. For most of its length the East Coast main line between Kings Cross and Edinburgh is particularly exposed to cross winds and I have personally experienced cases, when riding on the footplate of ordinary express trains when an eleven or twelve coach train was pulling like 'sixteen'. This was at no more than 65 to 70 mph, and one could well imagine how it could affect the Coronation, which had to run at 80 to 85 mph at least, on the open stretches of line. There were indeed several occasions when the southbound train was running so short of coal that they had to stop at Hitchin for assistance to get home!

Apart from occasional mischances, which affect every service at some time or another, the Coronation, both in its speed and in the elegance of its decor was one of the greatest British trains of the inter-war period; and some notes on a journey I enjoyed, southbound from Waverley to Kings Cross early in August 1937 will fittingly end this chapter and this book. Its departure at 4.30 pm was then as much of an Edinburgh spectacle as that of the Silver Jubilee had been in London two years earlier. Even though platform tickets in Scotland then cost three times as much as they did farther south the station was thronged with sightseers, of all ages and both sexes; but my recollection is that the railway 'buff' of the present day, lavishly equipped with cameras, cine and stills, and tape recording equipment was quite absent. Gliding away from Waverley behind an immaculately turned out *Commonwealth of Australia* we were soon sweeping along the Lothian coast through an unseasonable 'haar'. But though the mist

Preparation of engine 4490 Empire of India *for the Coronation Scot at Kings Cross shed.*

The crowd admiring No. 4491 Commonwealth of Australia, *before departure of the Coronation from Edinburgh (Waverley).*

rolling in from the sea was quite thick it did not appear to be interfering with the driver's sighting of the signals, and we kept up a fine pace. After Berwick-on-Tweed we had a spell in the observation car, and were fascinated to see the line receding from us, especially when we passed trains travelling in the opposite direction. We were in the observation car when the train reached Newcastle, and I was amused that interest, even greater than in Edinburgh, was almost entirely concentrated upon the head end.

On the fast non-stop run to Kings Cross speed was restrained at first because of the numerous restrictions on the line as far as York, and it was not until we were south of Doncaster that the driver of the *Commonwealth of Australia* really began to show his paces. Even so, a maximum of 95 mph descending to the Trent Valley was cut short by the need to slow to 70 mph over the water troughs near Newark. But recalling that the racing ground *par excellence*, from Stoke Tunnel down towards Peterborough, lay only just ahead, I thought again of the many fine records that had been made there: of 108 mph by the non-streamlined engine *Papyrus* in the trials prior to the building of the Silver Jubilee train; of 113 mph by the *Silver Fox* in the dynamometer car run of 1936, and then of 109½ mph on the demonstration run of this very train only a few weeks previously. What might we expect today? By this time Grantham had been passed and we were mounting the last stages of the rise to Stoke Tunnel at a steady 65 mph. We ran through, and then began the long descent towards Peterborough. The weather was now fine, clear and quite calm; and just after 9 o'clock on a summer evening conditions seemed ideal.

There was no question of pressing the engine to make a record maximum speed. She was going beautifully, steaming freely, and without changing the controls in any way she was allowed to run; and *run* we did! Little Bytham station was passed at 98 mph; shortly afterwards we reached 106, and from then onwards we ran at between 104 and 106 mph for nearly twelve miles. At this speed the motion of the train was uncannily smooth. During the course of the journey south several fellow passengers had become interested in my stop-watching, but now they frankly disbelieved my figures. The distance of 12·7 miles from Little Bytham station to Werrington Junction signal box was covered in 7 minutes 22 seconds, which works out at an average speed of 103·5 mph; and by Werrington we had already slowed up to 70 mph to take water at the troughs. No repetition of such thrilling speeds took place on the final run from Peterborough to Kings Cross; but we arrived with the engine in perfect mechanical order, and incidentally quite a lot of coal left on the tender. It was a wonderful memory of steam locomotion at its very finest, to take into the dark days of austerity that descended upon us in September 1939.